XNA 4.0 Game Development by Example – Visual Basic Edition

Beginner's Guide

Create your own exciting games with Visual Basic and Microsoft XNA 4.0

Kurt Jaegers

[PACKT]
PUBLISHING

BIRMINGHAM - MUMBAI

XNA 4.0 Game Development by Example – Visual Basic Edition
Beginner's Guide

First published: December 2011

Production Reference: 1161211

Published by Packt Publishing Ltd.
Livery Place
35 Livery Street
Birmingham B3 2PB, UK.

ISBN: 978-1-84969-240-3

www.packtpub.com

Cover Image by Vinayak Chittar (vinayak.chittar@gmail.com)

Credits

Author

Kurt Jaegers

Reviewers

Michael Schuld

Pedro Daniel Güida Vázquez

Acquisition Editor

Wilson D'souza

Development Editor

Wilson D'souza

Technical Editors

Lubna Shaikh

Ankita Shashi

Manasi Poonthottam

Project Coordinator

Kushal Bhardwaj

Proofreaders

Jonathan Todd

Lesley Harrison

Indexers

Tejal Daruwale

Hemangini Bari

Rekha Nair

Graphics

Conidon Miranda

Production Coordinator

Aparna Bhagat

Cover Work

Aparna Bhagat

About the Author

Kurt Jaegers is a database and network administrator, and a long-time hobbyist game developer, having built games for everything from the Commodore 64 to the Xbox 360. He is the owner of xnaresources.com and the author of the C# version of XNA Game Development by Example.

I would like to thank my parents George and Julie Jaegers for investing in a newfangled Atari 400 computer back in the 80s and encouraging my interest in computer programming from a very early age. As with my first book, thanks go to my wife Linda for proofreading, as well as my brother Jason for providing most of the graphics for the games.

About the Reviewers

Michael Schuld started his foray into game development using Managed DirectX 9, and after playing with the framework for a few months, decided that there wasn't enough beginner content out in the world to help people new to game development get started.

To fix this problem, he immediately set out writing a tutorial series that he kept up-to-date with the change from Managed DirectX to XNA, and all the updates to the XNA Framework since then. Along with these tutorials, he hosted a popular XNA Game Development forum and has helped hundreds of programmers new to game development get their feet wet. The site and tutorials have been listed by Microsoft and Game Informer as one of a select list of community resources for anyone wanting to learn the XNA Framework.

More recently, he has expanded his work into DirectX 11 and reviewing books in the game development arena. His recent work, tutorials, and reviews can all be found on http://www.thehazymind.com.

> I would like to thank David Bonner, Charles Humphrey, and Michael Quandt for their early interest and assistance with my tutorial series, both in reviewing the content for ease of use and helping out with the forums. I'm glad to have you guys around to keep things from getting too crazy.

Pedro Daniel Güida Vázquez is the owner of Pulsar Coders, an indie company that develops video games for many platforms. He enjoys working daily on everything related to video game development. Economist, System Analyst, Professor, Microsoft MVP for DirectX and XNA are some of the accomplishments obtained by him throughout his life. His skills cover many areas in the field, both technical and artistic, and he is always looking for interesting challenges to extend his personal and professional goals. You can find a comprehensive biography of this reviewer at http://www.linkedin.com/in/pedroguida.

www.PacktPub.com

Support files, eBooks, discount offers and more

You might want to visit www.PacktPub.com for support files and downloads related to your book.

Did you know that Packt offers eBook versions of every book published, with PDF and ePub files available? You can upgrade to the eBook version at www.PacktPub.com and as a print book customer, you are entitled to a discount on the eBook copy. Get in touch with us at service@packtpub.com for more details.

At www.PacktPub.com, you can also read a collection of free technical articles, sign up for a range of free newsletters and receive exclusive discounts and offers on Packt books and eBooks.

http://PacktLib.PacktPub.com

Do you need instant solutions to your IT questions? PacktLib is Packt's online digital book library. Here, you can access, read and search across Packt's entire library of books.

Why Subscribe?

- ◆ Fully searchable across every book published by Packt
- ◆ Copy and paste, print and bookmark content
- ◆ On demand and accessible via web browser

Free Access for Packt account holders

If you have an account with Packt at www.PacktPub.com, you can use this to access PacktLib today and view nine entirely free books. Simply use your login credentials for immediate access.

Table of Contents

Preface

The Microsoft XNA Framework provides a powerful set of tools to allow development teams of any size, from the individual developer to larger independent teams, to rapidly develop high-performance quality games for multiple Microsoft-related platforms.

This book will present a series of video games, utilizing Visual Basic and the XNA Framework, to delve into the world of 2D game development, targeting the Microsoft Windows environment. We will utilize XNA's 2D graphics capabilities to present our games to the player, and we will also look at the fundamental systems behind several game design challenges, such as pathfinding, collision detection, special effects, and more.

Each of the four games in this book cover a new gaming style and introduce progressively more advanced techniques and systems to provide a foundation for bringing your own creations to life.

What this book covers

Chapter 1, Introducing XNA Game Studio, begins by looking at the history of the XNA Framework and its predecessors and installing the Windows Phone SDK package that includes the version 4.0 release of the XNA tools. We wrap up this chapter by looking at the building blocks of an XNA game and putting together an XNA mini-game called SquareChase.

Chapter 2, Flood Control – Underwater Puzzling, introduces a board-based puzzle game called Flood Control. We introduce the XNA Content Pipeline and build a recursive function to determine the state of the game board while playing.

Chapter 3, Flood Control – Smoothing Out the Rough Edges, refines and completes the Flood Control game, adding animated rotation, movement, and fading of game pieces. We will implement a scoring system and cover displaying text to the screen.

Chapter 4, Asteroid Belt Assault – Lost in Space, begins by developing our second game. This time we put together a space-based shooter. We will create a basic moving star field, using a simple particle system, and introduce frame-based sprite animation. We will add moving asteroids to our star field and examine how to detect collisions between asteroids and make them respond realistically. We add a player-controlled spaceship and enemies that can fly across the screen following pre-defined waypoints.

Chapter 5, Asteroid Belt Assault – Special Effects, wraps up Asteroid Belt Assault. We implement collision detection between the player, enemies, asteroids, and bullets, and create particle-based explosions. Finally, we will look at loading and playing sound effects to bring life to our in-game events.

Chapter 6, Robot Rampage – Multi-Axis Mayhem, begins the construction of a tank-based game in which the player can move and fire independently using either an Xbox 360 controller or the keyboard. We build a tile-map-based game world and a camera class to view a screen-sized area of the larger world, and we implement player collision with the walls of the tile map.

Chapter 7, Robot Rampage—Lots and Lots of Bullets, completes Robot Rampage by expanding on our particle-based explosion system and adding enemies, player goals, and weapon upgrades to our tile map. We allow the player to fire at the enemies with several different weapons. Finally, we create an implementation of the A* pathfinding algorithm to allow the enemy tanks to track down the player.

Chapter 8, Gemstone Hunter - Put on Your Platform Shoes, introduces a side-scrolling, jump-and-run platform game. We start by evolving our tile-based mapping system to allow multiple layers of tiles, and we look at combining XNA and Windows Forms to produce a map editor for Gemstone Hunter. As part of this process, we will look at building more complex solutions that contain multiple projects, and we separate our game's tile engine into a Game Library project.

Chapter 9, Gemstone Hunter—Standing on your Own Two Pixels, concludes the Gemstone Hunter project by examining an alternative method for frame-based sprite animation, using player and enemy graphics from the XNA Platform Starter Kit. We implement platform physics and bring the game together by loading levels and reacting to their embedded code values.

What you need for this book

In order to install and use the Microsoft XNA 4.0 tools, you will need a Windows PC with either Microsoft Windows Vista or Microsoft Windows 7 and a video card supporting DirectX 9 or later. Shader Model 1.1 is required for XNA, but it is highly recommended that your video card support Shader Model 2.0 or later, as many of the XNA samples available online require 2.0 support.

Who this book is for

If you are an aspiring game developer who wants to take a shot at creating games for the Microsoft Windows platform with the XNA Framework, then this book is for you. Using this book, you can get started with creating games without any game development experience. Some knowledge of Visual Basic would be helpful to kick-start your game development experience.

Conventions

In this book, you will find several headings appearing frequently.

To give clear instructions of how to complete a procedure or task, we use:

Time for action – heading

1. Action 1
2. Action 2
3. Action 3

Instructions often need some extra explanation so that they make sense, so they are followed with:

What just happened?

This heading explains the working of tasks or instructions that you have just completed.

You will also find some other learning aids in the book, including:

Pop quiz – heading

These are short multiple choice questions intended to help you test your own understanding.

Have a go hero – heading

These set practical challenges and give you ideas for experimenting with what you have learned.

You will also find a number of styles of text that distinguish between different kinds of information. Here are some examples of these styles and an explanation of their meaning.

Code words in text are shown as follows: "We can include other contexts through the use of the `include` directive."

A block of code is set as follows:

```
Public ReadOnly Property RotationAmount As Single
    Get
        If Clockwise Then
            Return _rotationAmount
        Else
            Return (MathHelper.Pi * 2) - _rotationAmount
        End If
    End Get
End Property
```

When we wish to draw your attention to a particular part of a code block, the relevant lines or items are set in bold:

```
Public ReadOnly Property RotationAmount As Single
    Get
        If Clockwise Then
            Return _rotationAmount
        Else
            Return (MathHelper.Pi * 2) - _rotationAmount
        End If
    End Get
End Property
```

Any command-line input or output is written as follows:

```
#Region "Shot Management Methods"
```

New terms and **important words** are shown in bold. Words that you see on the screen, in menus or dialog boxes for example, appear in the text like this: "Click on the **Register. Now** link to go to the **Visual Studio Express** registration page".

Warnings or important notes appear in a box like this.

Tips and tricks appear like this.

Reader feedback

Feedback from our readers is always welcome. Let us know what you think about this book—what you liked or may have disliked. Reader feedback is important for us to develop titles that you really get the most out of.

To send us general feedback, simply send an e-mail to feedback@packtpub.com and mention the book title via the subject of your message.

If there is a topic that you have expertise in and you are interested in either writing or contributing to a book, see our author guide on www.packtpub.com/authors.

Customer support

Now that you are the proud owner of a Packt book, we have a number of things to help you to get the most from your purchase.

Downloading the example code and colored images

You can download the example code files and the colored images for all Packt books you have purchased from your account at http://www.PacktPub.com. If you purchased this book elsewhere, you can visit http://www.PacktPub.com/support and register to have the files e-mailed directly to you.

Errata

Although we have taken every care to ensure the accuracy of our content, mistakes do happen. If you find a mistake in one of our books—maybe a mistake in the text or the code—we would be grateful if you would report this to us. By doing so, you can save other readers from frustration and help us improve subsequent versions of this book. If you find any errata, please report them by visiting http://www.packtpub.com/support, selecting your book, clicking on the **errata submission form** link, and entering the details of your errata. Once your errata are verified, your submission will be accepted and the errata will be uploaded on our website, or added to any list of existing errata, under the Errata section of that title. Any existing errata can be viewed by selecting your title from http://www.packtpub.com/support.

Piracy

Piracy of copyright material on the Internet is an ongoing problem across all media. At Packt, we take the protection of our copyright and licenses very seriously. If you come across any illegal copies of our works, in any form, on the Internet, please provide us with the location address or website name immediately so that we can pursue a remedy.

Please contact us at `copyright@packtpub.com` with a link to the suspected pirated material.

We appreciate your help in protecting our authors and our ability to bring you valuable content.

Questions

You can contact us at `questions@packtpub.com` if you are having a problem with any aspect of the book, and we will do our best to address it.

1

Introducing XNA Game Studio

Since its initial release in 2006, the Microsoft XNA Framework has allowed C#
developers to harness the power of DirectX to create video games that can be
targeted to Windows, the Xbox 360, and Microsoft-based mobile devices such
as the Zune or the Windows Phone 7 platform.

XNA consists of the **XNA Framework***, which is a set of code libraries to perform*
common graphics, sound, and other game-related tasks, and **XNA Game**
Studio*, which is an extension of the Visual Studio interface that includes a*
number of project templates to make use of the XNA Framework.

The XNA project templates include an integrated game loop, easy-to-use (and
fast) methods to display graphics, full support for 3D models, and simple access
to multiple types of input devices.

With the summer 2011 release of the XNA 4.0 Refresh, Microsoft has provided
what has been cited as both the most requested feature for XNA and the most
requested feature of Visual Basic developers: the ability to use Visual Basic as
the backend for coding XNA projects.

What does XNA stand for, anyway?

According to the developers, XNA is an acronym for "XNA's
Not Acronymed".

In this introductory chapter, you will:

- ◆ Look at an overview of the games presented in this book
- ◆ Download and install the Windows Phone Developers Tools, which includes the
  Visual Studio Express and the XNA Extensions for Visual Studio

◆ Create a new Windows game project

◆ Modify the default Windows Game template to build your first XNA game

Overview of the games

Many beginning developers make the mistake of attempting to tackle far too large a project early on. Modern blockbuster video games are the result of the efforts of hundreds of programmers, designers, graphics artists, sound effects technicians, producers, directors, actors, and many other vocations, often working for years to create the game.

That does not mean that the efforts of a solo developer or small team need to be dull, boring, and unplayable. This book is designed to help you develop a solid understanding of 2D game development with XNA Game Studio. By the time you have completed the projects in this book, you will have the necessary knowledge to create games that you can complete without an army of fellow game developers at your back.

In this chapter, you will build your first XNA mini-game, chasing squares around the screen with your mouse cursor. In subsequent chapters, the following four more detailed games are presented:

◆ **Flood Control**: An explosion in one of the research laboratories has cracked the pressure dome protecting your underwater habitat. Work quickly to construct a series of pipes to pump water out of the habitat, before it floods. Flood Control is a board-based puzzle game with simple game mechanics and slowly increasing difficulty.

◆ **Asteroid Belt Assault**: After being separated from your attack fleet in hyperspace, you find yourself lost in an asteroid field without communications or navigation systems. Work your way through the chaos of the asteroid belt while combating alien pilots intent upon your destruction. A vertically-scrolling space shooter, Asteroid Belt Assault introduces scrolling backgrounds, along with player and computer-controlled characters.

◆ **Robot Rampage**: In the secret depths of a government defense facility, a rogue computer has taken control of robotic factories across the world, constructing an army of mechanical soldiers. Your mission—infiltrate these factories and shut down their network links to break the computer's control. A multi-axis shooter utilizing both of the analog control sticks on the Xbox 360 gamepad controller, Robot Rampage generates and manages dozens of on-screen sprites, and introduces world map construction.

◆ **Gemstone Hunter**: Explore the Australian wilderness, abandoned mines, and ancient caves in a search for fabulous treasures. In Gemstone Hunter, you will construct a classic platform-style game, including a Windows Forms-based level editor and a multi-map "world" to challenge the player.

The games are each presented over two chapters. In the first chapter, the basics are implemented to the point where the game is playable. In the second chapter, features and polish are added to the game.

Each game introduces both new concepts and expands on topics covered in the previous games. At the end of each game chapter, you will find a list of exercises challenging you to use your newly-gained knowledge, to enhance previous games in the book.

We will focus on Windows as our platform for the games presented in this book. That said, the code presented in this book requires very little in the way of changes for other XNA platforms, generally only requiring implementation of platform-specific controls (gamepads, touch screen, and so on), and consideration of the differences in display sizes and orientation on non-Windows devices.

System requirements

In order to develop games using XNA Game Studio, you will need a computer capable of running both Visual Studio 2010 and the XNA Framework extensions. The general requirements are listed in the following table:

Component	Minimum requirement	Notes
Operating System	Windows Vista SP2 or Windows 7 (all editions except Starter)	As of XNA 4.0, Windows XP is no longer officially supported.
Graphics Card	Shader Model 1.1 support and DirectX 9.0 support	Microsoft recommends Shader Model 2.0 support as it is required for many of the XNA Starter Kits and code samples. The projects in this book similarly require Shader Model 2.0 support.
Development Platform	Visual Studio 2010 or Visual Studio 2010 Express	You will install Visual Studio 2010 Express as part of the XNA installation later in this chapter.
Optional requirements		
Windows Phone	Windows Phone Development Tools, DirectX 10 or later, Compatible Video Card	Development tools include a Windows Phone emulator to test applications, without deployment to a physical device.
Xbox Live	Xbox Live Silver membership and XNA Creator's Club Premium membership	Xbox Live Silver is free. The XNA Creator's Club Premium membership costs $49 for 4 months or $99 for 1 year.

Installing XNA Game Studio

To get started developing games in XNA, you will need to download and install the software. You will need both Visual Studio and XNA extensions. With the release of XNA 4.0, the install packages have been consolidated, and both required components are included in the Windows Phone SDK package. The SDK was previously known as the Windows Phone Developers Tools prior to the release of the XNA 4.0 Refresh as part of the Windows Phone SDK 7.1 update.

XNA and the Windows Phone SDK

The October 2010 release of the Windows Phone 7 platform marked a shift in Microsoft's direction for XNA. Prior to Windows Phone, XNA was a separate download that included Visual C# Express. While still supporting the Windows and Xbox platforms as well as the Windows Phone, XNA is no longer available separately, and has been rolled into the Windows Phone SDK.

Time for action – installing XNA Game Studio

1. Visit `http://create.msdn.com/en-us/home/getting_started`, and download the latest version of the Windows Phone SDK package. Run the setup wizard and allow the installation package to complete.

2. Open **Visual Studio 2010 Express**. Click on the **Help** menu and select **Register Product**. Click on the **Register Now** link to go to the **Visual Studio Express** registration page. After you have completed the registration process, return to **Visual Studio 2010 Express** and enter the registration number into the registration dialog box.

3. Close **Visual Studio 2010 Express**.

4. Launch **Visual Studio 2010 Express**, and the **Integrated Development Environment** (**IDE**) will be displayed, as shown in the following screenshot:

Chapter 1

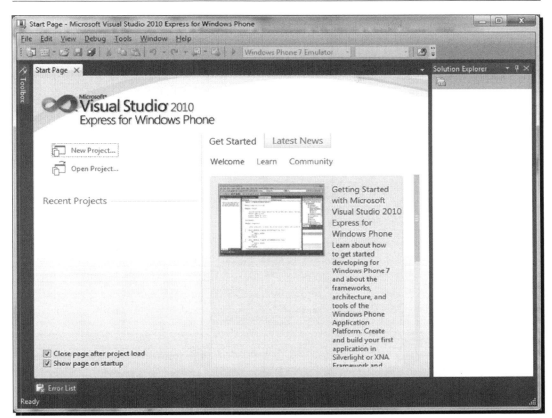

Other versions of Visual Studio and XNA

Different versions of Visual Studio and XNA can be installed on the same PC, without interfering with each other. If you wish to target the Zune platform, you will need to install Visual Studio 2008 Express and XNA 3.1 (which only supports the C# language). Additionally, Visual Studio Express and Visual Studio Professional can co-exist on the same PC, and XNA will integrate with both of them, if the Windows Phone SDK is installed after Visual Studio.

What just happened?

You have now successfully installed the Windows Phone SDK, which includes Visual Studio 2010 Express, the XNA Extensions for Visual Studio, and the re-distributable Font Pack provided by Microsoft for XNA developers.

Building your first game

XNA attempts to simplify many of the basic elements of game development by automatically handling things, such as the game update loop and presenting the current frame of graphical information to the display. To illustrate just how much of the background work is integrated into the XNA project templates, let's jump in straight away and create your first game within a few minutes of finishing the installation.

Visual Basic versus C# - tutorials and samples on the web

With a five-year headstart on Visual Basic developers, there are a host of XNA tutorials, code samples, and forum posts written for C# out on the Internet. In the interest of being able to utilize these resources, I will occasionally point out topics or sections of code and their equivalent in C# notation.

In **SquareChase**, we will generate randomly positioned squares of different colors while the user attempts to catch them with their mouse pointer before they disappear. While building the project, we will discuss each of the major code sections pre-defined by the XNA templates.

Time for action – creating a new Windows game project

1. In the **Visual Studio** window, open the **File** menu and select **New Project...**

2. Under **Project Type**, make sure **Visual Basic** is selected as the language and that the **XNA Game Studio 4.0** category is selected.

3. Under **Templates**, select **Windows Game (4.0)**.

4. Name the project `SquareChase` (this will automatically update the **Solution Name**).

5. Click on **OK**.

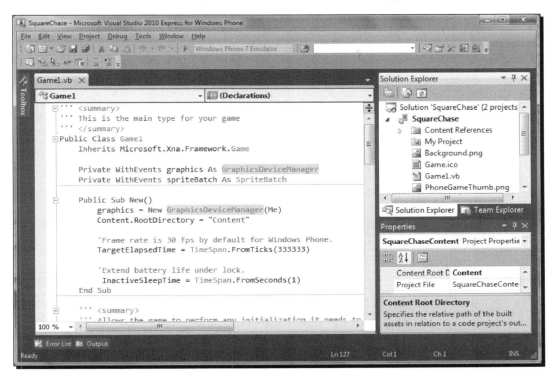

What just happened?

Each of the XNA project templates is a series of files and settings that get copied to your new project folder. Included in this set of files is the `Game1.vb` file, which is the heart of your XNA game.

Back up your projects

When you create your project, the **Location** field specifies where it will be saved. By default, Visual Studio creates a folder in your user documents area called Visual Studio 2010 to store both programs and configuration information. Under this folder is a **Projects** folder that contains subfolders for each new project you create. Make backups of your projects on a regular basis. You do not want to lose your hard work to a disk failure!

Anatomy of an XNA game

The most basic XNA game will have all of its code contained in the file called `Game1.vb`. This file is generated when you create a new project and contains override declarations for the methods used to manage your game. In addition to the `Game1` class' declarations area, there are five primary methods that you will customize for any XNA project.

The declarations area

Right below the class declaration for `Game1` is the class level declarations area. By default, this area contains two variables:

```
Private WithEvents graphics As GraphicsDeviceManager
Private WithEvents spriteBatch As SpriteBatch
```

The graphics object provides access to, not surprisingly, the system's video card. It can be used to alter the video mode, the size of the current viewport (the area that all drawing work will be clipped to if specified), and retrieve information about Shader Models the video card supports.

XNA provides the `SpriteBatch` class to allow you to (very quickly) draw 2D images (called **sprites**) to the screen. The `spriteBatch` variable is an instance of this class, which we will use for all of our drawing purposes in `SquareChase`.

The declarations area is the spot for any variables that need to be maintained outside of any of the individual methods discussed next, such as `LoadContent`, `Update`, and `Draw`. In practice, any data that you need to keep track of throughout your game will be referenced in some way in your declarations section.

Time for action – adding variables to the class declaration area

1. Right below the `Private WithEvents spriteBatch As SpriteBatch` line, add the following:

```
Private rand As New Random()
Private squareTexture As Texture2D
Private currentSquare As Rectangle
Private playerScore As Integer
Private timeRemaining As Single
Private Const TimePerSquare As Single = 0.75
Private colors() As Color = {Color.Red, Color.Green, Color.Blue}
```

What just happened?

These are all the variables you will need for the SquareChase MINI-GAME. Here is a quick breakdown:

- rand: This instance of the Random class is used to generate random numbers through the Next() method. You will use this to generate random coordinates for the squares that will be drawn to the screen.

- squareTexture: The Texture2D class holds a 2D image. We will define a small texture in memory to use when drawing the square.

- currentSquare: The XNA Framework defines a structure called **Rectangle** that can be used to represent an area of the display, by storing the x and y position of the upper-left corner along with a width and height. SquareChase will generate random squares and store the location in this variable.

- playerScore: Players will score one point each time they successfully "catch" a square by clicking on it with their mouse. Their score accumulates in this integer variable.

- timeRemaining: When a new square is generated, this float will be set to a value representing how many seconds it will remain active. When the counter reaches zero, the square will be removed and a new square generated.

- TimePerSquare: This constant is used to set the length of time that a square will be displayed before it "runs away" from the player.

- colors: This array of Color objects will be used when a square is drawn to cycle through the three colors in the array. The Color structure identifies a color by four components: red, green, blue, and alpha. Each of these components can be specified as a byte from 0 to 255, representing the intensity of that component in the color. Alpha represents how transparent the color is, allowing things already drawn behind it to show through. XNA drawing functions utilize pre-multiplied alpha, meaning that the alpha value has already been reflected in the other components of the color. We can accomplish this by simply creating a color with an RGB value and multiplying it by the desired alpha level we wish (between 0.0 and 1.0).

Data types

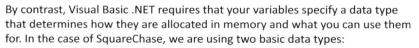

If your experience with Visual Basic is primarily VBScript-related, you may not be used to specifying data types (integer, single, Texture2D, and so on) to your variables. VBScript uses a generic "Variant" type that is interpreted by the runtime into a type that makes sense for what you are trying to do with it.

By contrast, Visual Basic .NET requires that your variables specify a data type that determines how they are allocated in memory and what you can use them for. In the case of SquareChase, we are using two basic data types:

Integer: It is a whole-number value between -2,147,483,648 and 2,147,483,647. This is equivalent to the C# type "int".

Single: This is a floating-point number. The numeric range for Singles depends on the digits of precision specified. This is equivalent to the C# type "float".

The Game1 class constructor

The XNA templates define an instance of the Microsoft.Xna.Framework.Game class with the default name Game1 as the primary component of your new game. Slightly more goes on behind the scenes, as we will see when we add an XNA game to a Windows form in *Chapter 8, Gemstone Hunter: Put on your Platform Shoes*, but for now, we can consider the Game1 constructor as the first thing that happens when our XNA game is executed. The class constructor is identified as Public Sub New(), and by default, the constructor contains only two lines:

```
graphics = New GraphicsDeviceManager(Me)
Content.RootDirectory = "Content"
```

For most of the games in this book, we will not need to make extensive modifications to the Game1 constructor, as its only job is to establish a link to the GraphicsDeviceManager object, and set the default directory for the Content object, which is used to load images, sound, and other game content.

Objects, classes, and methods

Many of the items that we define in our code will be classes. A **Class** is logical grouping of data and code. There are many built-in classes in Visual Basic and XNA, including things such as `Integer` and `SpritBatch`. Our `Game1` file is itself a class definition, based on the XNA Game class. We can define new classes either from scratch, or based on existing classes. When they are based on other classes, they are said to inherit from a base class. We create instances of our class in order to use them, called objects. In the previous code snippet, the `graphics` object is assigned a new instance of the `GraphicsDeviceManager` class.

The code portions of an object are called **Methods**. In Visual Basic, methods are either Subs or Functions. A class can have a special Sub called `New`, which is the class constructor. When an instance of the class is created, the constructor is run and can be passed values to initialize the new object to a known state.

The Initialize() method

After the constructor has finished and your XNA game begins to run, the `Initialize()` method is called. This method only runs once, and the default code created with a new project template simply calls the base version of the method. The `Initialize()` method is the ideal place to set up features, such as screen resolution, toggling full screen mode, and enabling the use of a mouse in a Windows project. Other game objects that do not rely on external content, such as graphics and sound resources, can also be initialized here.

Time for action – customizing the Initialize() method

1. Add the following before the call to `MyBase.Initialize()`:

```
Me.IsMouseVisible = True
```

What just happened?

By default, the mouse is not visible inside the XNA game window. Setting the `IsMouseVisible` property of the running instance of the `Game1` class enables the mouse cursor in Windows.

Input types on other platforms

The Xbox and Windows Phone do not have mice, so what happens when the code to enable the mouse runs on these platforms? Nothing! If a platform is not equipped to support a specific type of input, the request just returns the default values when no input is being received. It is also safe to ask other platforms about their non-existent keyboards and check the state of a gamepad on a Windows PC without one attached.

The LoadContent() method

Part of the responsibility of the base `Initialize()` method is to call `LoadContent()` when the normal initialization has completed. The method is used to read in any graphical and audio resources your game will need. The default `LoadContent()` method is also where the `spriteBatch` object gets initialized. You will use the `spriteBatch` instance to draw objects to the screen during execution of the `Draw()` method.

Time for action – creating the squareTexture

1. Open Microsoft Paint or your favorite image editor, create a new 16 x16 pixel image, and fill it with white.

2. Save the image as "`SQUARE.BMP`" in a temporary location.

3. Back in Visual Studio, right-click on **SquareChaseContent (Content)** in **Solution Explorer** (you may need to scroll down to see it) and select **Add | Existing Item**. Browse to the image you created and click on **Ok**.

4. Add the following code to the `LoadContent()` method after the `spriteBatch` initialization:

```
squareTexture = Content.Load(Of Texture2D)("SQUARE")
```

What just happened?

To load content, it must first exist. In *steps 1* and *2* mentioned previously, you created a bitmap image for the square texture. In *step 3*, you added the bitmap image as a piece of content to your project.

Powers of two

Very old graphics cards required that all texture images be sized to "powers of two" (2, 4, 8, 16, 32, 64, 128, 256, and so on). This limitation is largely non-existent with modern video hardware, especially for 2D graphics. In fact, the sample code in the XNA Platform Starter Kit uses textures that do not conform to the "powers of two" limitation. In our case, the size of the image we create is not critical, as we will be scaling the output when we draw squares to the screen.

Finally, in *step 4*, you used the `Content` instance of the `ContentManager` class to load the image from disk and into memory when your game runs. The Content object is established automatically by XNA for you when you create a new project. When we add content items, such as images and sound effects to our game project, the XNA Content Pipeline converts our content files into an intermediate format that we can read through the `Content` object. These XNB files get deployed alongside the executable for our game to provide their content data at runtime.

The `Content` object's `Load()` method requires us to specify what kind of data we are loading by including `Of` along with the data type in parenthesis before the parameters that are passed to the method. In this case, the content we are loading is a `Texture2D`, which represents a 2D image. Finally, we specify the asset name of the item we wish to load from the content project. The default asset name is the same as the filename, without the file extension.

Asset names

If you create subdirectories inside your `Content` project (as we will do in the other games in this book), the asset name will include the path to the file. If our `square.bmp` file were in a directory called `Textures`, the asset name would be `"Textures\Square"`.

The Update() method

Once `LoadContent()` has finished doing its job, an XNA game enters an endless loop in which it attempts to call the `Update()` method 60 times per second. This default update rate can be changed by setting the `TargetElapsedTime` property of the `Game1` object, but for our purposes, the default time step will be fine. If your `Update()` logic begins taking too long to run, your game will begin skipping calls to the `Draw()` method in favor of multiple calls to `Update()`, to attempt to catch up to the current game time.

All of your game logic gets built into the Update() method. It is here that you check for player input, move sprites, spawn enemies, track scores, and everything else except draw to the display. Update() receives a single parameter called gameTime, which can be used to determine how much time has elapsed since the previous call to Update() or to determine if your game is skipping Draw() calls by checking its IsRunningSlowly property.

The default Update() method contains code to exit the game if the player presses the **Back** button on the first gamepad controller.

Exiting a game under Windows

The default Update() code provides anyone with a gamepad a way to end the game, but what if you do not have a gamepad? Press *Alt + F4* on the keyboard or click on the standard Windows close button to exit your game when running in Windows.

Time for action – coding Update() for SquareChase

1. Add the following to Update() method right before MyBase.Update(gameTime):

```
If (timeRemaining = 0.0) Then
  currentSquare = New Rectangle(
    rand.Next(0, Me.Window.ClientBounds.Width - 25),
    rand.Next(0, Me.Window.ClientBounds.Height - 25),
  25, 25)
  timeRemaining = TimePerSquare
End If
Dim mouseInfo As MouseState = Mouse.GetState()
If (mouseInfo.LeftButton = ButtonState.Pressed) And
  (currentSquare.Contains(mouseInfo.X, mouseInfo.Y)) Then
  playerScore += 1
  timeRemaining = 0.0
End If
timeRemaining = MathHelper.Max(0, timeRemaining -
  CType(gameTime.ElapsedGameTime.TotalSeconds, Single))
Me.Window.Title = "Score : " & playerScore.ToString()
```

What just happened?

The first thing the Update() routine does is check to see if the current square has expired, by checking to see if timeRemaining has been reduced to zero. If it has, a new square is generated using the Next() method of the rand object. In this form, Next() takes two parameters: an (inclusive) minimum value and a (non-inclusive) maximum value. In this case, the minimum is set to 0, while the maximum is set to the size of the Me.Window. ClientBounds property minus 25 pixels. This ensures that the square will always be fully within the game window.

The square that is generated represents both the location and size of the square that we will draw shortly. Because we are drawing a solid color, the texture and the square do not need to be the same size. When we draw the square, XNA will stretch the `16x16` texture to fill the `25x25` square. If we were drawing a detailed image instead of a colored square, we would need to take this scaling into account to avoid visual artifacts or odd stretching when drawing the texture.

Next, the current position and button state of the mouse is captured into the `mouseInfo` variable through `Mouse.GetState()`. Both the `Keyboard` and the `GamePad` classes also use a `GetState()` method that captures all of the data about that input device when the method is executed.

> **Visual Basic versus C# - variable naming**
>
> C# is a case-sensitive language, so if we were to declare variables named "mouse", "Mouse" and "MOUSE", they would all represent different objects in memory. Visual Basic is case-insensitive, meaning that all three of these identifiers refer to the same variable. In fact, Visual Studio will change them all to match the way you type it when it is first declared in your code.
>
> It is common in C# to use a lower-case variable of the same name as the class or structure you are creating an instance of, so in C# "`mouse=Mouse.GetState();`" would be perfectly acceptable, but it would be problematic in Visual Basic. You might notice that the XNA template itself does this in a few cases (`spriteBatch`, `gameTime`), which are carried over from their C# counterparts. This ends up working out, because the `SpriteBatch` and `GameTime` classes do not have any methods or properties that can be accessed outside of an instance of the classes, while `Mouse` does.

If the mouse reports that the left button is pressed, the code checks with the `currentSquare` object by calling its `Contains()` method to determine if the mouse's coordinates fall within its area. If they do, then the player has "caught" the square and scores a point. The `timeRemaining` counter is set to `0`, indicating that the next time `Update()` is called, it should create a new square.

After dealing with the user input, the `MathHelper.Max()` method is used to decrease `timeRemaining` by an amount equal to the elapsed game time, since the last call to `Update()`. `Max()` is used to ensure that the value does not go below zero.

Finally, the game window title bar is updated to display the player's score.

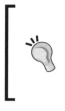

MathHelper

The Microsoft.Xna.Framework namespace provides a class called MathHelper that contains lots of goodies to make your life easier when dealing with numeric data, including converting degrees to and from radians, clamping values between a certain range, and generating smooth arcs between a starting and ending value.

The Draw() method

The final method in the default Game1.vb file is responsible, not surprisingly, for drawing the current game state to the display. Draw() is normally called once after each call to Update(), unless something is happening to slow down the execution of your game. In that case, Draw() calls may be skipped in order to call Update() more frequently. There will always be at least one call to Update() between calls to Draw(), however, as sequential Draw() calls would provide no benefit—nothing in the game state will have changed.

The default Draw() method simply clears the display window to the Cornflower Blue color.

Time for action – draw SquareChase!

1. Alter the GraphicsDevice.Clear(Color.CornflowerBlue) call and replace Color.CornflowerBlue with Color.Gray to make the game a bit easier on the eyes.

2. Add the following code after the call to clear the display:

```
spriteBatch.Begin()
spriteBatch.Draw(
   squareTexture,
   currentSquare,
   colors(playerScore Mod 3))
spriteBatch.End()
```

What just happened?

Any time you use a SpriteBatch object to draw to the display, you need to wrap the calls inside a Begin() and End() pair. Any number of calls to spriteBatch.Draw() can be included in a single batch, and it is common practice to simply start a Begin() at the top of your Draw() code, use it for all of your drawing, and then End() it right before the Draw() method exits. While not benefiting our SquareChase game, batching sprite drawing calls greatly speeds up the process of drawing a large number of images, by submitting them to the rendering system all at once instead of processing each image individually.

The `SpriteBatch.Draw()` method is used to draw a `Texture2D` object to the screen. There are a number of different options for how to specify what will be drawn. In this case, the simplest call requires a `Texture2D` object (`squareTexture`), a destination Rectangle (`currentSquare`), and a tint color to apply to the sprite. The expression "`playerScore Mod 3`" takes the player's score, divides it by 3, and returns the remainder. The result will always be 0, 1, or 2. This fits perfectly as an index to the elements in the colors array, allowing us to easily change the color of the square each time the player catches one.

Finally, the `spriteBatch.End()` tells XNA that we have finished queuing up sprites to draw and it should actually push them all out to the graphics card.

Time for action – play SquareChase!

1. Run your game by clicking on **Start Debugging** from the **Debug** menu or hitting *F5* on the keyboard.

2. Play an exciting game of `SquareChase`, by holding down the mouse button and trying to catch the squares with your mouse cursor:

What just happened?

You just finished your first XNA game, that's what!

Granted, it is not exactly the next blockbuster, but at only around 30 lines of code, it implements a simple game mechanic, user input, score tracking and display, and clock-based timing. Not bad for a few minutes' work.

Have a go hero

As simple as it is, here are a couple of enhancements you could make to SquareChase:

♦ Vary the size of the square, making it smaller every few times the player catches one, until you reach a size of 10 pixels.

♦ Start off with a higher setting for TimePerSquare and decrease it a little each time the player catches a square (*hint*: *you'll need to remove the* Const *declaration in front of* TimePerSquare *if you wish to change it at runtime*).

Summary

You now have a development environment set up for working on your XNA game projects, including Visual Studio 2010 Express and the XNA 4.0 Refresh extensions.

We also saw how the XNA game loop initializes, executes, and constructs an elementary game by expanding on the default methods provided by the Windows Game template.

It is time to dive headfirst into game creation with XNA. In the next chapter, we will begin building the puzzle game **Flood Control** in which the player is challenged to pump water out of their flooding underwater research station before the entire place really is underwater!

Flood Control – Underwater Puzzling

It was just another day on the bottom of the ocean, until an explosion in one of the storage bays cracked the protective dome around Deep Sea Research Lab Alpha. Now, the entire place is flooding, and the emergency pump system is a chaotic jumble of loose parts.

Designing a puzzle game

The Puzzler has always been a popular game genre. From old standbys such as Tetris, to modern crazes such as Bejeweled, puzzle games are attractive to players because they do not require a long-term time investment or a steep learning curve.

The game mechanic is the heart of any good puzzle game. This mechanic is usually very simple, with perhaps a few twists to keep the players on their toes.

In **Flood Control**, the player will be faced with a board containing 80 interactive pieces of pipe (the rows on the left and right are built into the background image, since they always stay the same). Some will be straight pipes and some will be curved. The objective of the game is to rotate the pipes to form a continuous line, to pump water from the left-side of the board to the right-side of the board.

Completing a section of pipe drains water out of the base and scores points for the player, but destroys the pipes used. New pipes will fall into place for the player to begin another row.

Flood Control focuses on the following concepts:

- Using the Content Pipeline to load textures from disk
- Creating classes to divide code into logical units
- Recursively evaluating the status of the game board to locate scoring chains
- Drawing textures using the `SpriteBatch.Draw()` method
- Utilizing some of the various .NET Collection classes (`List`, `Dictionary`, and `Queue`)
- Managing simple game states

Time for action – setting up the Flood Control project

1. Open Visual Studio Express Edition (if it is already open, select **Close Solution** from the **File** menu so that you are starting with an empty slate).

2. In the Visual Studio window, open the **File** menu and select **New Project...**.

3. Under **Project Type**, make sure **XNA Game Studio 4.0** is selected.

4. Under **Templates**, select **Windows Game (4.0)**.

5. Name the project `Flood Control`.

6. Click on **OK**.

7. Right-click on **Flood ControlContent (Content)** in the **Solution Explorer** window and select **Add | New Folder**. Name the folder Textures.

8. Add another folder under **Flood ControlContent (Content)** and name the folder Fonts.

9. Download the 2403_02_GRAPHICPACK.zip file from the book's companion website, and extract the files to a temporary folder.

10. Back in Visual Studio, right-click on **Textures** in the **Content** project and click on **Add | Existing Item**. Browse to the folder where you extracted the 2403_02_GRAPHICPACK files and highlight all of them. Click on **Add** to add them to your project.

What just happened?

You have now set up a workspace for building Flood Control and created a couple of folders for organizing game content. You have also imported the sample graphics for the Flood Control game into the project.

Introducing the Content Pipeline

The Flood Control Content (Content) project inside **Solution Explorer** is a special kind of project called a **Content Project**. Items in your game's content project are converted into .XNB resource files by **Content Importers** and **Content Processors**.

If you right-click on one of the image files you just added to the **Flood Control** project and select **Properties**, you will see that for both the Importer and Processor, the Content Pipeline will use **Texture – XNA Framework**. This means that the Importer will take the file in its native format (.PNG in this case) and convert it to a format that the processor recognizes as an image. The processor then converts the image into a .XNB file, which is a compressed binary format that XNA's content manager can read directly into a Texture2D object.

There are **Content Importer/Content Processor** pairs for several different types of content—images, audio, video, fonts, 3D models, and shader language effects files. All of these content types get converted to .XNB files, which can be used at runtime.

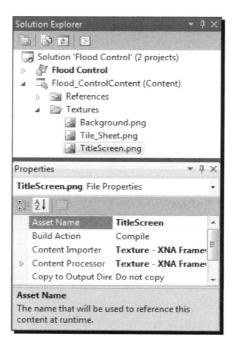

In order to see how to use the Content Pipeline at runtime, let's go ahead and write the code to read these textures into memory when the game starts:

Time for action – reading textures into memory

1. Double-click on `Game1.vb` in **Solution Explorer** to open it or bring it to the front if it is already open.

2. In the **Class Declarations** area of **Game1** (right below **Private WithEvents spriteBatch As SpriteBatch**), add:

```
Private playingPieces As Texture2D
Private background As Texture2D
Private titleScreen As Texture2D
```

3. Add code to load each of the `Texture2D` objects at the end of `LoadContent()`:

```
playingPieces = Content.Load(Of Texture2D)("Textures\Tile_Sheet")
background = Content.Load(Of Texture2D)("Textures\Background")
titleScreen = Content.Load(Of Texture2D)("Textures\TitleScreen")
```

What just happened?

In order to load the textures from disk, you need an in-memory object to hold them. These are declared as instances of the Texture2D class.

A default XNA project sets up the Content instance of the ContentManager class for you automatically. The Content object's Load() method is used to read .XNB files from disk and into the Texture2D instances declared earlier.

One thing to note here is that the Load() method requires a type identifier, specified in the first set of parenthesis using the Of notation, before the normal parameter list. Known in .Net programming as a **Generic**, many classes and methods support this kind of type specification to allow code to operate on a variety of data types. We will make more extensive use of Generics later when we need to store lists of objects in memory. The Load() method is used not only for textures, but also for all other kinds of content (sounds, 3D models, fonts, and so on) as well. It is important to let the Load() method know what kind of data you are reading, so that it knows what kind of object to return.

Sprites and sprite sheets

As far as XNA and the SpriteBatch classes are concerned, a **Sprite** is a 2D bitmapped image that can be drawn either with or without transparency information to the screen.

Sprites versus. textures

XNA defines a sprite as a 2D bitmap that is drawn directly to the screen. While these bitmaps are stored in Texture2D objects, the term **texture** is used when a 2D image is mapped onto a 3D object, providing a visual representation of the surface of the object. In practice, all XNA graphics are actually performed in 3D, with 2D sprites being rendered through special configurations of the XNA rendering engine.

The simple form of the SpriteBatch.Draw() call that you used in *Chapter 1, Introducing XNA Game Studio*, when drawing squares only needed two parameters: a Texture2D to draw a rectangle indicating where to draw it, and a Color to specify the tint to overlay onto the sprite.

Other overloads of the Draw() method, however, also allow you to specify a rectangle representing the source area within the Texture2D to copy from. If no source rectangle is specified, the entire Texture2D is copied and resized to fit the destination rectangle.

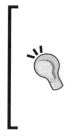

Overloads

When multiple versions of the same method are declared with either different parameters lists or different return values, each different declaration is called an **overload** of the method. Overloads allow methods to work with different types of data (for example, when setting a position, you could accept two separate X and Y coordinates or a Vector2 value), or leave out parameters that can then be assigned default values.

By specifying a source rectangle, however, individual pieces can be pulled from a large image. A bitmap with multiple sprites on it that will be drawn this way is called a sprite sheet.

The Tile_Sheet.png file for the Flood Control project is a sprite sheet containing 13 different sprites that will be used to represent the pieces of pipe used in the game. Each image is 40 pixels wide and 40 pixels high, with a one pixel border between each sprite and also around the entire image. When we call SpriteBatch.Draw(), we can limit what gets drawn from our texture to one of these 40x40 squares, allowing a single texture to hold all of the playing piece images that we need for the game:

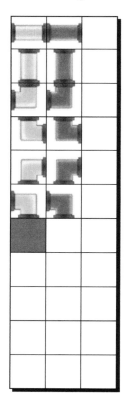

The `Tile_Sheet.png` file was created with alpha-based transparency. When it is drawn to the screen, the alpha level of each pixel will be used to merge that pixel with any color that already occupies that location on the screen.

Using this fact, you can create sprites that do not look like they are rectangular. Internally, you will still be drawing rectangles, but visually, the image can be of any shape.

What we really need now to be able to work with the playing pieces is a way to reference an individual piece, knowing not only what to draw to the screen, but what ends of the pipe connect to adjacent squares on the game board.

Alpha blending

Each pixel in a sprite can be fully opaque, fully transparent, or partially transparent. Fully opaque pixels are drawn directly, while fully transparent pixels are not drawn at all, leaving whatever has already been drawn to that pixel on the screen unchanged. In the 32-bit color mode, each channel of a color (Red, Green, Blue, and Alpha) are represented by 8 bits, meaning that there are 256 different degrees of transparency between fully opaque (255) and fully transparent (0). Partially transparent pixels are combined with the current pixel color at that location to create a mixed color, as if the pixels below were being seen through the new color. As briefly mentioned in *Chapter 1, Introducing XNA Game Studio*, because XNA uses pre-multiplied alpha, simply creating a transparent color by specifying an Alpha component will not produce the results you might expect. To create a transparent color, create the color as a solid color and then multiply it by the desired alpha value between 0 (fully transparent) and 1 (fully opaque).

Classes used in Flood Control

While it would certainly be possible to simply pile all of the game code into the `Game1` class, the result would be difficult to read and manage later on. Instead, we need to consider how to logically divide the game into classes that can manage themselves and help to organize our code.

A good rule of thumb is that a class should represent a single thing or type of thing. If you can say, *This object is made up of these other objects*, or, *This object contains these objects*, consider creating classes to represent those relationships.

The Flood Control game contains a game board made up of 80 pipe pieces. We can abstract these pipes as a class called `GamePiece` and provide it with the code it needs to handle rotation, and provide the code that will display the piece with a rectangle that can be used to pull the sprite off the sprite sheet.

The game board itself can be represented by a `GameBoard` class, which will handle managing individual `GamePiece` objects and be responsible for determining which pieces should be filled with water and which ones should be left empty.

The GamePiece class

The `GamePiece` class represents an individual pipe on the game board. One `GamePiece` has no knowledge of any other game pieces (that is, the responsibility of the `GameBoard` class), but it will need to be able to provide information about the pipe to objects that use the `GamePiece` class. Our class has the following requirements:

- Identify the sides of each piece that contain pipe connectors
- Differentiate between game pieces, which are filled with water and which are empty
- Allow game pieces to be updated
- Automatically handle rotation, by changing the piece type to the appropriate new piece type
- Given one side of a piece, provide the other sides of the piece in order to facilitate determining how water can flow through the game board
- Provide a rectangle that will be used when the piece is drawn to locate the graphic for the piece on the sprite sheet

Identifying a GamePiece

While the sprite sheet contains 13 different images, only 12 of them are actual game pieces (the last one is an empty square). Of the 12 remaining pieces, only six of them are unique pieces. The other six are the water-filled versions of the first six images.

Each of the game pieces can be identified by which sides of the square contain a connecting pipe. This results in two straight pieces and four pieces with 90 degree bends in them.

Instead of treating filled pieces as separate piece types, a second value can be tracked to determine if the piece is filled with water or not.

Time for action – build a GamePiece class - declarations

1. Switch back to your **Visual Studio** window if you have your image editor open.

2. Right-click on the **Flood Control** project in **Solution Explorer** and select **Add | Class...**.

3. Name the class `GamePiece.vb`, and click on **Add**.

4. Add the following declarations to the (currently empty) class:

```
Public Shared PieceTypes() As String =
  {
    "Left,Right",
    "Top,Bottom",
    "Left,Top",
    "Top,Right",
    "Right,Bottom",
    "Bottom,Left",
    "Empty"
  }

  Public Const PieceHeight As Integer = 40
  Public Const PieceWidth As Integer = 40

  Public Const MaxPlayablePieceIndex As Integer = 5
  Public Const EmptyPieceIndex As Integer = 6

  Private Const textureOffsetX As Integer = 1
  Private Const textureOffsetY As Integer = 1
  Private Const texturePaddingX As Integer = 1
  Private Const texturePaddingY As Integer = 1

  Private _pieceType As String = ""
  Private _pieceSuffix As String = ""
```

5. Add two properties to retrieve information about the piece:

```
Public ReadOnly Property PieceType As String
  Get
    Return _pieceType
  End Get
End Property

Public ReadOnly Property PieceSuffix As String
  Get
    Return _pieceSuffix
  End Get
End Property
```

What just happened?

Our new class file begins containing only the class declaration (`Public Class GamePiece`) and the `End Class` statements. Inside the class, you have added an array called `PieceTypes` that gives a name to each of the different types of game pieces that will be added to the game board. There are two straight pieces, four angled pieces, and an empty tile with a background image on it, but no pipe. The array is declared as `Shared`, because all instances of the `GamePiece` class will share the same array. A `Shared` member can be updated at execution time, but all members of the class will see the same changes.

Second, you have declared two integer constants that specify the height and width of an individual playing piece in pixels, along with two variables that specify the array index of the last piece that can be placed on the board (`MaxPlayablePieceIndex`) and of the fake `Empty` piece.

Next are four integers that describe the layout of the texture file you are using. There is a one-pixel offset from the left and top edge of the texture (the one-pixel border), and a single pixel of padding between each sprite on the sprite sheet.

> **Constants versus numeric literals**
>
> Why create constants for things, such as `PieceWidth` and `PieceHeight`, and have to type them out when you could simply use the number 40 in their place? If you need to go back and resize your pieces later, you only need to change the size in one place, instead of hoping that you find each place in the code where you entered 40, and change them all to something else. Even if you do not change the number in the game you are working on, you may re-use the code for something else later, as having easily changeable parameters will make the job much easier.

There are only two pieces of information that each instance of `GamePiece` will track about itself—the **type** of the piece and any **suffix** associated with the piece. The instance members `_pieceType` and `_pieceSuffix` store these values. We will use the suffix to determine if the pipe that the piece represents is empty or filled with water.

However, these members are declared as `private`, in order to prevent code outside the class from directly altering the values. To allow them to be read but not written to, we create a pair of read-only properties (`PieceType` and `Suffix`), which contain `get` blocks but no `set` blocks. This makes these values accessible in a read-only mode to code outside the `GamePiece` class.

Visual Basic versus C# - property names

It is a common convention in C# code to create a `private` member variable of a class with a lowercase first letter and a `public` property with the same name and an uppercase letter. In the C# version of the GamePiece class, the `_pieceType` and `_pieceSuffix` would be named simply `pieceType` and `suffix`. In Visual Basic, this would clash with the `PieceType` and `Suffix` property names, so the leading underscore (_) is used to differentiate the names.

This naturally leads to the question: *what is a property, anyway*? In some respects, a property behaves like a variable. It can return a value, and some properties can be assigned values like a variable. Under the hood, though, they are a bit more powerful. When the value of a property is set or checked, code can be executed to compute a return value, validate the stored value, or take any number of other actions. Whenever we want our class to provide data to the outside world, properties provide a method to control how that data is presented and modified, while simple `public` variables would not. The two properties we use here are declared `ReadOnly`, meaning we can read the values, but we cannot assign new values to them.

Creating a GamePiece

The only information we need to create an instance of `GamePiece` are the piece type and, potentially, the suffix.

Time for action – building a GamePiece class – constructors

1. Add two constructors to your `GamePiece.vb` file after the declarations:

```
Public Sub New(type As String, suffix As String)
  _pieceType = type
  _pieceSuffix = suffix
End Sub

Public Sub New(type As String)
  _pieceType = type
  _pieceSuffix = ""
End Sub
```

What just happened?

A constructor is run when an instance of the `GamePiece` class is created. By specifying two constructors, we will allow future code to create a `GamePiece`, by specifying a piece type with or without a suffix. If no suffix is specified, an empty suffix is assumed.

Updating a GamePiece

When a GamePiece is updated, you can change the piece type, the suffix, or both.

Time for action – GamePiece class methods – part 1 – updating

1. Add the following methods to the GamePiece class:

```
Public Sub SetPiece(type As String, suffix As String)
  _pieceType = type
  _pieceSuffix = suffix
End Sub

Public Sub SetPiece(type As String)
  SetPiece(type, "")
End Sub

Public Sub AddSuffix(suffix As String)
  If Not _pieceSuffix.Contains(suffix) Then
    _pieceSuffix &= suffix
  End If
End Sub

Public Sub RemoveSufix(suffix As String)
  _pieceSuffix = _pieceSuffix.Replace(suffix, "")
End Sub
```

The first two methods are overloads with the same name, but different parameter lists. In a manner similar to the GamePiece constructors, code that wishes to update a GamePiece can pass it a piece type and, optionally, a suffix.

Additional methods have been added to modify suffixes without changing the pieceType associated with the piece. The AddSuffix() method first checks to see if the piece already contains the suffix. If it does, nothing happens. If it does not, the suffix value passed to the method is added to the _pieceSuffix member variable.

The RemoveSuffix() method uses the Replace() method of the String class to remove the passed suffix from the _pieceSuffix variable.

Rotating pieces

The heart of the Flood Control play mechanic is the ability of the player to rotate pieces on the game board to form continuous pipes. In order to accomplish this, we can build a table that, given an existing piece type and a rotation direction, supplies the name of the piece type after rotation. We can then implement this code as a switch statement:

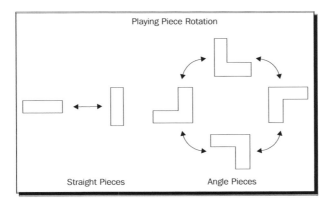

Time for action – GamePiece class methods – part 2 – rotation

1. Add the `RotatePiece()` method to the `GamePiece` class:

```
Public Sub RotatePiece(clockwise As Boolean)
  Select Case _pieceType
    Case "Left,Right"
      _pieceType = "Top,Bottom"
    Case "Top,Bottom"
      _pieceType = "Left,Right"
    Case "Left,Top"
      If (clockwise) Then
        _pieceType = "Top,Right"
      Else
        _pieceType = "Bottom,Left"
      End If
    Case "Top,Right"
      If (clockwise) Then
        _pieceType = "Right,Bottom"
      Else
        _pieceType = "Left,Top"
      End If
    Case "Right,Bottom"
      If (clockwise) Then
        _pieceType = "Bottom,Left"
      Else
```

```
                _pieceType = "Top,Right"
            End If
        Case "Bottom,Left"
            If clockwise Then
                _pieceType = "Left,Top"
            Else
                _pieceType = "Right,Bottom"
            End If
    End Select
End Sub
```

What just happened?

The only information the `RotatePiece()` method needs is a rotation direction. For straight pieces, rotation direction does not matter (a left/right piece will always become a top/bottom piece and vice-versa).

For angled pieces, the piece type is updated based on the rotation direction and the previous screenshot.

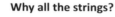

Why all the strings?

It would certainly be reasonable to create constants that represent the various piece positions, instead of fully spelling out things, such as `Bottom,Left` as strings. However, because the Flood Control game is not taxing on the system, the additional processing time required for string manipulation will not impact the game negatively and helps clarify how the logic works, especially when we get to determine which pipes are filled with water.

Pipe connectors

Our `GamePiece` class will need to be able to provide information about the connectors it contains (top, bottom, left, and right) to the rest of the game. Since we have represented the piece types as simple strings, a string comparison will determine what connectors the piece contains.

Time for action – GamePiece class methods – part 3 – connection methods

1. Add the `GetOtherEnds()` method to the `GamePiece` class:

```
Public Function GetOtherEnds(startingEnd As String) As String()
    Dim Opposites As List(Of String) = New List(Of String)()

    For Each pipeEnd As String In _pieceType.Split(CChar(","))
```

```
        If pipeEnd <> startingEnd Then
          Opposites.Add(pipeEnd)
        End If
    Next

  Return Opposites.ToArray()
End Function
```

2.   Add the `HasConnector()` method to the `GamePiece` class:

```
Public Function HasConnector(direction As String) As Boolean
  Return _pieceType.Contains(direction)
End Function
```

What just happened?

The `GetOtherEnds()` method creates an empty `List` object for holding the ends we want to return to the calling code. It then uses the `Split()` method of the `String` class to get each end listed in the `_pieceType`. For example, the `Top,Bottom` piece will return an array with two elements. The first element will contain `Top`, and the second will contain `Bottom`. The comma delimiter will not be returned with either string.

If the end in question is not the same as the `startingEnd` parameter that was passed to the method, it is added to the list. After all of the items in the string have been examined, the list is converted to an array and returned to the calling code.

Type conversion

The `Split()` method of the `String` class accepts a `Char` value, but if we simply supply the comma that we use within quotes (`Split(",")`, for example), the result is itself a `String` value. This would produce a compiler warning, informing us that we have an *implicit conversion from string to char*. We need to be careful that we are passing the right types of values to methods, so we are specifically casting the string to a char value using the `CChar` built-in function. There are a number of these type-conversion functions in Visual Basic that support conversion to various data types, including a `CType` method that accepts the type you wish to convert to as a parameter.

In the previous example, requesting `GetOtherEnds("Top")` from a `GamePiece` with a `_pieceType` value of `Top,Bottom` will return a string array with a single element containing `Bottom`.

We will need this information in a few moments when we have to figure out which pipes are filled with water and which are empty.

The second function, `HasConnector()`, simply returns `true` if the `_pieceType` string contains the string value passed in as the direction parameter. This will allow code outside the `GamePiece` class to determine if the piece has a connector facing in any particular direction.

Sprite sheet coordinates

Because we set up the `PieceTypes` array listing the pieces in the same order they exist on the sprite sheet texture, we can calculate the position of the rectangle to draw from based on the `_pieceType`.

Time for action – GamePiece class methods – part 4 – GetSourceRect

1. Add the `GetSourceRect()` method to the `GamePiece` class:

```
Public Function GetSourceRectangle() As Rectangle
    Dim x As Integer = textureOffsetX
    Dim y As Integer = textureOffsetY

    If _pieceSuffix.Contains("W") Then
      x += PieceWidth + texturePaddingX
    End If

    y += (Array.IndexOf(PieceTypes, _pieceType) *
      (PieceHeight + texturePaddingY))

    Return New Rectangle(x, y, PieceWidth, PieceHeight)
End Function
```

What just happened?

Initially, the x and y variables are set to the `textureOffsets` that are listed in the `GamePiece` class declaration. This means they will both start with a value of 1.

Because the sprite sheet is organized with a single type of pipe on each row, the x coordinate of the rectangle is the easiest to determine. If the `_pieceSuffix` variable does not contain a W (signifying that the piece is filled with water), the x coordinate will simply remain 1.

If `_pieceSuffix` does contain the letter W (indicating the pipe is filled), the width of a piece (40 pixels), along with the padding between the pieces (1 pixel), are added to the x coordinate of the source rectangle. This shifts the x coordinate from a 1 to a value of 1 + 40 + 1, or 42, which corresponds to the second column of images on the sprite sheet.

To determine the y coordinate for the source rectangle, `Array.IndexOf(PieceTypes, _pieceType)` is used to locate the `_pieceType` within the `PieceTypes` array. The index that is returned represents the position of the tile on the sprite sheet (because the array is organized in the same order as the pieces on the image). For example, `Left,Right` returns `0`, while `Top,Bottom` returns `1`, and `Empty` returns `6`.

The value of this index is multiplied by the height of a game piece plus the padding between pieces. For our sprite sheet, an index of `2` (the `Left,Top` piece) would be multiplied by `41` (`PieceHeight` of `40` plus `texturePaddingY` of `1`), resulting in a value of `82` being added to the y variable.

Finally, the new rectangle is returned, comprised of the calculated x and y coordinates and the pre-defined width and height of a piece:

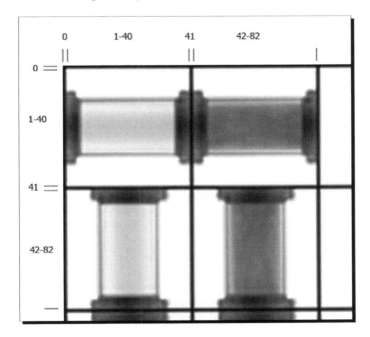

The GameBoard class

Now that we have a way to represent pieces in memory, the next logical step is to create a way to represent an entire board of playing pieces.

The game board is a two-dimensional array of `GamePiece` objects, and we can build in some additional functionality to allow our code to interact with pieces on the game board by their `X` and `Y` coordinates.

The GameBoard class needs to:

◆ Store a GamePiece object for each square on the game board

◆ Provide methods for code using the GameBoard to update individual pieces, by passing calls through to the underlying GamePiece instances

◆ Randomly assign a piece type to a GamePiece

◆ Set and clear the "Filled with water" flags on individual GamePieces

◆ Determine which pipes should be filled with water, based on their position and orientation, and mark them as filled

◆ Return lists of potentially scoring water chains to code using the GameBoard

Time for action – creating the GameBoard.cs class

1. As you did to create the GamePiece class, right-click on **Flood Control** in **Solution Explorer** and select **Add | Class...**. Name the new class file GameBoard.vb.

2. Add the following declarations to the GameBoard class:

```
Private rand As New Random()

Public Const GameBoardWidth As Integer = 7
Public Const GameBoardHeight As Integer = 9

Private playingPieces As Texture2D
Private emptyPiece As Rectangle

Private boardSquares(GameBoardWidth, GameBoardHeight) As GamePiece

Private waterTracker As New List(Of Vector2)()
```

What just happened?

We used the Random class in SquareChase to generate random numbers. Since we will need to randomly generate pieces to add to the game board, we need an instance of Random in the GameBoard class.

The Texture2D (playingPieces) and the Rectangle (emptyPiece) will be passed in when the class is created and hold the sprite sheet used to draw the board and the location of the sheet's empty piece square.

The two constants and the `boardSquares` array provide the storage mechanism for the `GamePiece` objects that make up the `8x10` piece board. Note that since arrays start counting at `0` instead of `1`, we use numbers for the width and height that are one lower than the actual number of board squares. This is a personal preference, but we will be doing a lot of looping over the items in the `boardSquares` array, and we can either add a `-1` to all of the references to our width and height, or declare them as one item smaller to take zero-based arrays into account.

> **Visual Basic arrays**
>
> Visual Basic arrays are a bit quirky in order to maintain some compatibility with pre-.NET versions of VB. In prior versions of VB, arrays could be designated as starting with either element 0 or element 1. If you declared an array with 5 elements when you had your `Option Base` set to 0, you actually got 6 elements, numbered 0 through 5. Visual Basic .NET no longer allows arrays to be one-based, but does continue to allocate the extra array element at the end of the array just like older versions did. For this reason, our code will not actually fail if we had our width and height set to 8 and 10, but it would produce some strange results. Go ahead and try it out after you have completed the chapter!

Finally, a list of `Vector2` objects is declared that we will use to identify scoring pipe combinations. The `List` class is one of the .NET Framework's generic collection classes – classes that support the `Of` notation that we first saw when loading a texture for `SquareChase`. Each of the `Collection` classes can be used to store multiple items of the same type, with different methods to access the entries in the collection. We will use several of the `Collection` classes in our projects. The `List` class is much like an array, except that we can add any number of values at runtime, and remove values in the `List`, if necessary.

A `Vector2` is a structure defined by the XNA framework that holds two floating point (single) values, `X` and `Y`. Together, the two values represent a vector pointing in any direction from an imaginary origin (`0, 0`) point. We will use `Vector2` structures to represent the locations on our game board in Flood Control and off-setting all of our additional drawing based on this location.

Creating the game board

If we were to try to use any of the elements in the `boardSquares` array at this point, we would get a `Null Reference` exception, because none of the `GamePiece` objects in the array have actually been created yet.

Time for action – initializing the game board

1. Add a constructor to the `GameBoard` class:

```
Public Sub New(pieceTexture As Texture2D, emptyArea As Rectangle)
  playingPieces = pieceTexture
  emptyPiece = emptyArea
  ClearBoard()
End Sub
```

2. Add the `ClearBoard()` helper method to the `GameBoard` class:

```
Public Sub ClearBoard()
  Dim x, y As Integer
  For x = 0 To GameBoardWidth
    For y = 0 To GameBoardHeight
      boardSquares(x, y) = New GamePiece("Empty")
    Next
  Next
End Sub
```

What just happened?

When a new instance of the `GameBoard` class is created, we store the texture and rectangle values that we will need for drawing, and the constructor calls the `ClearBoard()` helper method, which simply creates 80 empty game pieces and assigns them to each element in the array.

Helper methods

Why not simply put the two `for` loops that clear the board into the `GameBoard` constructor? Splitting work up into methods that accomplish a single purpose greatly helps to keep your code both readable and maintainable. Additionally, by splitting `ClearBoard()` out as its own method, we can call it separately from the constructor. When we add increasing difficulty levels in *Chapter 3, Flood Control - Smoothing Out the Rough Edges*, we will make use of this call when a new level starts.

Updating GamePieces

The `boardSquares` array in the `GameBoard` class is declared as a `private` member, meaning that code that uses the `GameBoard` will not have direct access to the pieces contained on the board.

In order for code in our `Game1` class to interact with a `GamePiece`, we will need to create `public` methods in the `GameBoard` class that expose the pieces in `boardSquares`.

Time for action – manipulating the GameBoard

1. Add `public` methods to the `GameBoard` class to interact with `GamePieces`:

```
Public Sub RotatePiece(x As Integer, y As Integer,
  clockwise As Boolean)
    boardSquares(x, y).RotatePiece(clockwise)
End Sub


Public Function GetSourceRect(
  x As Integer,
    y As Integer) As Rectangle
    Return boardSquares(x, y).GetSourceRectangle()
End Function


Public Function GetSquare(x As Integer, y As Integer) As String
    Return boardSquares(x, y).PieceType
End Function


Public Sub SetSquare(x As Integer, y As Integer,
  pieceType As String)
    boardSquares(x, y).SetPiece(pieceType)
End Sub


Public Function HasConnector(x As Integer, y As Integer,
  direction As String) As Boolean
    Return boardSquares(x, y).HasConnector(direction)
End Function


Public Sub RandomPiece(x As Integer, y As Integer)
    boardSquares(x, y).SetPiece(GamePiece.PieceTypes(
      rand.Next(0, GamePiece.MaxPlayablePieceIndex + 1)))
End Sub
```

What just happened?

`RotatePiece()`, `GetSourceRect()`, `GetSquare()`, `SetSquare()`, and
`HasConnector()` methods simply locate the appropriate `GamePiece` within the
`boardSquares` array and pass on the function request to the piece.

The `RandomPiece()` method uses the `rand` object to get a random value from the
`PieceTypes` array and assigns it to a `GamePiece`. It is important to remember that with
the `Random.Next()` method overload used here, the second parameter is non-inclusive. In
order to generate a random number from 0 through 5, the second parameter needs to be 6.

Subs, functions, and methods

Method is the generic term for a callable code block inside a class. Both **Subs** and **Functions** are methods. The difference between the two is that a Function returns a value, while a Sub does not.

Filling in the gaps

Whenever the player completes a scoring chain, the pieces in that chain are removed from the board. Any pieces above them fall down into the vacated spots and new pieces are generated.

Time for action – filling in the gaps

1. Add the `FillFromAbove()` method to the `GameBoard` class.

```
Public Sub FillFromAbove(x As Integer, y As Integer)
  Dim rowLookup As Integer = y - 1

  Do While (rowLookup >= 0)
    If GetSquare(x, rowLookup) <> "Empty" Then
      SetSquare(x, y, GetSquare(x, rowLookup))
      SetSquare(x, rowLookup, "Empty")
      rowLookup = -1
    End If
    rowLookup -= 1
  Loop
End Sub
```

What just happened?

Given a square to fill, `FillFromAbove()` looks at the piece directly above to see if it is marked as `Empty`. If it is, the method will subtract one from `rowLookup` and start over until it reaches the top of the board. If no non-empty pieces are found when the top of the board is reached, the method does nothing and exits.

When a non-empty piece is found, it is copied to the destination square, and the copied piece is changed to an empty piece. The `rowLookup` variable is set to -1 to ensure that the loop does not continue to run.

Generating new pieces

We can create a single method that will fill any empty spaces on the game board, use it when the game begins, and when pieces are removed from the board after scoring.

Time for action – generating new pieces

1. Add the `GenerateNewPieces()` method to the `GameBoard` class:

```
Public Sub GenerateNewPieces(dropSquare As Boolean)
  Dim x, y As Integer

  If dropSquare Then
    For x = 0 To GameBoardWidth
      For y = GameBoardHeight To 0 Step -1
        If GetSquare(x, y) = "Empty" Then
          FillFromAbove(x, y)
        End If
      Next
    Next
  End If

  For y = 0 To GameBoardHeight
    For x = 0 To GameBoardWidth
      If GetSquare(x, y) = "Empty" Then
        RandomPiece(x, y)
      End If
    Next
  Next

End Sub
```

What just happened?

When `GenerateNewPieces()` is called with `true` passed as `dropSquares`, the looping logic processes one column at a time from the bottom up. By using the *step 1* in the `for` loop for the Y coordinate, we can make the loop run backwards instead of the default forward direction. When it finds an empty square, it calls `FillFromAbove()` to pull a filled square from above into that location.

The reason the processing order is important here is that by filling a lower square from a higher position, that higher position will become empty. It, in turn, will need to be filled from above.

After the holes are filled (or if `dropSquares` is set to `false`), `GenerateNewPieces()` examines each square in `boardSquares` and asks it to generate random pieces for each square that contains an empty piece.

Water-filled pipes

Whether or not a pipe is filled with water, it is managed separately from its orientation. Rotating a single pipe could change the water-filled status of any number of other pipes, without changing their rotation.

Instead of filling and emptying individual pipes, it is easier to empty all of the pipes and then re-fill the pipes that need to be marked as having water in them.

Time for action – water in the pipes

1. Add a method to the `GameBoard` class to clear the water marker from all pieces:

```
Public Sub ResetWater()
  Dim x, y As Integer
  For x = 0 To GameBoardWidth
    For y = 0 To GameBoardHeight
      boardSquares(x, y).RemoveSufix("W")
    Next
  Next
End Sub
```

2. Add a method to the `GameBoard` class to fill an individual piece with water:

```
Public Sub FillPiece(x As Integer, y As Integer)
  boardSquares(x, y).AddSuffix("W")
End Sub
```

What just happened?

The `ResetWater()` method simply loops through each item in the `boardSquares` array and removes the `W` suffix from the `GamePiece`. Similarly, to fill a piece with water, the `FillPiece()` method adds the `W` suffix to the `GamePiece`. Recall that by having a `W` suffix, the `GetSourceRect()` method of `GamePiece` shifts the source rectangle one tile to the right on the sprite sheet, returning the image for a pipe filled with water, instead of an empty pipe.

Propagating water

Now that we can fill individual pipes with water, we can write the logic to determine which pipes should be filled depending on their orientation.

Time for action – making the connection

1. Add the `PropagateWater()` method to the `GameBoard` class:

```
Public Sub PropagateWater(x As Integer, y As Integer,
  fromDirection As String)

    If (y >= 0) And (y <= GameBoardHeight) And
      (x >= 0) And (x <= GameBoardWidth) Then
      If boardSquares(x, y).HasConnector(fromDirection) And
        Not (boardSquares(x, y).PieceSuffix.Contains("W")) Then
        FillPiece(x, y)
        waterTracker.Add(New Vector2(x, y))
        For Each pipeEnd As String In
          boardSquares(x, y).GetOtherEnds(fromDirection)
          Select Case pipeEnd
            Case "Left"
              PropagateWater(x - 1, y, "Right")
            Case "Right"
              PropagateWater(x + 1, y, "Left")
            Case "Top"
              PropagateWater(x, y - 1, "Bottom")
            Case "Bottom"
              PropagateWater(x, y + 1, "Top")
          End Select
        Next
      End If
    End If
End Sub
```

2. Add the `GetWaterChain()` method to the `GameBoard` class:

```
Public Function GetWaterChain(y As Integer) As List(Of Vector2)
  waterTracker.Clear()
  PropagateWater(0, y, "Left")
  Return waterTracker
End Function
```

What just happened?

Together, `GetWaterChain()` and `PropagateWater()` are the keys to the entire Flood Control game, so understanding how they work is vital. When the game code wants to know if the player has completed a scoring row, it will call the `GetWaterChain()` method once for each row on the game board:

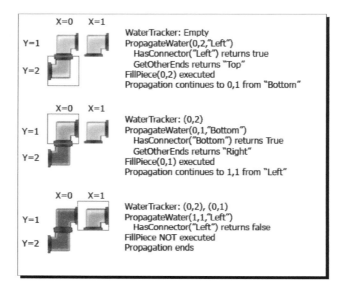

The `WaterTracker` list is cleared and `GetWaterChain()` calls `PropagateWater()` for the first square in the row, indicating that the water is coming from the `Left` direction.

The `PropagateWater()` method checks to make sure that the x and y coordinates passed to it exist within the board and, if they do, it checks to see if the piece at that location has a connector matching the `fromDirection` parameter and that the piece is not already filled with water. If all of these conditions are met, that piece gets filled with water and added to the `WaterTracker` list.

Finally, `PropagateWater()` gets a list of all other directions that the piece contains (in other words, all directions the piece contains that do not match `fromDirection`). For each of these directions `PropagateWater()` recursively calls itself, passing in the new x and y location as well as the direction the water is coming from.

Building the game

We now have the component classes we need to build the Flood Control game, so it is time to bring the pieces together in the `Game1` class.

Declarations

We only need a handful of game-wide declarations to manage things, such as the game board, the player's score, and the game state.

Time for action – Game1 declarations

1. Double click on the `Game1.vb` file in **Solution Explorer** to reactivate the `Game1.vb` code file window.

2. Add the following declarations to the `Game1` class member declaration area:

    ```
    Private _gameBoard As GameBoard
    Private gameBoardDisplayOrigin As New Vector2(70, 89)
    Private playerScore As Integer = 0

    Private Enum GameStates
      TitleScreen
      Playing
    End Enum

    Private gameState As GameStates = GameStates.TitleScreen

    Private EmptyPiece As Rectangle = New Rectangle(1, 247, 40, 40)

    Private Const MinTimeSinceLastInput As Single = 0.25
    Private timeSinceLastInput As Single = 0
    ```

What just happened?

The `_gameBoard` instance of `GameBoard` will hold all of the playing pieces, while the `gameBoardDisplayOrigin` vector points to where on the screen the board will be drawn. Using a vector like this makes it easy to move the board in the event that you wish to change the layout of our game screen.

As we did in `SquareChase`, we store the player's score and will display it in the window title bar.

In order to implement a simple game state mechanism, we define two game states. When in the `TitleScreen` state, the game's title image will be displayed and the game will wait until the user presses the *Space* bar to start the game. The state will then switch to `Playing`, which will display the game board and allow the user to play.

Enumerations (Enums)

An Enum, or enumeration, is a list of named values that we are using to build a custom type. Variables of this type can then be declared and assigned any of the values from the enumerator list. Using an enumerator instead of, say, assigning numbers to each state (that is, 1 is at the `Title Screen`, 2 is `Playing`) allows you to keep your code more readable. It also provides some basic error detection, because you will get a compiler error if you try to assign a value not on the enumerator list to the variable.

If you look at the sprite sheet for the game, the pipe images themselves do not cover the entire `40x40` pixel area of a game square. In order to provide a background, an empty tile image will be drawn in each square first. The `EmptyPiece` rectangle is a convenient pointer to where the empty background is located on the sprite sheet.

Just as we used an accumulating timer in `SquareChase` to determine how long to leave a square in place before moving it to a new location, we will use the same timing mechanism to make sure that a single-click by the user does not send a game piece spinning unpredictably. Remember that the `Update()` method will be executing up to `60`-times-each-second, so slowing the pace of user input is necessary to make the game respond in a way that feels natural.

Initialization

Before we can use the `_gameBoard` instance, it needs to be initialized. We will also need to enable the mouse cursor.

Time for action – updating the Initialize() method

1. Update the `Initialize()` method to include the following:

```
Me.IsMouseVisible = True
Me.graphics.PreferredBackBufferWidth = 800
Me.graphics.PreferredBackBufferHeight = 600
graphics.ApplyChanges()
```

2. Update the `LoadContent()` method to include the following after three texture files have been loaded:

```
_gameBoard = New GameBoard(playingPieces, EmptyPiece)
```

What just happened?

After making the mouse cursor visible, we set the size of the BackBuffer to 800x600 pixels. On Windows, this will size the game window to 800x600 pixels as well.

The constructor for the GameBoard class calls the ClearBoard() method, so each of the pieces on the _gameBoard instance will be set to Empty.

The Draw() method – the title screen

In the declarations section, we established two possible game states. The first (and default) state is GameStates.TitleScreen, indicating that the game should not be processing actual game play, but should instead be displaying the game's logo and waiting for the user to begin the game.

Time for action – drawing the screen – the title screen

1. Modify the Draw() method of Game1 to include the code necessary to draw the game's title screen after GraphicsDevice.Clear(Color.CornflowerBlue):

```
If gameState = GameStates.TitleScreen Then
  spriteBatch.Begin()
  spriteBatch.Draw(titleScreen,
    New Rectangle(0, 0,
      Me.Window.ClientBounds.Width,
      Me.Window.ClientBounds.Height),
    Color.White)
  spriteBatch.End()
End If
```

2. Run the game and verify that the title screen is displayed. You will not be able to start the game yet, however, as we have not written the Update() method yet.

3. Stop the game by pressing *Alt + F4*.

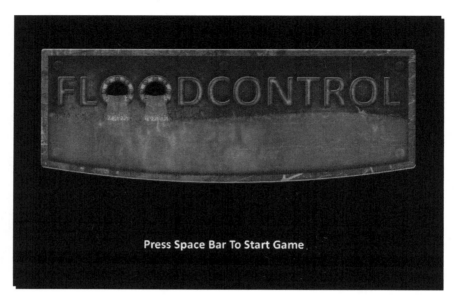

What just happened?

The title screen is drawn with a single call to the Draw() method of the spriteBatch object. Since the title screen will cover the entire display, a rectangle is created that is equal to the width and height of the game window.

The Draw() method – the play screen

Finally, we are ready to display the playing pieces on the screen. We will accomplish this by using a simple loop to display all of the playing pieces in the _gameBoard object.

Time for action – drawing the screen – the play screen

1. In the GameBoard class, add the Draw() method to allow the game board to draw itself:

```
Public Sub Draw(
    spriteBatch As SpriteBatch,
    DisplayOrigin As Vector2)

    Dim x As Integer, y As Integer

    For x = 0 To GameBoardWidth
```

```
            For y = 0 To GameBoardHeight
              Dim pixelX As Integer =
                CInt(DisplayOrigin.X +
                (x * GamePiece.PieceWidth))
              Dim pixelY As Integer =
                CInt(DisplayOrigin.Y +
                (y * GamePiece.PieceHeight))

              spriteBatch.Draw(
                playingPieces,
                New Rectangle(
                  pixelX,
                  pixelY,
                  GamePiece.PieceWidth,
                GamePiece.PieceHeight),
                EmptyPiece,
              Color.White)

              spriteBatch.Draw(
                playingPieces,
                New Rectangle(
                  pixelX,
                  pixelY,
                  GamePiece.PieceWidth,
                GamePiece.PieceHeight),
              GetSourceRect(x, y),
            Color.White)
          Next
        Next
      End Sub
```

2. Update the `Draw()` method of the `Game1` class to add the code to call the `Draw()` method of `GameBoard`. Place this code after the code that draws the title screen:

```
If gameState = GameStates.Playing Then
  spriteBatch.Begin()
  spriteBatch.Draw(background,
        New Rectangle(0, 0,
                      Me.Window.ClientBounds.Width,
                      Me.Window.ClientBounds.Height),
        Color.White)
    _gameBoard.Draw(spriteBatch, gameBoardDisplayOrigin)

    Me.Window.Title = playerScore.ToString()

    spriteBatch.End()
End If
```

What just happened?

The `GameBoard` class will be responsible for drawing itself, so we begin by creating a `Draw()` method that accepts a `SpriteBatch` to use for drawing, and a `Vector2` pointing to the upper-left corner of the drawing area. The method loops through each of the squares on the `gameboard` and calculates the `X` and `Y` location, where the piece should be drawn.

Since both `x` and `y` begin at `0`, the `(x * GamePiece.PieceWidth)` and `(y * GamePiece.PieceHeight)` will also be equal to `0`, resulting in the first square being drawn at the location specified by the `gameBoardDisplayOrigin` vector.

As `x` increments, each new piece is drawn `40` pixels further to the right than the previous piece. After a row has been completed, the `y` value increments, and a new row is started `40` pixels below the previous row.

The first `spriteBatch.Draw()` call uses `Rectangle(pixelX, pixelY, GamePiece.PieceWidth, GamePiece.PieceHeight)` as the destination rectangle and `EmptyPiece` as the source rectangle. Recall that we added this rectangle to our declarations area as a shortcut to the location of the empty piece on the sprite sheet.

The second `spriteBatch.Draw()` call uses the same destination rectangle, overlaying the playing piece image onto the empty piece that was just drawn. It asks `_gameBoard` to provide the source rectangle for the piece it needs to draw.

The `Game1` portion of the code to draw the game board begins exactly like the code to draw the title screen. Since we are using a background image that takes up the full screen, we draw it exactly the same way as the title screen. After the background has been displayed, we call the method we just created in the `GameBoard` class to draw the board.

The player's score is displayed in the window title bar, and `spriteBatch.End()` is called to finish up the `Draw()` method.

Keeping score

Longer chains of filled water pipes score the player more points. However, if we were to simply assign a single point to each piece in the pipe chain, there would be no scoring advantage to making longer chains versus quickly making shorter chains.

Time for action – scores and scoring chains

1. Add a method to the `Game1` class to calculate a score based on the number of pipes used:

```
Private Function DetermineScore(squareCount As Integer) As Integer
    Return CInt(
```

```
            ((Math.Pow((squareCount / 5), 2) + squareCount) * 10))
      End Function
```

2. Add a method to evaluate a chain to determine if it scores and process it:

```
Private Sub CheckScoringChain(WaterChain As List(Of Vector2))
   If (WaterChain.Count > 0) Then
      Dim LastPipe As Vector2 = WaterChain(WaterChain.Count - 1)

      If LastPipe.X = gameBoard.GameBoardWidth Then
        If _gameBoard.HasConnector(
           CInt(LastPipe.X),
           CInt(LastPipe.Y),
         "Right") Then
           playerScore += DetermineScore(WaterChain.Count)
           For Each thisPipe As Vector2 In WaterChain
             _gameBoard.SetSquare(
               CInt(thisPipe.X),
               CInt(thisPipe.Y),
             "Empty")
           Next
         End If
       End If
     End If
End Sub
```

What just happened?

`DetermineScore()` accepts the number of squares in a scoring chain and returns a score value for that chain. The number of squares in the chain is divided by 5, and that number is squared. The initial number of squares is added to the result, and the final amount is multiplied by 10.

```
   Score = (((Squares / 5) ^ 2) + Squares) * 10
```

For example, a minimum scoring chain would be 8 squares (forming a straight line across the board). This chain would result in *1 squared plus 8 times 10*, or 90 points. If a chain had 18 squares, the result would be *3 squared plus 18 times 10*, or 270 points. This scoring equation makes longer scoring chains (especially increments of five squares) award much higher scores than a series of shorter chains.

The `CheckScoringChain()` method makes sure that there are entries in the `WaterChain` list, and then examines the last piece in the chain and checks to see if it has an X value of 7 (the right-most column on the board). If it does, the `HasConnector()` method is checked to see if the last pipe has a connector to the right, indicating that it completes a chain across the board.

After updating `playerScore` for the scoring row, `CheckScoringChain()` sets all of the pieces in the scoring chain to `Empty`. They will be refilled by a subsequent call to the `GenerateNewPieces()` method.

Input handling

The player interacts with Flood Control using the mouse. For readability reasons, we will create a helper method that deals with mouse input and call it when appropriate from the `Update()` method.

Time for action – handling mouse input

1. Add the `HandleMouseInput()` helper method to the `Game1` class:

```
Private Sub HandleMouseInput(mouseInfo As MouseState)
  Dim x, y As Integer

  x = mouseInfo.X - CInt(gameBoardDisplayOrigin.X)
  y = mouseInfo.Y - CInt(gameBoardDisplayOrigin.Y)

  x = x \ GamePiece.PieceWidth
  y = y \ GamePiece.PieceHeight

  If (x >= 0) And (x <= GameBoard.GameBoardWidth) And
    (y >= 0) And (y <= GameBoard.GameBoardHeight) Then
    If mouseInfo.LeftButton = ButtonState.Pressed Then
      _gameBoard.RotatePiece(x, y, False)
      timeSinceLastInput = 0
    End If
    If mouseInfo.RightButton = ButtonState.Pressed Then
      _gameBoard.RotatePiece(x, y, True)
      timeSinceLastInput = 0
    End If
  End If
End Sub
```

What just happened?

The `MouseState` class reports the X and Y position of the mouse relative to the upper-left corner of the window. What we really need to know is what square on the game board the mouse was over.

We break the mouse position into X and Y components and subtract the corresponding parts of `gameBoardDisplayOrigin` from them. Next, we use the **Integer Division** operator (\) to divide the result by the size of a game board square.

If the resulting X and Y locations fall within the game board, the left and right mouse buttons are checked. If the left button is pressed, the piece is rotated counter clockwise. The right button rotates the piece clockwise. In either case, the input delay timer is reset to 0, since input was just processed.

Letting the player play!

Only one more section to go and you can begin playing Flood Control. We need to code the Update() method to tie together all of the game logic we have created so far.

Time for action – letting the player play

1. Modify the Update() method of Game1.vb, by adding the following before the call to MyBase.Update(gameTime):

```
Select Case gameState
  Case GameStates.TitleScreen
    If Keyboard.GetState().IsKeyDown(Keys.Space) Then
      _gameBoard.ClearBoard()
      _gameBoard.GenerateNewPieces(False)
      playerScore = 0
      gameState = GameStates.Playing
    End If

    Case GameStates.Playing
      timeSinceLastInput +=
      (CSng(gameTime.ElapsedGameTime.TotalSeconds))

      If timeSinceLastInput >= MinTimeSinceLastInput Then
        HandleMouseInput(Mouse.GetState())
      End If

      _gameBoard.ResetWater()

      Dim y As Integer

      For y = 0 To GameBoard.GameBoardHeight
        CheckScoringChain(_gameBoard.GetWaterChain(y))
      Next

      _gameBoard.GenerateNewPieces(True)
  End Select
```

What just happened?

The Update() method performs two different functions, depending on the current gameState value. If the game is in TitleScreen state, Update() examines the keyboard, waiting for the *Space* bar to be pressed. When it is, Update() clears the _gameBoard, generates a new set of pieces, resets the player's score, and changes gameState to Playing.

While in the Playing state, Update() accumulates time in timeSinceLastInput in order to pace the game play properly. If enough time has passed, the HandleMouseInput() method is called to allow the player to rotate game pieces.

Update() then calls ResetWater() to clear the water flags for all pieces on the game board. This is followed by a loop that processes each row, starting at the top and working downward, using CheckScoringChain() and GetWaterChain(), to fill any pieces that should have water in them and check the results of each row for completed chains.

Finally, GenerateNewPieces() is called with the true parameter for dropSquares, which will cause GenerateNewPieces() to fill the empty holes from the squares above, and then generate new pipes to replace the empty squares.

Play the game

You now have all of the components assembled and can run Flood Control and play!

Summary

You now have a working Flood Control game. In this chapter, we have looked at:

- Adding content objects to your project and loading them into textures at runtime using an instance of the ContentManager class
- Dividing code up into classes that represent objects in the game
- Building a recursive method
- Using the SpriteBatch.Draw() method to display images
- Dividing the Update() and Draw() code into different units, based on the current game state

In *Chapter 3*, *Flood Control - Smoothing Out the Rough Edges*, we will spruce up the Flood Control game, adding animation by modifying the parameters of the SpriteBatch.Draw() method and creating text effects in order to make the game visually more appealing.

3
Flood Control – Smoothing Out the Rough Edges

While playable, **Flood Control** *in its current form is rather rough. When the player clicks on game pieces, they simply flop to their new orientation. Completed rows vanish without a trace, being filled in so rapidly that it is hard to tell if they actually disappeared at all. The game never ends! Once you have started, you can play forever, not worrying about the underwater research lab actually filling up with water.*

In this chapter, we will address these issues by:

- Animating the rotation of pieces when manipulated by the player
- Gradually fading out pieces of completed scoring chains
- Animating the falling of pieces into place on the board
- Implementing the flooding of the dome and adding increasing difficulty levels
- Adding a `SpriteFont` to the game and displaying the current level and score in their appropriate positions on the screen

All of these enhancements will give the player a better game experience, as well as give us the opportunity to learn more about how the `SpriteBatch` class can be used for animation and text display.

Animated pieces

We will define three different types of animated pieces: rotating, falling, and fading. The animation for each of these types will be accomplished by altering the parameters of the `SpriteBatch.Draw()` call.

Classes for animated pieces

In order to represent the three types of animated pieces, we will create three new classes. Each of these classes will inherit from the `GamePiece` class, meaning they will contain all of the methods and members of the `GamePiece` class but will add additional information to support the animation.

Child classes

Child classes inherit all of their parent's members and methods. The `RotatingPiece` class can refer to the `_pieceType` and `_pieceSuffix` of the piece, without recreating them within `RotatingPiece` itself. Additionally, child classes can extend the functionality of their base class, adding new methods and properties, or overriding old ones. In fact, `Game1` itself is a child of the `Micrsoft.Xna.Game` class, which is why all of the methods we use (`Update()`, `Draw()`, `LoadContent()`, and so on) are declared with the `Overrides` modifier.

Let's begin by creating the class we will use for rotating pieces.

Time for action – rotating pieces

1. Open your existing **Flood Control** project in Visual Studio, if it is not already active.

2. Add a new class to the project called `RotatingPiece`.

3. Under the class declaration (`Public Class RotatingPiece`), add the following line:

   ```
   Inherits GamePiece
   ```

4. Add the following declarations to the `RotatingPiece` class:

   ```
   Public Clockwise As Boolean
   Public Shared RotationRate As Single = (MathHelper.PiOver2/10)
   Private _rotationAmount As Single
   Public rotationTicksRemaining As Single = 10
   ```

5. Add a property to retrieve the current `RotationAmount`:

```
Public ReadOnly Property RotationAmount As Single
    Get
        If Clockwise Then
            Return _rotationAmount
        Else
            Return (MathHelper.Pi * 2) - _rotationAmount
        End If
    End Get
End Property
```

6. Add a constructor for the `RotatingPiece` class as follows:

```
Public Sub New(type As String, clockwise As Boolean)
    MyBase.New(type)
    Me.Clockwise = clockwise
End Sub
```

7. Add a method to update the piece as follows:

```
Public Sub UpdatePiece()
    _rotationAmount += RotationRate
    rotationTicksRemaining =
        CInt(MathHelper.Max(0, rotationTicksRemaining - 1))
End Sub
```

What just happened?

In *step 3*, we modified the `RotatingPiece` class by adding `Inherits GamePiece` on the line after the class declaration. This indicates to Visual Basic that the `RotatingPiece` class is a child of the `GamePiece` class.

The `Clockwise` variable stores a true value if the piece will be rotating clockwise, and false if the rotation is counter clockwise.

When a game piece is rotated, it will turn a total of 90 degrees (or pi/2 radians) over 10 animation frames. The `MathHelper` class provides a number of constants to represent commonly used numbers, with `MathHelper.PiOver2` being equal to the number of radians in a 90 degree angle. We divide this constant by 10 and store the result as the `rotationRate` for use later. This number will be added to the `_rotationAmount` `single`, which will be referenced when the animated piece is drawn.

Working with radians

All angular math is handled in radians in XNA. A complete (360 degree) circle contains 2*pi radians. In other words, one radian is equal to about 57.29 degrees. We tend to relate to circles more often in terms of degrees (a right angle being 90 degrees, for example), so if you prefer to work with degrees, you can use the `MathHelper.ToRadians()` method to convert your values when supplying them to XNA classes and methods.

The final declaration, `rotationTicksRemaining`, is reduced by one, each time the piece is updated. When this counter reaches zero, the piece has finished animating.

When the piece is drawn, the `RotationAmount` property is referenced by a `spriteBatch.Draw()` call and returns either the `_rotationAmount` variable (in the case of a clockwise rotation), or 2*pi (a full circle) minus the `_rotationAmount` if the rotation is counter clockwise.

The constructor in *step 6* illustrates how the parameters passed to a constructor can be forwarded to the class' parent constructor via the `MyBase` call. Since the `GamePiece` class has a constructor that accepts a piece type, we can pass that information along to its constructor, while using the second parameter (`clockwise`) to update the `clockwise` member that does not exist in the `GamePiece` class. In this case, since both the `Clockwise` member variable and the `clockwise` parameter have identical names, we specify `Me.Clockwise` to refer to the `clockwise` member of the `RotatingPiece` class. Simply, `clockwise` in this scope refers only to the parameter passed to the constructor.

Me notation

You can see that it is perfectly valid for Visual Basic code to have method parameter names that match the names of class variables, thus potentially hiding the class variables from being used in the method (since referring to the name inside the method will be assumed to refer to the parameter). To ensure that you can always access your class variables even when a parameter name conflicts, you can preface the variable name with `Me.` when referring to the class variable. `Me.` indicates to Visual Basic that the variable you want to use is part of the class and not a local method parameter. In C#, a similar type of notation is used, prefacing class-level members with `this.` to access a hidden variable.

Lastly, the `UpdatePiece()` method simply increases the `_rotationAmount` member, while decreasing the `rotationTicksRemaining` counter (using `MathHelper.Max()` to ensure that the value does not fall below zero).

Time for action – falling pieces

1. Add a new class to the **Flood Control** project called `FallingPiece`.

2. Add the `Inherits` line after the class declaration as follows:

   ```
   Inherits GamePiece
   ```

3. Add the following declarations to the `FallingPiece` class:

   ```
   Public VerticalOffset As Integer
   Public Shared FallRate As Integer = 5
   ```

4. Add a constructor for the `FallingPiece` class:

   ```
   Public Sub New(type As String, verticalOffset As Integer)
       MyBase.New(type)
       Me.VerticalOffset = verticalOffset
   End Sub
   ```

5. Add a method to update the piece:

   ```
   Public Sub UpdatePiece()
       VerticalOffset =
           CInt(MathHelper.Max(0, VerticalOffset - FallRate))
   End Sub
   ```

What just happened?

Simpler than a `RotatingPiece`, a `FallingPiece` is also a child of the `GamePiece` class. A `FallingPiece` has an offset (how high above its final destination it is currently located) and a falling speed (the number of pixels it will move per update).

As with a `RotatingPiece`, the constructor passes the type parameter to its base class constructor, and uses the `verticalOffset` parameter to set the `VerticalOffset` member. Again, we use the `Me.` notation to differentiate the two identifiers of the same name.

Lastly, the `UpdatePiece()` method subtracts `FallRate` from `VerticalOffset`, again using the `MathHelper.Max()` method to ensure that the offset does not fall below zero.

Time for action – fading pieces

1. Add a new class to the **Flood Control** project called `FadingPiece`.

2. Add the following line to indicate that `FadingPiece` also inherits from `GamePiece`:

```
Inherits GamePiece
```

3. Add the following declarations to the `FadingPiece` class:

```
Public AlphaLevel As Single = 1.0
Public Shared AlphaChangeRate As Single = 0.02
```

4. Add a constructor for the `FadingPiece` class as follows:

```
Public Sub New(type As String, suffix As String)
    MyBase.New(type, suffix)
End Sub
```

5. Add a method to update the piece:

```
Public Sub UpdatePiece()
    AlphaLevel = MathHelper.Max(0, AlphaLevel - AlphaChangeRate)
End Sub
```

What just happened?

The simplest of our animated pieces, the `FadingPiece` only requires an alpha value (which always starts at `1.0f`, or fully opaque) and a rate of change. The `FadingPiece` constructor simply passes the parameters along to the base constructor.

When a `FadingPiece` is updated, `alphaLevel` is reduced by `alphaChangeRate`, making the piece more transparent.

Managing animated pieces

Now that we can create animated pieces, it will be the responsibility of the `GameBoard` class to keep track of them. In order to do that, we will define a `Dictionary` object for each type of piece.

A `Dictionary` is a collection object similar to a `List`, except that instead of being organized by an index number, a `Dictionary` consists of a set of key and value pairs. In an array or a `List`, you might access an entity by referencing its index as in `dataValues(2) = 12`. With a `Dictionary`, the index is replaced with your desired key type. Most commonly, this will be a string value. This way, you can do something like `fruitColors("Apple")="red"`.

Time for action – updating GameBoard to support animated pieces

1. In the declarations section of the GameBoard class, add three Dictionaries, shown as follows:

```
Public FallingPieces As Dictionary(Of String, FallingPiece) =
    New Dictionary(Of String, FallingPiece)
Public RotatingPieces As Dictionary(Of String, RotatingPiece) =
    New Dictionary(Of String, RotatingPiece)
Public FadingPieces As Dictionary(Of String, FadingPiece) =
    New Dictionary(Of String, FadingPiece)
```

2. Add methods to the GameBoard class to create new falling piece entries in the Dictionaries:

```
Public Sub AddFallingPiece(x As Integer, y As Integer,
                           type As String, verticalOffset As
Integer)
    FallingPieces.Add(
        x.ToString() + "_" + y.ToString(),
        New FallingPiece(type, verticalOffset))
End Sub


Public Sub AddRotatingPiece(x As Integer, y As Integer,
                            type As String, clockwise As Boolean)
    RotatingPieces.Add(
        x.ToString() + "_" + y.ToString(),
        New RotatingPiece(type, clockwise))
End Sub


Public Sub AddFadingPiece(x As Integer, y As Integer, type As
String)
    FadingPieces.Add(
        x.ToString() + "_" + y.ToString(),
        New FadingPiece(type, "W"))
End Sub
```

3. Add the ArePiecesAnimating() method to the GameBoard class:

```
Public Function ArePiecesAnimating() As Boolean
    If (FallingPieces.Count +
        FadingPieces.Count +
        RotatingPieces.Count) = 0 Then
        Return False
    Else
```

```
            Return True
        End If
    End Function
```

4. Add the `UpdateFadingPieces()` method to the `GameBoard` class:

```
Public Sub UpdateFadingPieces()
    Dim RemoveKeys As Queue(Of String) = New Queue(Of String)

    For Each thisKey As String In FadingPieces.Keys
        FadingPieces(thisKey).UpdatePiece()
        If FadingPieces(thisKey).AlphaLevel = 0 Then
            RemoveKeys.Enqueue(thisKey)
        End If
    Next

    While RemoveKeys.Count > 0
        FadingPieces.Remove(RemoveKeys.Dequeue())
    End While
End Sub
```

5. Add the `UpdateFallingPieces()` method to the `GameBoard` class:

```
Public Sub UpdateFallingPieces()
    Dim RemoveKeys As Queue(Of String) = New Queue(Of String)

    For Each thisKey As String In FallingPieces.Keys
        FallingPieces(thisKey).UpdatePiece()
        If FallingPieces(thisKey).VerticalOffset = 0 Then
            RemoveKeys.Enqueue(thisKey)
        End If
    Next

    While RemoveKeys.Count > 0
        FallingPieces.Remove(RemoveKeys.Dequeue())
    End While
End Sub
```

6. Add the `UpdateRotatingPieces()` method to the `GameBoard` class as follows:

```
Public Sub UpdateRotatingPieces()
    Dim RemoveKeys As Queue(Of String) = New Queue(Of String)

    For Each thisKey As String In RotatingPieces.Keys
        RotatingPieces(thisKey).UpdatePiece()
        If RotatingPieces(thisKey).rotationTicksRemaining = 0 Then
            RemoveKeys.Enqueue(thisKey)
```

```
            End If
      Next

      While RemoveKeys.Count > 0
            RotatingPieces.Remove(RemoveKeys.Dequeue())
      End While
End Sub
```

7. Add the `UpdateAnimatedPieces()` method to the `GameBoard` class as follows:

```
Public Sub UpdateAnimatedPieces()
      If (FadingPieces.Count = 0) Then
            UpdateFallingPieces()
            UpdateRotatingPieces()
      Else
            UpdateFadingPieces()
      End If
End Sub
```

What just happened?

After declaring the three `Dictionary` objects, we have three methods used by the `GameBoard` class to create them when necessary. In each case, the key is built in the form `X_Y`, so an animated piece in column 5 on row 4 will have a key of `5_4`. Each of the three Add... methods simply pass the parameters along to the constructor for the appropriate piece types, after determining the key to use.

When we begin drawing the animated pieces, we want to be sure that animations finish playing before responding to other input or taking other game actions (like creating new pieces). The `ArePiecesAnimating()` method returns `true` if any of the `Dictionary` objects contain entries. If they do, we will not process any more input or fill empty holes on the game board until they have completed.

The `UpdateAnimatedPieces()` method will be called from the game's `Update()` method and is responsible for calling the previous three different update methods (`UpdateFadingPiece()`, `UpdateFallingPiece()`, and `UpdateRotatingPiece()`) for any animated pieces currently on the board. The first line in each of these methods declares a `Queue` object called `RemoveKeys`. We will need this because Visual Basic does not allow you to modify a `Dictionary` (or `List`, or any of the similar *generic collection* objects) while a `for each` loop is processing them.

A `Queue` is yet another generic collection object that works like a line at the bank. People stand in a line and await their turn to be served. When a bank teller is available, the first person in the line transacts his/her business and leaves. The next person then steps forward. This type of processing is known as **FIFO (First In, First Out)**.

Using the `Enqueue()` and `Dequeue()` methods of the `Queue` class, objects can be added to the `Queue` (`Enqueue()`), where they await processing. When we want to deal with an object, we `Dequeue()` the oldest object in the `Queue`, and handle it. `Dequeue()` returns the first object waiting to be processed, which is the oldest object added to the `Queue`.

Collection classes

The .NET Framework provides a number of different *collection* classes, such as the `Dictionary`, `Queue`, `List`, and `Stack` objects. Each of these classes provide different ways to organize and reference the data in them. For information on the various *collection* classes and when to use each type, see the following MSDN entry: `http://msdn.microsoft.com/en-us/library/6tc79sx1(v=VS.100).aspx`

Each of the update methods loops through all of the keys in its own `Dictionary`, and in turn calls the `UpdatePiece()` method for each key. Each piece is then checked to see if its animation has completed. If it has, its key is added to the `RemoveKeys` queue. After all of the pieces in the `Dictionary` have been processed, any keys that were added to `RemoveKeys` are then removed from the `Dictionary`, eliminating those animated pieces.

If there are any `FadingPieces` currently active, those are the only animated pieces that `UpdateAnimatedPieces()` will update. When a row is completed, the scoring tiles fade out, the tiles above them fall into place, and new tiles fall in from above. We want all of the fading to finish before the other tiles start falling (or it would look strange as the new tiles pass through the fading old tiles).

Fading pieces

In the discussion of `UpdateAnimatedPieces()`, we stated that fading pieces are added to the board whenever the player completes a scoring chain. Each piece in the chain is replaced with a fading piece.

Time for action – generating fading pieces

1. In the `Game1` class, modify the `CheckScoringChain()` method by adding the following call inside the `for each` loop, before the square is set to `Empty`:

```
_gameBoard.AddFadingPiece(
    CInt(thisPipe.X),
    CInt(thisPipe.Y),
    _gameBoard.GetSquare(
        CInt(thisPipe.X),
        CInt(thisPipe.Y)))
```

What just happened?

Adding fading pieces is simply a matter of getting the type of piece currently occupying the square that we wish to remove (before it is replaced with an empty square) and adding it to the `FadingPieces` dictionary. We need to use the `CInt` typecasts because the `thisPipe` variable is a `Vector2` value, which stores its `X` and `Y` components as `Singles`.

Falling pieces

Falling pieces are added to the game board in two possible locations: from the `FillFromAbove()` method when a piece is being moved from one location on the board to another, and in the `GenerateNewPieces()` method when a new piece falls in from the top of the game board.

Time for action – generating falling pieces

1. Modify the `FillFromAbove()` method of the `GameBoard` class by adding a call to generate falling pieces right before the `rowLookup = -1` line (inside the `If` block):

```
AddFallingPiece(x, y, GetSquare(x, y),
    GamePiece.PieceHeight * (y - rowLookup))
```

2. Update the `GenerateNewPieces()` method by adding the following call, right after the `RandomPiece(x,y)` line as follows:

```
AddFallingPiece(x, y, GetSquare(x, y),
    GamePiece.PieceHeight * (GameBoardHeight + 1))
```

What just happened?

When `FillFromAbove()` moves a piece downward, we now create an entry in the `FallingPieces` dictionary that is equivalent to the newly moved piece. The vertical offset is set to the height of a piece (40 pixels) times the number of board squares the piece was moved. For example, if the empty space was at location 5, 5 on the board, and the piece above it (5, 4) is being moved down one block, the animated piece is created at 5, 5 with an offset of 40 pixels (5-4 = 1, times 40).

When new pieces are generated for the board, they are added with an offset equal to the height (in pixels) of the game board (recall that we specified the height as one less than the real height, to account for the allocation of the extra element in the `boardSquares` array), determined by multiplying the `GamePiece.PieceHeight` value by `GameBoardHeight` +1. This means they will always start above the playing area and fall into it.

Rotating pieces

The last type of animated piece that we need to deal with adding during the play is the rotation piece. This piece type is added whenever the user clicks on a game piece.

Time for action – modify Game1 to generate rotating pieces

1. Update the `HandleMouseInput()` method in the `Game1` class to add rotating pieces to the board by adding the following inside the "`if mouseInfo. LeftButton = ButtonState.Pressed`" block, before `_gameBoard. RotatePiece()` is called:

```
_gameBoard.AddRotatingPiece(x, y,
    _gameBoard.GetSquare(x, y), False)
```

2. Still in `HandleMouseInput()`, add the following in the same location inside the `if` block for the right-mouse button:

```
_gameBoard.AddRotatingPiece(x, y,
    _gameBoard.GetSquare(x, y), True)
```

What just happened?

Recall that the only difference between a clockwise rotation and a counter-clockwise rotation (from the standpoint of the `AddRotatingPiece()` method) is a true or false in the final parameter. Depending on which button is clicked, we simply add the current square (before it gets rotated, otherwise the starting point for the animation would be the final position) and true for right-mouse clicks or false for left-mouse clicks.

Calling UpdateAnimatedPieces()

In order for the `UpdateAnimatedPieces()` method of the `GameBoard` class to run, the game's `Update()` method needs to be modified to call it.

Time for action – updating Game1 to update animated pieces

1. Modify the `Update()` method of the `Game1` class by replacing the current case statement for the `GameState.Playing` state with the following:

```
Case GameStates.Playing
    timeSinceLastInput +=
        (CSng(gameTime.ElapsedGameTime.TotalSeconds))

    If _gameBoard.ArePiecesAnimating() Then
        _gameBoard.UpdateAnimatedPieces()
```

```
            Else
                _gameBoard.ResetWater()
                Dim y As Integer
                For y = 0 To GameBoard.GameBoardHeight
                    CheckScoringChain(_gameBoard.GetWaterChain(y))
                Next
                _gameBoard.GenerateNewPieces(True)
                If (timeSinceLastInput >= MinTimeSinceLastInput) Then
                    HandleMouseInput(Mouse.GetState())
                End If
            End If
        End If
```

What just happened?

This method is very similar to its previous incarnation. In this instance, we check to see if there are outstanding animated pieces to process. If there are, then `UpdateAnimatedPieces()` will run. If no animated pieces currently exist, the previous behavior of the `GameStates.Playing` case is executed.

Drawing animated pieces

Our animated pieces are almost completed. In fact, they all function right now, but you cannot see them because we have not yet updated `Draw()` to take them into account.

Time for action – update Game1 to draw animated pieces

1. Add methods to the `GameBoard` class to draw each potential type of game piece (empty, animated, and non-animated):

```
Private Sub drawEmptyPiece(
    spriteBatch As SpriteBatch,
    pixelX As Integer, pixelY As Integer)

  spriteBatch.Draw(
      playingPieces,
      New Rectangle(pixelX, pixelY,
          GamePiece.PieceWidth, GamePiece.PieceHeight),
      EmptyPiece,
      Color.White)
End Sub

Private Sub drawStandardPiece(
    spriteBatch As SpriteBatch,
    x As Integer, y As Integer,
    pixelX As Integer, pixelY As Integer)
```

```
        spriteBatch.Draw(
            playingPieces,
            New Rectangle(pixelX, pixelY,
                GamePiece.PieceWidth, GamePiece.PieceHeight),
            GetSourceRect(x, y),
            Color.White)
    End Sub

    Private Sub drawFallingPiece(
        spriteBatch As SpriteBatch,
        pixelX As Integer, pixelY As Integer,
        position As String)
      spriteBatch.Draw(
            playingPieces,
            New Rectangle(
              pixelX,
              pixelY - FallingPieces(position).VerticalOffset,
                GamePiece.PieceWidth, GamePiece.PieceHeight),
            FallingPieces(position).GetSourceRectangle(),
            Color.White)
    End Sub

    Private Sub drawFadingPiece(
        spriteBatch As SpriteBatch,
        pixelX As Integer, pixelY As Integer,
        position As String)

      spriteBatch.Draw(
            playingPieces,
            New Rectangle(pixelX, pixelY,
                GamePiece.PieceWidth, GamePiece.PieceHeight),
            FadingPieces(position).GetSourceRectangle(),
            Color.White * FadingPieces(position).AlphaLevel)
    End Sub

    Private Sub drawRotatingPiece(
        spriteBatch As SpriteBatch,
        pixelX As Integer, pixelY As Integer,
        position As String)

      spriteBatch.Draw(
        playingPieces,
        New Rectangle(
```

```
              pixelX + (GamePiece.PieceWidth \ 2),
              pixelY + (GamePiece.PieceHeight \ 2),
              GamePiece.PieceWidth, GamePiece.PieceHeight),
          RotatingPieces(position).GetSourceRectangle(),
          Color.White,
          RotatingPieces(position).RotationAmount,
          New Vector2(GamePiece.PieceWidth / 2, GamePiece.PieceHeight /
    2),
          SpriteEffects.None,
              0)
    End Sub
```

2. Modify the `Draw()` method of the `GameBoard` class by replacing the `for` loop that currently draws the playing pieces with the following:

```
For x = 0 To GameBoard.GameBoardWidth
    For y = 0 To GameBoard.GameBoardHeight
        Dim pixelX As Integer =
          CInt(DisplayOrigin.X +
            (x * GamePiece.PieceWidth))
        Dim pixelY As Integer =
          CInt(DisplayOrigin.Y +
            (y * GamePiece.PieceHeight))

        drawEmptyPiece(spriteBatch, pixelX, pixelY)

        Dim pieceDrawn As Boolean = False

        Dim position As String = x.ToString() + "_" + y.ToString

        If RotatingPieces.ContainsKey(position) Then
            drawRotatingPiece(spriteBatch, pixelX, pixelY,
    position)
            pieceDrawn = True
        End If

        If FadingPieces.ContainsKey(position) Then
            drawFadingPiece(spriteBatch, pixelX, pixelY, position)
            pieceDrawn = True
        End If

        If FallingPieces.ContainsKey(position) Then
            drawFallingPiece(spriteBatch, pixelX, pixelY,
    position)
            pieceDrawn = True
        End If
```

```
        If Not pieceDrawn Then
            drawStandardPiece(spriteBatch, x, y, pixelX, pixelY)
        End If
    Next
Next
```

3. Try it out! Run your game and complete a few rows.

What just happened?

To keep things organized, we have split the drawing of each of the different potential piece types into its own small method. These methods (drawEmptyPiece(), drawStandardPiece(), drawFallingPiece(), drawFadingPiece(), and drawRotatingPiece()) each contain only a single statement to draw the piece.

Before we look at how each of the pieces is actually drawn, let's examine the way we determine which of these methods to call when drawing a piece. The structure of the drawing loop is still the same as it was before we added animated pieces: each square on the board is looped through, with a blank square being drawn first in each position.

After the blank space, a new Boolean value called pieceDrawn is declared and set to false. If an animated piece occupies a square, only the animated piece will be drawn, and not the underlying game piece.

The reason for this is that when the user clicks on the mouse button to rotate a piece, in memory the piece is rotated immediately. The animated piece that the user sees is inserted into the drawing process, so it looks like the piece is turning. If both the animated piece and the real underlying piece were to be drawn, the final rotation position would be visible overlaid on top of the rotating piece while the rotation animation was playing.

The positionName string contains the dictionary key for the space we are currently drawing (in X_Y format). We use this to check each of the animated piece dictionaries to see if they contain an entry for that key.

If they do, the animated piece is drawn, and the pieceDrawn variable is set to true. If the piece still has not been drawn after all of the dictionaries have been checked, the base piece is drawn just as it was before.

SpriteBatch overloads

Both falling and fading pieces are drawn using the SpriteBatch.Draw() overload that we are already familiar with; where a Texture2D, destination Rectangle, source Rectangle, and Color are specified when drawing. By multiplying our base drawing color (white) by the alpha value for a fading piece, we cause the whole piece to be drawn partially transparent. As the time passes, the alpha value will reach zero, and the piece will be fully transparent.

However, rotated pieces need to use an overload of the `SpriteBatch.Draw()` method. The first four parameters are the same as our existing `Draw()` calls. To these parameters, we add a `Single` for the rotation amount, a `Vector2` for the origin around which the rotation takes place, a `SpriteEffects` property (set to `SpriteEffects.None` in this case), and a sorting depth (set to 0, or the top-level).

When using a rotation with this form of the `SpriteBatch.Draw()` call, it is necessary to specify the point around which the sprite should be rotated. If we were to set the origin to `Vector2.Zero` (equivalent to `0, 0`), the sprite would rotate around the upper-left corner of the image, swinging into the spaces of other tiles on the board. The center point of the sprite is specified in local sprite coordinates (as opposed to screen coordinates, or even coordinates within the texture the sprite is being pulled from). The local coordinates of the sprite range from `0, 0` in the upper-left corner to the height and width of the sprite in the lower-right corner. In our case, the lower-right corner of the sprite is `GamePiece.PieceWidth`, `GamePiece.PieceHeight`, or `40, 40`.

By specifying `Vector2(GamePiece.PieceWidth/2, GamePiece.PieceHeight/2)`, we are setting the origin to the center of the sprite, meaning it will rotate in place as expected.

SpriteFonts

Unlike a Windows Forms application, XNA cannot use the `TrueType` fonts that are installed on your computer. In order to use a font, it must first be converted into a `SpriteFont`, a bitmap-based representation of the font in a particular size that can be drawn with the `SpriteBatch.DrawString()` command.

Technically, any Windows font can be turned into a `SpriteFont`, but licensing restrictions on most fonts will prevent you from using them in your XNA games. Along with the other tools, the Windows Phone Developers Tools installed in *Chapter 1, Introducing XNA Game Studio* is a collection of fonts provided by Microsoft to address this problem and give XNA developers a range of usable fonts that can be included in XNA games. The following are the samples of each of the redistributable fonts included:

Kootenay	
Lindsey	
Miramonte	**Miramonte Bold**
PERICLES	PERICLES LIGHT
Pescadero	**Pescadero Bold**

Time for action – add SpriteFonts to Game1

1. Right-click on the **Fonts** folder in the **Content** project in **Solution Explorer**, and select **Add | New Item**.

2. From the **Add New Item** dialog, select `SpriteFont`.

3. Name the font as `Pericles36.spritefont`. After adding the font, the `SpriteFont` file will open in the editor window.

4. In the `SpriteFont` file, change `<Fontname>Segoe UI Mono</Fontname>` to `<Fontname>Pericles</Fontname>`.

5. Change `<Size>14</Size>` to `<Size>36</Size>`.

6. Add the following declaration to the `Game1` class:

   ```
   Private pericles36Font as SpriteFont
   ```

7. Update the `LoadContent()` method of the `Game1` class to load the `SpriteFont`, by adding the following:

   ```
   pericles36Font = Content.Load(Of SpriteFont)("Fonts\Pericles36")
   ```

What just happened?

Adding a `SpriteFont` to your game is very similar to adding a texture image. Since both are managed by the Content Pipeline, working with them is identical from a code standpoint. In fact, `SpriteFonts` are really just specialized sprite sheets, similar to what we used for our game pieces, and are drawn via the same `SpriteBatch` class we use to draw our sprites.

The `.spritefont` file that gets added to your project is actually an XML document, containing information that the Content Pipeline uses to create the `.XNB` file that holds the bitmap information for the font when you compile your code. The `.spritefont` file is copied from a template, so no matter what you call it, the XML will always default to 14 point Segoe UI Mono. In *step 4* and *step 5*, we edited the XML to generate 36 point Pericles instead.

Just as with a `Texture2D`, we declare a variable (this time a `SpriteFont`) to hold the Pericles 36 point font. The `Load()` method of the `Content` object is used to load the font.

SpriteFonts and extended characters

When a `SpriteFont` is built by the Content Processor, it actually generates bitmap images for each of the characters in the font. The range of characters generated is controlled by the `<CharacterRegions>` section in the SpriteFont's XML description. If you attempt to output a character not covered by this range, your game will crash. You can avoid this by removing the HTML comment characters (`<!--`and `-->`) from around the `<DefaultCharacter>` definition in the XML file. Whenever an unknown character is the output, the character defined in `<DefaultCharacter>` will be used in its place. This is particularly important if you are allowing the user to input text, or displaying text from an outside source (such as the web), because you won't necessarily have control over what might be displayed.

Score display

Displaying the player's score with our new `SpriteFont` is simply a matter of calling the `SpriteBatch.DrawString()` method.

Time for action – drawing the score

1. Add a new `Vector2` to the declarations area of `Game1` to store the screen location where the score will be drawn:

   ```
   Private scorePosition as Vector2 = new Vector2(605, 215)
   ```

2. In the `Draw()` method, remove `Me.Window.Title = playerScore.ToString()` and replace the line with the following:

   ```
   spriteBatch.DrawString(pericles36Font,
       playerScore.ToString(),
       scorePosition,
       Color.Black)
   ```

What just happened?

Using named vectors to store things like text positions allows you to easily move them around later, if you decide to modify the layout of your game screen. It also makes code more readable, as we have the name `scorePosition` instead of a hardcoded vector value in the `spriteBatch.DrawString()` call. Since our window size is set to 800 x 600 pixels, the location we have defined previously will place the score into the pre-defined score box on our background image texture.

The `DrawString()` method accepts a font to draw with (`pericles36Font`), a string to output (`playerScore.ToString()`), a `Vector2` specifying the upper-left corner of the location to begin drawing (`scorePosition`), and a color for the text to be drawn in (`Color.Black`).

ScoreZooms

Simply drawing the player's score is not very exciting, so let's add another use for our `SpriteFont`. In some puzzle games when the player scores, the number of points earned is displayed in the center of the screen, rapidly growing larger and expanding until it flies off the screen toward the player.

We will implement this functionality with a class called `ScoreZoom` that will handle scaling the `font002E`.

Time for action – creating the ScoreZoom class

1. Add a new class file called `ScoreZoom.vb` to the **Flood Control** project.

2. Add the following declarations to the `ScoreZoom` class:
```
Public Text As string
Public DrawColor As Color
Private displayCounter As Integer
Private maxDisplayCount As Integer = 30
Private _scale As Single = 0.4
Private lastScaleAmount As Single = 0.0
Private scaleAmount As Single = 0.4
```

3. Add the `Scale` read-only property to the `ScoreZoom` class:
```
Public ReadOnly Property Scale as Single
    Get
        Return (scaleAmount * displayCounter)
    End Get
End Property
```

4. Add a `Boolean` property to indicate when the `ScoreZoom` has finished displaying:
```
Public ReadOnly Property IsCompleted as Boolean
    Get
        Return (displayCounter > maxDisplayCount)
    End Get
End Property
```

5. Create a constructor for the `ScoreZoom` class:

```
Public Sub New(displayText as String, fontColor as Color)
    Text = displayText
    DrawColor = fontColor
    displayCounter = 0
End Sub
```

6. Add an `Update()` method to the `ScoreZoom` class:

```
Public Sub Update()
    _scale += lastScaleAmount + scaleAmount
    lastScaleAmount += scaleAmount
    displayCounter += 1
End Sub
```

What just happened? The `ScoreZoom` class holds some basic information about a piece of text and how it will be displayed to the screen. The number of frames the text will be drawn for are determined by `displayCounter` and `maxDisplayCount`.

To manage the scale, three variables are used: `_scale` contains the actual scale size that will be used when drawing the text, `lastScaleAmount` holds the amount the scale was increased by during the previous frame, and `scaleAmount` determines the growth in the scale factor during each frame.

You can see how this is used in the `Update()` method. The current scale is increased by both the `lastScaleAmount` and `scaleAmount`. `lastScaleAmount` is then increased by the `scaleAmount`. This results in the scale growing in an exponential fashion, instead of increasing linearly by a `scaleAmount` for each frame. This will give the text a zooming effect as it starts growing slowly and then speeds up rapidly to fill the screen.

Time for action – updating and displaying ScoreZooms

1. Add a `Queue` object to the `Game1` class to hold active `ScoreZooms`:

```
Private ScoreZooms as Queue(Of ScoreZoom) = new Queue(Of
ScoreZoom)()
```

2. Add a new helper method to the `Game1` class to update the `ScoreZooms` queue:

```
Private Sub UpdateScoreZooms()
    Dim dequeueCounter as Integer = 0
    For Each zoom as ScoreZoom in ScoreZooms
        Zoom.Update()
```

```
            If (zoom.IsCompleted) Then
                dequeueCounter += 1
            End If
        Next
        For d as Integer = 0 to dequeueCounter - 1
            ScoreZooms.Dequeue()
        Next
    End Sub
```

3. In the `Update()` method, inside the case section for `GameState.Playing`, add the call to update any active `ScoreZooms`. This can be placed right before the case's `End Select` statement:

```
UpdateScoreZooms()
```

4. Add the following to the `CheckScoringChain()` method to create a `ScoreZoom` when the player scores. Add this right after the `playerScore` is increased:

```
ScoreZooms.Enqueue(new ScoreZoom("+" +
    DetermineScore(WaterChain.Count).ToString(),
    new Color(255, 0, 0) * 0.4))
```

5. Modify the `Draw()` method of the `Game1` class by adding the following, right after the `SpriteBatch.DrawString()` call, which draws the player's score:

```
For Each zoom as ScoreZoom in ScoreZooms
    spriteBatch.DrawString(pericles36Font, zoom.Text,
        new Vector2(CSng(Me.Window.ClientBounds.Width / 2),
            CSng(Me.Window.ClientBounds.Height / 2)),
        zoom.DrawColor, 0.0,
        new Vector2(pericles36Font.MeasureString(zoom.Text).X / 2,
            pericles36Font.MeasureString(zoom.Text).Y / 2),
        zoom.Scale, SpriteEffects.None, 0.0)
Next
```

What just happened?

Since all `ScoreZoom` objects *live* for the same amount of time, we can always be certain that the first one we create will finish before any created during a later loop. This allows us to use a simple `Queue` to hold `ScoreZooms`, since a `Queue` works in a first-in-first-out manner.

When `UpdateScoreZooms()` is executed, the `dequeueCounter` holds the number of `ScoreZoom` objects that have finished updating during this cycle. It starts at zero, and while the `for each` loop runs, any `ScoreZoom` that has an `IsCompleted` property of true increments the counter. When the `for each` has completed, `ScoreZooms.Dequeue()` is run a number of times equal to `dequeueCounter`.

Adding new `ScoreZoom` objects is accomplished in *step 4*, with the `Enqueue()` method. A new `ScoreZoom` object is passed to the `Enqueue()` method, which is constructed with a plus sign (+), and the score being added, followed by a red color multiplied by an alpha value of 0.4, making it a little more than halfway transparent.

Just as the `SpriteBatch.Draw()` method has multiple overloads, so does the `SpriteBatch.DrawString()` method, and in fact, they follow much the same pattern. This form of the `DrawString()` method accepts the `SpriteFont` (`pericles36Font`), the text to display, a location vector, and a draw color just like the previous call.

For the draw location in this case, we use `Me.Window.ClientBounds` to retrieve the width and height of the game window. By dividing each by two, we get the coordinates of the center of the screen.

The remaining parameters are the same as those of the extended `Draw()` call that we used to draw rotated pieces. After the color value is rotation, which we have set to `0. 0`, followed by the origin point for that rotation. We have used the `MeasureString()` method of the `SpriteFont` class to determine both the height and width of the text that will display and divide the value by two to determine the center point of the text. Why do this when there is no rotation happening? Despite what the order of the parameters might indicate, this origin also impacts the next parameter: the scale.

When the scale is applied, it sizes the text around the origin point. If we were to leave the origin at the default (0, 0), the upper-left corner of the text would remain in the center of the screen, and it would grow towards the bottom-right corner. By setting the origin to the center of the text, the scale is applied evenly in all directions, shown as follows:

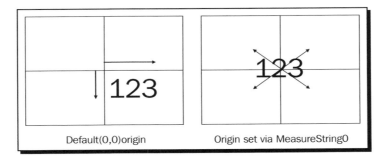

Default(0,0)origin   Origin set via MeasureString0

Just as with the extended `Draw()` method earlier, we will use `SpriteEffects.None` for the `spriteEffects` parameter, and `0. 0` for the layer depth, indicating that the text should be drawn on top of whatever has been drawn already.

Adding the GameOver game state

Now that we can draw text, we can add a new game state in preparation for actually letting the game end when the facility floods.

Time for action – game over

1. Modify the declaration of the GameStates Enum in the Game1 class to include the GameOver state as follows:

```
Private Enum GameStates
    TitleScreen
    Playing
    GameOver
End Enum
```

2. Add the following declarations to the Game1 class:

```
Private gameOverLocation as Vector2 = new Vector2(200, 260)
Private gameOverTimer as Single
```

3. Modify the Update() method of Game1 by adding a new case section for the GameState.GameOver state:

```
Case GameStates.GameOver
    gameOverTimer -= CSng(gameTime.ElapsedGameTime.TotalSeconds)
    If gameOverTimer <= 0 Then
        gameState = GameStates.TitleScreen
    End If
```

4. Modify the if statement in the Draw() method of Game1 for the GameState.Playing state from if (gameState = GameStates.Playing) Then to the following:

```
If (gameState = GameStates.Playing) Or
   (gameState = GameStates.GameOver) Then
```

5. Add a new if statement for the GameState.GameOver state to the Draw() method, right before the call to MyBase.Draw(gameTime):

```
If (gameState = GameStates.GameOver) Then
    spriteBatch.Begin()
    spriteBatch.DrawString(pericles36Font,
        "G A M E   O V E R!",
        gameOverLocation,
        Color.Yellow)
    spriteBatch.End()
End If
```

What just happened?

With the addition of GameOver, we now have a complete cycle of game states. When the program is started, the game begins in the TitleScreen state. Pressing the *Space bar* switches from TitleScreen to Playing state. When the game ends, the state moves to GameOver.

The Update() method handles the GameOver state by decreasing the gameOverTimer value until it reaches zero, at which point the state is set back to TitleScreen.

While the Update() method handles each of the game states in a mutually exclusive manner (the update code for Playing will never run when in the GameOver state), the Draw() method handles things differently.

When in the GameOver state, we want to display the text **G A M E O V E R!** on top of the game board. The location of the text, defined as (200, 260) in our declarations area, places it in the upper half of the screen, covering the center horizontally. We need to execute the drawing code for the Playing state in both the Playing and GameOver states, as well as an additional section of code only for GameOver.

The flood

The background story of the game centers on an underwater research laboratory that is slowly flooding, with the player trying to empty out the flood waters before the place fills up.

Up to this point, we do not have a representation of that flood in the game, or any incentive for the player to think quickly to find scoring chains.

Time for action – tracking the flood

1. Add the following declarations to the Game1 class:

```
Private Const MaxFloodCounter As Single = 100.0
Private floodCount As Single = 0.0
Private timeSinceLastFloodIncrease As Single = 0.0
Private timeBetweenFloodIncreases As Single = 1.0
Private floodIncreaseAmount As Single = 0.5
```

2. In the Update() method of Game1.vb, add the following code to keep track of the increasing flood waters, right after the timeSinceLastInput variable is updated in the GameState.Playing case section:

```
timeSinceLastFloodIncrease +=
    CSng(gameTime.ElapsedGameTime.TotalSeconds)
```

```
If timeSinceLastFloodIncrease >= timeBetweenFloodIncreases Then
    floodCount += floodIncreaseAmount
    timeSinceLastFloodIncrease = 0.0
    If (floodCount >= MaxFloodCounter) Then
        gameOverTimer = 8.0
        gameState = GameStates.GameOver
    End If
End If
```

3. Update the `CheckScoringChain()` method of the `Game1` class by adding the following to decrease the flood counter when the player scores. Place this code right after `playerScore += DetermineScore(WaterChain.Count)`:

```
floodCount = MathHelper.Clamp(CSng(floodCount -
    (DetermineScore(WaterChain.Count)/10)), 0.0, 100.0)
```

What just happened?

The flood itself is represented as a percentage. When the `floodCount` reaches `100` (`MaxFloodCounter`), the laboratory has completely flooded and the game is over. In addition to these two declarations, we also need to track how rapidly the flood increases (`timeSinceLastFloodIncrease` and `timeBetweenFloodIncreases`), and the rate at which the water rises (`floodIncreaseAmount`).

The timing on the flood increases is handled the same way input pacing is handled: a timer is incremented, based on the elapsed game time, until it reaches a threshold value. When it does, the timer is reset, and the `floodCount` variable is increased by the `floodIncreaseAmount` value.

When this increase takes place, we check to see if the `floodCount` has reached `MaxFloodCount`, indicating that the facility is flooded. If it has, then an eight-second timer is set for `gameOverTimer`, and the game state is set to `GameOver`. Recall that in the `GameOver` handler, the `gameOverTimer` determines how long the **G A M E O V E R!** text will be displayed before the game switches back to the title screen.

Finally, in *step 3*, the `floodCount` variable needs to be decreased each time the player completes a scoring chain. `MathHelper.Clamp()` is used to subtract the score value (divided by 10) from the `floodCount`, while keeping the value between `0. 0` and `100. 0`.

Displaying the flood

If you open the `Background.png` file in an image viewer, you will see that there is a full water tank floating inside the space on the playfield, where game pieces get displayed. Since we always draw opaque game piece backgrounds over this area, so far we have not seen this portion of the image during game play.

We can use `SpriteBatch.Draw()` to cut out pieces of this full water tank and superimpose it over the empty tank on the right-side of the game screen as the facility fills with water. The deeper the water gets, the more of the hidden water tank image we transfer to the visible tank on the screen, working our way up from the bottom, as shown in the following image:

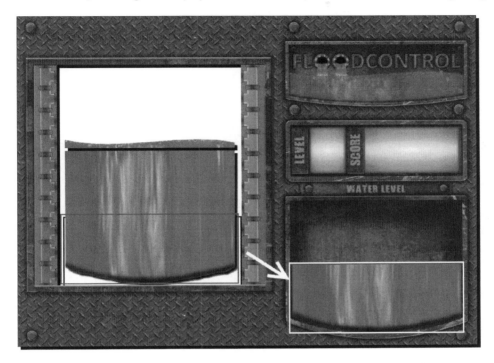

Time for action – displaying the flood

1. Add the following declarations to the `Game1` class:

   ```
   Private Const MaxWaterHeight As Integer = 244
   Private Const WaterWidth As Integer = 297

   Private waterOverlayStart As Vector2 = new Vector2(85, 245)
   Private waterPosition As Vector2 = new Vector2(478, 338)
   ```

2. Modify the `Draw()` method of the `Game1` class by adding the following, right after the `SpriteBatch.DrawString()` call that displays the player's score:

   ```
   Dim waterHeight As Integer

   waterHeight = CInt(MaxWaterHeight * (floodCount / 100))
   ```

```
spriteBatch.Draw(background,
    new Rectangle(
        CInt(waterPosition.X),
        CInt(waterPosition.Y + (MaxWaterHeight - waterHeight)),
        WaterWidth,
        waterHeight),
    new Rectangle(
        CInt(waterOverlayStart.X),
        CInt(waterOverlayStart.Y + (MaxWaterHeight -
waterHeight)),
        WaterWidth,
        waterHeight),
    new Color(255, 255, 255, 180))
```

3. Try it out! You should now be able to watch the flood slowly increase in the flood tank. When it reaches the top, the game should switch to the `GameOver` state, and after an eight-second delay, back to the title screen. You will not be able to play a second round at this point, however.

What just happened?

The two integer values, `MaxWaterHeight` and `WaterWidth`, refer to the size of the water image hidden inside the game board. It is 297 pixels wide, and the full water image is 244 pixels high.

Two vectors are used to store the location of the filled water image (`85, 245`) and the location that it will be drawn to on the screen (`478, 338`).

In order to draw the water in the water tank, the `MaxWaterHeight` is multiplied by the percentage of water currently in the tank and stored in the `waterHeight` variable. This results in the number of pixels of water that need to be drawn into the tank.

When determining the source and destination rectangles, the `X` coordinates are dependant only on the location of the overlay and the drawing position, since they will not change.

The `Y` coordinates must be modified to pull pixels from the bottom of the image and expand upwards. In order to accomplish this, the current `waterHeight` is subtracted from the `MaxWaterHeight`, and this value is added to the `Y` coordinate of both vectors.

Difficulty levels

Now that the game can end, we need some way to make the game more difficult so the player plays for longer.

After the player has completed 10 scoring chains, the water tank will be emptied, a new set of game pieces will be generated, and the flood will increase faster.

Time for action – adding difficulty levels

1. Add the following declarations to the `Game1` class:

```
Private currentLevel As Integer = 0
Private linesCompletedThisLevel As Integer = 0

Private Const floodAccelerationPerLevel As Single= 0.5

Private levelTextPosition As Vector2 = new Vector2(512, 215)
```

2. Add the `StartNewLevel()` method to the `Game1` class:

```
Private Sub StartNewLevel()
    currentLevel += 1
    floodCount = 0.0
    linesCompletedThisLevel = 0
    floodIncreaseAmount += floodAccelerationPerLevel
    _gameBoard.ClearBoard()
    _gameBoard.GenerateNewPieces(false)
End Sub
```

3. Modify the `Update()` method of the `Game1` class by replacing the case section for `GameState.TitleScreen` with the following:

```
Case GameStates.TitleScreen
    If (Keyboard.GetState().IsKeyDown(Keys.Space)) Then
        playerScore = 0
        currentLevel = 0
        floodIncreaseAmount = 0.0
        StartNewLevel()
        gameState = GameStates.Playing
    End If
```

4. Modify the `CheckScoringChain()` method to increment the `linesCompletedThisLevel` variable, right after `playerScore += DetermineScore(WaterChain.Count)`:

```
linesCompletedThisLevel += 1
```

5. Still in the `CheckScoringChain()` method, add the following to call the `StartNewLevel()` method if necessary. Place this code directly after the `for each` loop that fades out tiles on the board:

```
If (linesCompletedThisLevel >= 10) Then
    StartNewLevel()
End If
```

6. Update the `Draw()` method to display the current level in the appropriate location on the screen. Place this code right after the `spriteBatch.DrawString()` call that displays the player's score as follows:

```
spriteBatch.DrawString(pericles36Font,
    currentLevel.ToString(),
    levelTextPosition,
    Color.Black)
```

7. Play! **Flood Control** is now completed, so try it out!

What just happened?

The current game level and the number of lines the player has completed in the current level are tracked as integers (`currentLevel` and `linesCompletedThisLevel`). The two constants, `baseFloodAmount` and `floodAccelerationPerLevel`, determine how much water is added to the facility every time the flood is updated. Finally, the `levelTextPosition` vector points to the location on the screen where the level number will be displayed.

The `StartNewLevel()` method increases the `currentLevel` and clears the `floodCount` and `lineCompletedThisLevel` variables. It increases the `floodIncreaseAmount` by the value of `floodAccelerationPerLevel`, and then clears the game board. Finally, new pieces are generated for each square on the board.

When beginning a new game (the updates in *step 3*), we can simply set `currentLevel` and `floodIncreaseAmount` to zero, and then call the `StartNewLevel()` method. Since both of these variables are increased by `StartNewLevel()`, the first level of a new game will begin with the appropriate values.

Step 4 increases the counter that tracks the number of lines the player has completed on the current level every time a scoring chain results in points. *Step 5* checks to see if the player has completed 10 or more lines. If they have, a new level is started.

Finally, drawing the level number is a call to the simple form of `SpriteBatch.DrawString()`, just as we did for displaying the player's score.

Have a go hero

There are a number of different things you could do to spruce up **Flood Control**. Here are a few suggestions to try using the knowledge you have gained over these two chapters:

◆ Basic—add a `Paused` game state that displays an indication that the game is paused and how to resume play. To prevent cheating, the game board should either not be visible or be obscured in some way while the game is paused.

◆ Intermediate—the **G A M E O V E R!** screen is not very exciting. Create a new bitmap image indicating the aftermath of the flooded facility, and display that image instead of the simple **G A M E O V E R!** text. You will need to load the image via the `LoadContent()` method, and display it when appropriate.

◆ Advanced—create an additional *suffix* for pieces that are locked down and cannot be turned. You'll need to expand the `Tile_Sheet.png` file by adding an additional (fourth) column, and then copying the first two columns to columns three and four. Draw bolts in the four corners of each of the 12 new piece images, and modify the draw code to add an additional 40 pixels to the `X` value of the source `Rectangle`, if the piece contains the locked suffix. Grant extra points for using locked pieces in a scoring chain.

Summary

This chapter has looked at ways to add some polish to the basic **Flood Control** game that was presented in *Chapter 2, Flood Control – Underwater Puzzling*. We have looked at the following:

◆ Creating classes that inherit from existing classes to extend their functionality

◆ Using the advanced overloads of the `SpriteBatch.Draw()` method to add basic animations to the **Flood Control** game

◆ Adding `SpriteFonts` to the project, and using them to draw text to the screen

◆ Expanding the basic Game State system used in *Chapter 2, Flood Control – Underwater Puzzling*, to allow for a complete **Title | Playing | Game Over** cycle

◆ Adding increasing levels of difficulty as the player progresses through the game

4
Asteroid Belt Assault – Lost in Space

Mid-way through the hyperspace jump to the rim territories, something went wrong. Your hyper-drive engine shut down, and you found yourself suddenly back in normal space, in the middle of a massive asteroid field.

To make matters worse, the field appears to have been a hiding spot for a group of enemy fighters, intercepting communications from the Earth Fleet.

In this chapter, we will begin the construction of Asteroid Belt Assault by:

- Creating the base **Asteroid Belt Assault** project and structure
- Creating a class for frame-based animated sprite handling
- Building a scrolling sprite-based star field background
- Creating asteroids that can collide with each other
- Building a `ShotManager` class that will track projectiles fired by both the player and enemy ships
- Adding a player-controlled star fighter
- Adding enemy fighters that fly a set of waypoints across the screen

Creating the project

We will need a new Windows Game project for **Asteroid Belt Assault**. To create this project, we need to add the graphics package that we will use for the game.

Time for action – creating the Asteroid Belt Assault project

1. Visit `http://www.PacktPub.com` and download the `0669_04_GRAPHICPACK.ZIP` file. Extract the file to a temporary location.

2. Open **Visual Studio Express Edition**, and create a new **XNA 4.0 Windows Game** project called **Asteroid Belt Assault**.

3. In the **Asteroid Belt AssaultContent** project, right-click on the project name, select **Add | New Folder**, and add a folder called **Textures**. Add another folder called **Fonts**.

4. Right-click on **Textures**, and add the `SpriteSheet.png` and `TitleScreen.png` files from the graphics pack to the project.

5. Add declarations to the `Game1` class for game states and textures as follows:

```
Public Enum GameStates
    TitleScreen
    Playing
    PlayerDead
    GameOver
End Enum
Private gameState As GameStates = GameStates.TitleScreen
Private titleScreen As Texture2D
Private spriteSheet As Texture2D
```

6. Update the `LoadContent()` method to load the sprite sheet:

```
titleScreen = Content.Load(Of Texture2D)("Textures\TitleScreen")
spriteSheet = Content.Load(Of Texture2D)("Textures\spriteSheet")
```

7. Add a basic structure for the `Update()` method, before the call to `MyBase.Update()`:

```
Select Case gameState
    Case GameStates.TitleScreen

    Case GameStates.Playing

    Case GameStates.PlayerDead

    Case GameStates.GameOver

End Select
```

8. Add a basic structure for the `Draw()` method, before the call to `MyBase.Draw()`:

```
spriteBatch.Begin()

If (gameState = GameStates.TitleScreen)
    spriteBatch.Draw(titleScreen,
        new Rectangle(0, 0, Me.Window.ClientBounds.Width,
            Me.Window.ClientBounds.Height),
            Color.White)
End If

If ((gameState = GameStates.Playing) or
    (gameState = GameStates.PlayerDead) or
    (gameState = GameStates.GameOver))

End If

If (gameState = GameStates.GameOver)

End If

spriteBatch.End()
```

9. Execute your project to verify that the title screen is displayed. Since the `Update()` method is just a shell at this point, hit *Alt + F4* to close the game window.

What just happened?

The basic project setup and loading of content should be familiar by now. We have added the skeleton of our `Update()` and `Draw()` methods, which we will flesh out as we build our game.

Another definition for sprite

The term *sprite* predates XNA itself, and it can be used to refer to any method of displaying a bitmap over an existing background. In **Asteroid Belt Assault**, we will expand our use of the term *sprite* to include a class that stores both the bitmap image associated with the sprite, information about its current location on the screen, animation frames, and the code necessary to update and draw the object.

Building the Sprite class

The `Sprite` class will be used as the basis for all of the objects drawn in **Asteroid Belt Assault**. It will support collision detection and frame-based animation.

Time for action – declarations for the Sprite class

1. Add a new class file to the project, called `Sprite.vb`.

2. Add the following declarations to the `Sprite` class:

```
Public Texture as Texture2D
Protected frames As List(Of Rectangle) = new List(Of Rectangle)
Private frameWidth As Integer = 0
Private frameHeight As Integer = 0
Private currentFrame As Integer
Private _frameTime As Single = 0.1
Private timeForCurrentFrame As Single = 0.0

Private _tintColor As Color = Color.White
Private _rotation As Single = 0.0

Public CollisionRadius As Integer = 0
Public BoundingXPadding As Integer = 0
Public BoundingYPadding As Integer = 0

Protected _location As Vector2 = Vector2.Zero
Protected _velocity As Vector2 = Vector2.Zero
```

What just happened?

All of the animation frames for any individual sprite will be stored on the same sprite sheet, identified by the `Texture` variable. The frames list will hold a single `Rectangle` object for each animation frame defined for the sprite, while `currentFrame` stores the frame that is being displayed at any given time.

In order to control the animation, each frame is displayed for a pre-determined amount of time. This time, stored in `_frameTime`, will be compared to `timeForCurrentFrame` to determine when `currentFrame` should be incremented. This is the same timing mechanism we used in **Flood Control** to pace input. The `frameWidth` and `frameHeight` variables will be assigned, when the first frame of animation is established to provide shortcuts to these values.

The `_tintColor` and `_rotation` members store the implied information that will be used when the sprite is drawn to influence its appearance.

`CollisionRadius`, `BoundingXPadding`, and `BoundingYPadding` will all be used when we implement collision detection. We'll support both bounding circle and bounding box collisions. The `CollisionRadius` defines how large a circle to consider when determining if this sprite has collided with other sprites, while the padding values are used to *shrink* the frame size for collision detection, providing a cushion around the edges of the bounding box for collision purposes.

Finally, the location of the sprite on the screen is tracked via the `_location` vector, while the speed and direction at which the sprite is moving is stored in `_velocity`. The `_velocity` vector represents the distance (in pixels) that the sprite will travel in one second of game time.

Time for action – Sprite constructor

1. Add a constructor to the `Sprite` class as follows:

```
Public Sub New(
        location As Vector2,
        texture As Texture2D,
        initialFrame As Rectangle,
        velocity As Vector2)

    Me.Texture = texture
    _location = location
    _velocity = velocity

    frames.Add(initialFrame)
    frameWidth = initialFrame.Width
    frameHeight = initialFrame.Height
End Sub
```

What just happened?

The constructor for the `Sprite` class, sets the `Texture`, `_location`, and `_velocity` members to the passed parameter values, using the `Me` notation for `Texture`. since its name will otherwise collide with the parameter name. It adds the first frame to the frames list, and then sets the `frameWidth` and `frameHeight` variables by extracting that information from the `Rectangle`.

Time for action – basic Sprite properties

_1._ Add the following public properties to allow access to the `Sprite` class' members:

```
Public Property Location As Vector2
    Get
        return _location
    End Get

    Set(value As Vector2)
        _location = value
    End Set
End Property

Public Property Velocity as Vector2
    Get
        return _velocity
    End Get

    Set(value as Vector2)
        _velocity = value
    End Set
End Property

Public Property TintColor as Color
    Get
        return _tintColor
    End Get

    Set(value as Color)
        _tintColor = value
    End Set
End Property

Public Property Rotation as Single
    Get
        return _rotation
    End Get

    Set(value as Single)
        _rotation = value Mod MathHelper.TwoPi
    End Set
End Property
```

What just happened?

The `Location`, `Velocity`, and `TintColor` properties are simple pass-throughs for their underlying private members, as no additional code or checks need to be done when these values are manipulated.

When `Rotation` is set, the value is divided by `MathHelper.TwoPi`, and the remainder of the result is stored in the rotation member. This is a shorthand way of keeping the value between 0 and 2*pi. If a value within this range is passed into `Rotation`, the remainder of the division will equal the passed value. If the value is larger than 2*pi, any full rotations will be removed by the division, leaving only the partial rotation value as the remainder. This method allows external code to increment the value beyond a full rotation, and have the `Sprite` class correct the value appropriately.

Time for action – animation and drawing properties

1. Add the following public properties to allow access to the `Sprite` class' members:

```
Public Property Frame As Integer
    Get
        Return currentFrame
    End Get

    Set(value as Integer)
        currentFrame = CInt(MathHelper.Clamp(value, 0,
            frames.Count - 1))
    End Set
End Property

Public Property FrameTime As Single
    Get
        return _frameTime
    End Get

    Set(value as Single)
        _frameTime = MathHelper.Max(0, value)
    End Set
End Property

Public ReadOnly Property Source As Rectangle
    Get
        return frames(currentFrame)
    End Get
End Property
```

```
Public ReadOnly Property Destination As Rectangle
    Get
        return new Rectangle(
            CInt(location.X),
            CInt(location.Y),
            frameWidth,
            frameHeight)
    End Get
End Property
Public ReadOnly Property Center As Vector2
    Get
        return _location +
            new Vector2(CSng(frameWidth) / 2, CSng(frameHeight) /
2)
    End Get
End Property
```

What just happened?

The set portion of the `Frame` property, uses `MathHelper.Clamp()` to ensure that when it is set, the value stored in `currentFrame` is valid for the frames list of `Rectangles`. This will prevent, for example, setting the frame number to 10 for a sprite with 5 animation frames. The `FrameTime` property allows the speed at which the animation plays to be updated, using `MathHelper.Max()` to ensure the value is greater than or equal to zero. A `FrameTime` of zero will result in an animation that updates its frame during every `Update()` cycle.

The `Source` property returns the `Rectangle` associated with the current frame from the frames list, while the `Destination` property builds a new `Rectangle` based on the sprite's current screen location, and the width and height of a frame. Because we will be supporting rotation of the sprite, we will not use the `Destination Rectangle`, when drawing directly from the `Sprite` class, but it will be available for external code to determine the area containing the sprite on the screen, without the padding modifiers of the collision bounding box rectangle, which we will see in a moment.

In order to support both rotation and bounding circle collision detection, we will need to be able to determine the screen coordinates of the center of the sprite, so the `Center` property returns the `_location` member, offset by half of the width and height of the sprite.

Collision detection

Generally, when two objects in our game world come into contact with each other, we will need some way to know that they have collided, so we can take an appropriate action. It might be a player-fired bullet hitting an alien ship, or an asteroid hitting the player, or a number of other events.

Asteroid Belt Assault's `Sprite` class will have support for both bounding box and bounding circle collisions. In both cases, we define a basic shape (a box or a circle) that encompasses the area occupied by the sprite. A similar shape is defined for other objects in the game. When we need to check for collisions, we will compare the bounding shapes of each object with that of each other object. If any of them overlap, we know that a collision has taken place.

Because our sprites will often not fill the entire area allocated to them (otherwise they would simply be a square of color), the `Sprite` class' bounding box collision detection will support padding values around the edges of the sprite. By shrinking the rectangle around the object by the padding value, we allow for a cushion around the outer edges of a sprite, where collisions will be ignored. This is shown in the following image:

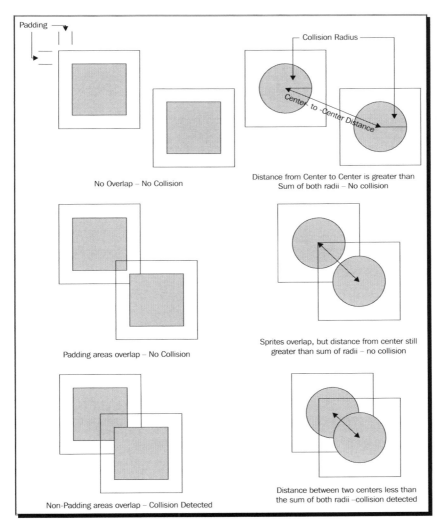

No Overlap – No Collision

Distance from Center to Center is greater than Sum of both radii – No collision

Padding areas overlap – No Collision

Sprites overlap, but distance from center still greater than sum of radii – no collision

Non-Padding areas overlap – Collision Detected

Distance between two centers less than the sum of both radii –collision detected

Time for action – supporting collision detection

1. Add the following properties and methods needed to support collision detection to the `Sprite` class:

```
Public ReadOnly Property BoundingBoxRect As Rectangle
    Get
        return new Rectangle(
            CInt(_location.X) + BoundingXPadding,
            CInt(_location.Y) + BoundingYPadding,
            frameWidth - (BoundingXPadding * 2),
            frameHeight - (BoundingYPadding * 2))
    End Get
End Property

Public Function IsBoxColliding(OtherBox as Rectangle) As Boolean
    return BoundingBoxRect.Intersects(OtherBox)
End Function

Public Function IsCircleColliding(
    otherCenter As Vector2, otherRadius As Single) As Boolean
    If (Vector2.Distance(Center, otherCenter) <
        (CollisionRadius + otherRadius)) Then
        return true
    Else
        return false
    End If
End Function
```

What just happened?

The `BoundingBoxRect` property provides a `Rectangle` object equivalent to the location and size of the sprite, accounting for the padding values around the edges. There is already a `BoundingBox` class as part of the XNA Framework, and while Visual Basic will not have a problem with us declaring a parameter with the name of an existing class, we are appending `Rect` to the end of the name here simply to avoid confusion.

When checking for a bounding box collision, the `IsBoxColliding()` method accepts another bounding box and returns true, if the two rectangles overlap at any point. The `Rectangle` class' `Intersects()` method contains the logic to check for this overlap.

When performing bounding circle collisions, the `IsCircleColliding()` method accepts a `Vector2`, representing the center of the object that the sprite will be compared against, and the other object's radius. If the distance between the two centers is less than the sum of the radii of both the objects, then the two circles overlap.

Animation and movement

In order to play an animation, we need to be able to add `frames` to the `frames` list, which requires a simple method.

Time for action – adding animation frames

1. Add the `AddFrame()` method to the `Sprite` class:

```
Public Sub AddFrame(frameRectangle As Rectangle)
    frames.Add(frameRectangle)
End Sub
```

What just happened?

Adding a frame to the sprite's animation is as simple as adding the corresponding `Rectangle` to the `frames` list. When the animation is updated, the frame value will be compared to the number of entries in `frames` (via `frames.Count`), eliminating the need to store the number of animation frames as a separate value.

Time for action – updating the Sprite

1. Add the `Update()` method to the `Sprite` class:

```
Public Overridable Sub Update(gameTime as GameTime)
    Dim elapsed as Single
    elapsed = CSng(gameTime.ElapsedGameTime.TotalSeconds)

    timeForCurrentFrame += elapsed

    If (timeForCurrentFrame >= FrameTime) Then
        currentFrame = (currentFrame + 1) Mod (frames.Count)
        timeForCurrentFrame = 0.0
    End If

    _location += (_velocity * elapsed)
End Sub
```

What just happened?

When `Update()` is called for the sprite, the standard timing mechanism, we have been using is implemented to determine when the frame should be updated. When it is, the frame is set to `(currentFrame + 1) Mod (frames.Count)`. This is a short-hand method of saying, "Add 1 to the current frame, divide the total by the number of frames in the animation and return the remainder.".

As an example, consider an animation with five frames (numbered zero through four). When `currentFrame` needs to go from zero to one, the assignment looks like the following:

```
currentFrame = ( 0 + 1 ) Mod 5
```

One divided by five is zero, with one as the remainder. When the `currentFrame` has reached the last frame of the animation (frame four), the assignment looks like the following:

```
currentFrame = ( 4 + 1 ) Mod 5
```

Five divided by five is one, with zero as the remainder. Since the remainder is what we are using as the new `currentFrame`, this causes `currentFrame` to be reset back to zero to begin the animation loop again.

After `currentFrame` has been updated, `timeForCurrentFrame` is reset to `0.0`, to begin the animation timing loop over again.

Finally, the `Update()` method adds the sprite's `_velocity` (adjusted for the time elapsed since the last frame) to the sprite's `_location`. Since, `_velocity` is stored as the change over one second, multiplying it by the `gameTime.ElapsedGameTime.TotalSeconds` (which will, if the game is not running slowly, be equal to 1/60th of a second—the default update rate for an XNA game) determines the distance moved over a single frame.

Why not just specify the velocity in pixels per frame? In many cases, that may work out just fine, but since you cannot be sure that your game will be running on hardware that can support a full 60 frames per second, if you did not scale your movements to actual elapsed time, your objects would move differently, when the game is running at different frame rates, potentially producing a jerky motion.

Overridable

The `Update()` method here is declared as `Overridable`, meaning that other classes we create based on the `Sprite` class can declare their own `Update()` methods that override (run in place of) this one. From the new `Update()` method, we can call `MyBase.Update()`, if we wish to run this underlying code. This is the same mechanism that the pre-defined methods of the `Game1` class use to allow us to update, draw, and load content, while still maintaining the built-in functionality of the methods.

Time for action – drawing the Sprite

1. Add the `Draw()` method to the `Sprite` class:

```
Public Overridable Sub Draw(spriteBatch As SpriteBatch)
    spriteBatch.Draw(
        Texture,
        Center,
        Source,
        tintColor,
        rotation,
        new Vector2(CSng(frameWidth / 2), CSng(frameHeight / 2)),
        1.0,
        SpriteEffects.None,
        0.0)
End Sub
```

What just happened?

The `Draw()` method consists of a single call to the `SpriteBatch.Draw()` method, using an overload of the method that allows for rotation and scaling.

Because we are specifying a rotation, we need to identify a center point for the rotation to be based around (`new Vector2(CSng(frameWidth / 2), CSng(frameHeight / 2))`). Instead of specifying a destination rectangle, we specify a vector that points to the center of the area, the object will occupy on the screen (the `Center` property of the `Sprite` class).

A Sprite-based star field

Let's put our new `Sprite` class to use by creating a scrolling star field. On the `SpriteSheet.png` file, we added to the project earlier, there is a 50 by 50 pixel empty white square located at 0,450 in the image. As we saw in the introductory `SquareChase` game, we can use an empty white sprite in combination with the `TintColor` parameter of the `SpriteBatch.Draw()` method to draw squares of any color we wish. We will make use of this ability to create slight color variations in the stars in the star field to make them look more realistic than if they were simply uniformly colored squares.

In order to create the star field, we will create 200 sprites and place them on the screen randomly. They will have a velocity that will slowly draw them down the screen. The `StarField` class will be responsible for monitoring the stars, and determining when they fall off the bottom of the screen. When this happens, they will be placed back at the top of the screen in a random location.

Time for action – creating the StarField class

1. Add a new class file called `StarField.vb` to the **Asteroid Belt Assault** project.

2. Add the following declarations to the `StarField` class:

```
Private stars As List(Of Sprite) = new List(Of Sprite)
Private screenWidth As Integer = 800
Private screenHeight As Integer = 600
Private rand As Random = new Random()
Private colors As Color() = { Color.White, Color.Yellow,
                              Color.Wheat, Color.WhiteSmoke,
                              Color.SlateGray}
```

3. Add a constructor to the `StarField` class:

```
Public Sub New(
        screenWidth As Integer,
        screenHeight As Integer,
        starCount As Integer,
        starVelocity As Vector2,
        texture As Texture2D,
        frameRectangle As Rectangle)
    Me.screenWidth = screenWidth
    Me.screenHeight = screenHeight
    For x As Integer = 0 to starCount
        stars.Add(new Sprite(
            new Vector2(CSng(rand.Next(0,screenWidth)),
                CSng(rand.Next(0,screenHeight))),
            texture,
            frameRectangle,
            starVelocity))
        Dim starColor As Color = colors(rand.Next(0, colors.
Count()))
        starColor *= CSng((rand.Next(30, 80) / 100))
        stars(stars.Count() - 1).TintColor = starColor
    Next
End Sub
```

What just happened?

Each star in the `StarField` will be stored in the `stars` list, making it simple to update and draw them using a `For Each` loop. When the stars are created, a color will be selected randomly from the `colors` array.

The class constructor assigns the `screenWidth` and `screenHeight` values to their local counterparts, and then begins creating star sprites. Each sprite is assigned a random location and passed the `texture`, `frameRectangle`, and `starVelocity` parameters. Next, `starColor` is assigned a random color from the `colors` array. The color is then multiplied by a random value between `0.30` and `0.79`, making the star semi-transparent. This color is then assigned to the `TintColor` property of the star that was just added to the `stars` list.

Time for action – updating and drawing the StarField

1. Add the `Update()` and `Draw()` methods to the `StarField` class:

```
Public Sub Update(gameTime As GameTime)
    For Each star As Sprite in Stars
        star.Update(gameTime)
        If (star.Location.Y > screenHeight) Then
            star.Location = new Vector2(
                CSng(rand.Next(0, screenWidth)), 0)
        End If
    Next
End Sub

Public Sub Draw(spriteBatch As SpriteBatch)
    For Each star As Sprite in stars
        star.Draw(spriteBatch)
    Next
End Sub
```

What just happened?

When the `StarField` needs to be updated, a `For Each` loop processes each item in the `stars` list, running the sprite's `Update()` method. The method then checks the star's `Location` property's Y component to determine if the star has moved off the bottom of the screen. If it has, the star is assigned a new `Location` with a random X component and a Y component of zero, placing the star at a random location along the top of the screen.

The `StarField.Draw()` method simply passes along the `spriteBatch` object to each of the individual stars in the `stars` list, and instructs them to draw themselves.

Time for action – viewing the StarField in action

1. Add the following declaration to the `Game1` class:

```
Private _starField as StarField
```

2. In the declarations area of the `Game1` class, temporarily modify the declaration for `gameState` from `GameStates.TitleScreen` to `GameStates.Playing`:

```
Private gameState as GameStates = GameStates.Playing
```

3. Update the `LoadContent()` method of the `Game1` class to initialize the `_starField` object. Be sure to place this code, after the `spriteSheet` texture is loaded:

```
_starField = new StarField(
    Me.Window.ClientBounds.Width,
    Me.Window.ClientBounds.Height,
    200,
    new Vector2(0, 30),
    spriteSheet,
    new Rectangle(0, 450, 2, 2))
```

4. In the `Upate()` method, add the following line to the `GameStates.Playing` section of the `Select..Case` statement you created earlier:

```
_starField.Update(gameTime)
```

5. In the `Draw()` method, change the background color from `Color.CornflowerBlue` to `Color.Black`.

6. Still in the `Draw()` method, add the following line to the `if` block containing `GameStates.Playing`:

```
_starField.Draw(spriteBatch)
```

7. Run the game by hitting *F5*, and observe the `StarField`. Exit the game by pressing *Alt + F4* on the keyboard.

What just happened?

Using our `StarField` class is simply a matter of creating an instance of the class, and then calling its `Update()` and `Draw()` methods during the game's corresponding methods. When the `_starField` object is constructed, we pass in the size of the screen, and specify that 200 stars will be created. Each star is assigned a velocity of (`0, 30`), meaning that in one second the star will move 30 pixels downward on the screen. With a screen height of 600 pixels, each star will take 20 seconds to travel from the top of the screen to the bottom.

The `spriteSheet` texture is specified, and the rectangle specifies an area on the textures that contains white pixels, as we indicated previously. The resulting sprite contains a single frame that is 2 by 2 pixels, located at (0, 450) on the `SpriteSheet`.

Animated sprites – asteroids

The asteroids we create for **Asteroid Belt Assault** are included on the `SpriteSheet.png` texture as the top row of 50 by 50 pixel images. There are 20 individual animation frames for the asteroid, spinning through space. This is shown in the following image:

Much like we did with the `StarField` class, we will create a class that will automatically manage the game's asteroids for us, including their initial positioning, handling what happens when they collide with each other, and repositioning them, when they have moved off the screen.

Time for action – building the AsteroidManager class

1. Add a new class called `AsteroidManager` to the **Asteroid Belt Assault project**.

2. Add the following declarations to the `AsteroidManager` class:

```
Private screenWidth As Integer = 800
Private screenHeight As Integer = 600
Private screenPadding As Integer = 10

Private initialFrame As Rectangle
Private asteroidFrames As Integer
Private texture As Texture2D

Public Asteroids As List(Of Sprite) = new List(Of Sprite)()
Private minSpeed As Integer = 60
Private maxSpeed As Integer = 120

Private rand As Random = new Random()
```

3. Add a `helper` method that will be used in the `AsteroidManager` constructor:

```
Public Sub AddAsteroid()
    Dim newAsteroid As Sprite = new Sprite(
        new Vector2(-500, -500),
        texture,
```

```
            initialFrame,
            Vector2.Zero)
        for X as Integer = 1 to asteroidFrames - 1
            newAsteroid.AddFrame(new Rectangle(
                CInt(initialFrame.X) + (initialFrame.Width * x),
                CInt(initialFrame.Y),
                initialFrame.Width,
                initialFrame.Height))
        Next

        newAsteroid.Rotation =
            MathHelper.ToRadians(CSng(rand.Next(0, 360)))
        newAsteroid.CollisionRadius = 15
        Asteroids.Add(newAsteroid)
    End Sub
```

4. Add a second `helper` function to the `AsteroidManager` class:

```
Public Sub Clear()
    Asteroids.Clear()
End Sub
```

5. Add a constructor for the `AsteroidManager` class:

```
Public Sub New(
        asteroidCount As Integer,
        texture As Texture2D,
        initialFrame As Rectangle,
        asteroidFrames As Integer,
        screenWidth As Integer,
        screenHeight As Integer)

    Me.texture = texture
    Me.initialFrame = initialFrame
    Me.asteroidFrames = asteroidFrames
    Me.screenWidth = screenWidth
    Me.screenHeight = screenHeight
    for X As Integer = 1 to asteroidCount
        AddAsteroid()
    Next
End Sub
```

What just happened?

Asteroids will be stored in the Asteroids list object. The AddAsteroid() method provides a way to generate a new asteroid when necessary. As the game becomes increasingly more difficult, more Asteroids can be added to make them harder to avoid.

When an asteroid is generated, its position is set to (-500, -500), placing it well off the screen. Off screen, Asteroids will be repositioned during the Update() method, so instead of duplicating the code to position the asteroid, we will simply start it off in a position that will force it to be moved during the first update cycle. The same is true for the asteroid's velocity. When the asteroid is positioned, it will be assigned a random velocity, so initially we simply set velocity to (0, 0).

While the initial frame is added to the asteroid sprite during the sprite's construction, the other 19 frames need to be added in order for the animation to play properly. The For loop inside AddAsteroid(), accomplishes this by pushing the X value of the rectangle representing the frame, the width of one frame to the right, for each added frame.

SpriteSheet organization

All of the animated sprites, we will create for **Asteroid Belt Assault** are intentionally laid out on the SpriteSheet.png file, so that each frame is located along a horizontal line in the file. This makes adding the subsequent animation frames as simple as moving the frame rectangle to the right, by the width of the rectangle for each frame. The loop utilized in the AddAsteroid() method will be implemented for all of our animated game objects, requiring just an initial frame rectangle and a frame count to build all of the animation frames.

Finally, right before the asteroid is added to the Asteroids list, the sprite's rotation value is set randomly by generating a value in degrees, and using MathHelper.ToRadians() to set the actual rotation value, and the asteroid's collision radius is assigned.

The constructor method copies all of the passed parameters to local variables, and then executes the AddAsteroid() method a number of times, equal to the asteroidCount parameter.

Positioning the asteroids

Asteroids will be flying all over the screen, while the game is running, and while we could generate new Asteroids every time one is needed, and remove it when it leaves the screen, we are going to cheat a little. When an asteroid leaves the screen, we will simply generate a new (off screen) location for the asteroid, a new velocity, and let it fly.

What if it goes straight off the screen again? That is ok too. It will be repositioned as soon as it does.

Cheating

Do not shy away from cheating in your game design! Remember that the goal is to make the game appear to behave naturally, and not to write a realistic simulator. There are several instances of faking things to make them look good in **Asteroid Belt Assault**, including the random rotation set on each asteroid, when it is generated to make it appear that there are several different asteroid graphics, and also the way we will create explosions in *Chapter 5*. Something that looks good and behaves properly, because doing a little cheating is just as good (sometimes better!) than a complicated simulation.

Time for action – positioning the asteroids

1. Add methods to generate random locations and velocities to the AsteroidManager class:

```
Private Function randomLocation() As Vector2
    Dim location As Vector2 = Vector2.Zero
    Dim locationOK As Boolean = True
    Dim tryCount As Integer = 0

    Do
        locationOK = True
        Select Case (rand.Next(0,3))
            Case 0
                location.X = -initialFrame.Width
                location.Y = rand.Next(0, screenHeight)

            Case 1
                location.X = screenWidth
                location.Y = rand.Next(0, screenHeight)

            Case 2
                location.X = rand.Next(0, screenWidth)
                location.Y = -initialFrame.Height
        End Select

        For Each asteroid As Sprite in Asteroids
            If (asteroid.IsBoxColliding(
                New Rectangle(
                    CInt(location.X),
                    CInt(location.Y),
```

```
                              initialFrame.Width,
                              initialFrame.Height))) Then
                    locationOK = False
                End If
            Next

            tryCount += 1
            If ((tryCount > 5) And locationOK = False) Then
                location = New Vector2(-500, -500)
                locationOK = True
            End If
        Loop While locationOK = False

        Return location
    End Function

    Private Function randomVelocity() As Vector2
        Dim velocity As Vector2 = New Vector2(
            rand.Next(0, 101) - 50,
            rand.Next(0, 101) - 50)
        velocity.Normalize()
        velocity *= rand.Next(minSpeed, maxSpeed)
        Return velocity
    End Function
```

What just happened?

When a random location is generated, we want to make sure that it is not already colliding with an existing asteroid. In order to perform this check, a do...while loop surrounds the switch statement, which randomly determines which side of the screen to use for the location. Here, we have chosen the left side of the screen (Case 0), the right side of the screen (Case 1), or the top of the screen (Case 2). We have chosen not to have Asteroids appear directly from the bottom of the screen, in order to give the player a little warning that they are coming, since the player ship will be near that area of the screen.

Each existing asteroid is checked to see if it would collide (using the Sprite class' IsBoxColliding() method) with a rectangle equal to the width and height of the asteroid frame placed at a location. If it does collide with any asteroid, the locationOK Boolean is set to false, causing the loop to repeat. If the check has failed more than 5 times (determined by comparing against tryCount), the location is set to a distant off-screen location, and the check is automatically passed, in order to prevent the game getting stuck when trying to place too many Asteroids in the limited off-screen area available. This is simply a safety measure. If we were to generate more than about 30 Asteroids at the same time, it may become impossible for the code to place them all so that none of them are too close together. This would result in the game trying forever and locking up.

In order to generate a velocity, the `randomVelocity()` method creates a vector with both the `X` and `Y` components set randomly to a number between `-50` and `50`. That vector is then normalized, resulting in a vector that is exactly 1 unit long, but pointing in a random direction. The vector is multiplied by a random scaling factor, resulting in the final velocity, which determines how far the asteroid moves in a single second of game time.

Time for action – checking the asteroid's position

1. Add the `isOnScreen()` helper method to the `AsteroidManager` class:

```
Private Function isOnScreen(asteroid As Sprite) As Boolean
    If (asteroid.Destination.Intersects(
            new Rectangle(
                -screenPadding,
                -screenPadding,
                ScreenWidth + screenPadding,
                screenHeight + screenPadding)
                )
            ) Then
        Return True
    Else
        Return False
    End If
End Function
```

What just happened?

The `isOnScreen()` method checks the passed asteroid to determine if its destination rectangle (where the sprite would be drawn to the screen) intersects a rectangle, generated by expanding the screen by `screenPadding` pixels in all directions. This padding allows the asteroid to move several pixels off the screen, before the game determines that it has actually left the playfield.

Time for action – updating and drawing Asteroids

1. Add the `Update()` and `Draw()` methods to the `AsteroidManager` class:

```
Public Sub Update(gameTime As GameTime)
    For Each asteroid As Sprite In Asteroids
        asteroid.Update(gameTime)
        If Not isOnScreen(asteroid) Then
            asteroid.Location = randomLocation()
            asteroid.Velocity = randomVelocity()
        End If
```

```
        Next
    End Sub

    Public Sub Draw(spriteBatch As SpriteBatch)
        For Each asteroid As Sprite In Asteroids
            asteroid.Draw(spriteBatch)
        Next
    End Sub
```

2. Add a declaration for the AsteroidManager in the declarations section of the Game1 class:

```
Private _asteroidManager As AsteroidManager
```

3. In the Game1 class' LoadContent() method, initialize _asteroidManager, after the initialization of the _starField object:

```
_asteroidManager = New AsteroidManager(
    10,
    spriteSheet,
    new Rectangle(0, 0, 50, 50),
    20,
    Me.Window.ClientBounds.Width,
    Me.Window.ClientBounds.Height)
```

4. Add the following line to Game1's Update() method, immediately after the _starField.Update(gameTime) line:

```
_asteroidManager.Update(gameTime)
```

5. Add the following line to the Draw() method of Game1, right after the _starField.Draw(spriteBatch) line:

```
_asteroidManager.Draw(spriteBatch)
```

6. Execute the game to see the Asteroids flying above the StarField.

What just happened?

The Update() method passes the update along to each asteroid, and then checks to see if the asteroid is still on the screen. If the asteroid has moved off the screen, it is assigned a new random location and velocity.

As with the StarField class, the AsteroidManager class simply passes the Draw call along to each of its component sprites when drawing.

Colliding Asteroids

`Asteroids` fly nicely around the screen, but they do not interact with each other. When two `Asteroids` collide, they simply pass right through each other and continue on their way. We will implement a simple elastic collision system, allowing the `Asteroids` to bounce off of each other in a fairly realistic manner.

When two objects meet in an elastic collision, they rebound off of each other and preserve the total kinetic energy contained in the two `Asteroids` after the impact. Energy may be transferred from one asteroid to the other, but the net energy will remain the same. While not perfectly realistic, this type of collision will suit our needs nicely, because any individual asteroid is only visible to the player for a short time. When an asteroid leaves the screen and is repositioned, it is considered a new asteroid.

We will be implementing a special case, elastic collision for our `AsteroidManager` class, in which all of the `Asteroids` have equal mass, which simplifies the method involved in determining the velocities of the two `Asteroids` after the collision.

Time for action – bouncing Asteroids – part 1

1. Add the `BounceAsteroids()` method to the `AsteroidManager` class:

```
Private Sub BounceAsteroids(asteroid1 As Sprite, asteroid2 As
Sprite)
    Dim cOfMass As Vector2 = (asteroid1.Velocity +
        asteroid2.Velocity) / 2

    Dim normal1 As Vector2 = asteroid2.Center - asteroid1.Center
    normal1.Normalize()
    Dim normal2 As Vector2 = asteroid1.Center - asteroid2.Center
    normal2.Normalize()

    asteroid1.Velocity -= cOfMass
    asteroid1.Velocity =
        Vector2.Reflect(asteroid1.Velocity, normal1)
    asteroid1.Velocity += cOfMass

    asteroid2.Velocity -= cOfMass
    asteroid2.Velocity =
        Vector2.Reflect(asteroid2.Velocity, normal2)

    asteroid2.Velocity += cOfMass
End Sub
```

What just happened?

We begin by calculating the velocity of the center of mass for the collision, represented by the `cOfMass` vector variable. This value is determined by adding the velocities of the two colliding objects, and then dividing by the total mass of the objects. In our special case, we are assuming both `Asteroids` to have a mass of one, resulting in the vector sum being divided by two. If the two colliding objects hit each other and get stuck together, this `cOfMass` velocity is the velocity that the resulting composite object would have. This is shown in the following image:

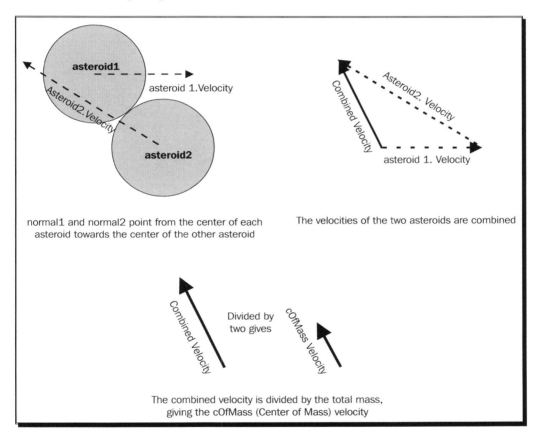

normal1 and normal2 point from the center of each asteroid towards the center of the other asteroid

The velocities of the two asteroids are combined

The combined velocity is divided by the total mass, giving the cOfMass (Center of Mass) velocity

The two vectors, `normal1` and `normal2` are generated by subtracting the locations of the centers of each asteroid from each other. This can be confusing because both vectors are **normalized normals**. In vector terminology, a **normalized** vector (produced in XNA by the `Normalize()` method) is a vector, whose length is exactly one unit. When a vector is normalized, it points in the same direction it initially pointed, but its length is increased or reduced to make it one unit long. In the following image, **V** is a **Vector: (1, -1)**. The **Length** of the vector is equal to **1.414** units. Vector **Vn** is a normalized vector that points in the same direction, but is one unit long:

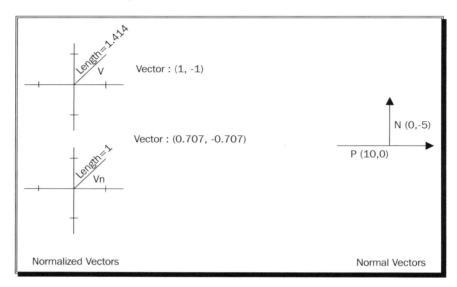

Normalized Vectors   Normal Vectors

Vector normalization

XNA vectors support a `Length` property, returning the length of the vector as a `Single`. Since, all vectors can be thought of as the hypotenuse of a right-angled triangle, the length can be obtained by the Pythagorean Theorem, a2 + b2 = c2, with c being the length of the vector, while a and b represent the X and Y components. When a vector is normalized, it is simply divided by its length, scaling the X and Y components appropriately.

A **normal** vector is a vector that is perpendicular to another vector. In the previous image, vector **N** is a normal vector to vector **P**. They are at right angles to each other. When used in calculations, such as collision detection, it is often convenient for the normal vectors to also be normalized, because multiplications involving the length of the vector end up multiplying by one, leaving the value unchanged.

In our code, `normal1` and `normal2` represent normalized (length of 1) vectors that are normal (perpendicular) to the plane, along which the two `Asteroids` are colliding, as in the following image:

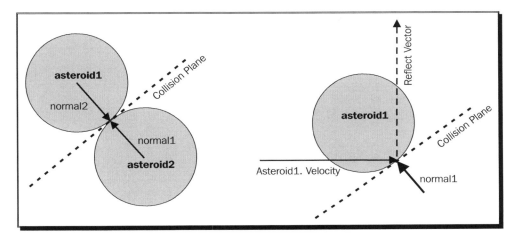

In order to calculate the final velocity vector of an individual asteroid after the collision, the `cOfMass` vector is subtracted from the asteroid's velocity. The `Vector2` class' `Reflect()` method is then used to find the reflection vector between the asteroid's velocity (without the center of mass velocity), and the vector that is normal to the collision plane. Given a vector that is normal to the surface, a vector is colliding with, `Reflect()` returns the result of that vector *bouncing off* the surface, as illustrated in the previous image.

This bit of vector magic produces a vector that points along the direction that the asteroid would move in, if it had hit a solid, immobile plane. Since, it is not impacting an immobile plane, but rather another moving object, the `cOfMass` vector is added back to the asteroid's velocity to represent the influence that the relative velocity of the other object has on the final direction, and speed of the asteroid after the collision.

Time for action – bouncing Asteroids – part 2

1. Replace the current `Update()` method of the `AsteroidManager` class:

```
Public Sub Update(gameTime As GameTime)
    For Each asteroid as Sprite in Asteroids
        asteroid.Update(gameTime)
        If Not isOnScreen(asteroid) Then
            asteroid.Location=randomLocation()
            asteroid.Velocity=randomVelocity()
        End If
    Next
```

```
        For x as Integer = 0 to Asteroids.Count -1
            For y as Integer = x+1 to Asteroids.Count -1
                If (Asteroids(x).IsCircleColliding(
                    Asteroids(y).Center,
                        Asteroids(y). CollisionRadius)) Then
                    BounceAsteroids(Asteroids(x), Asteroids(y))
                End If
            Next
        Next
    End Sub
```

2. Execute the game and watch the `Asteroids` bounce off of each other.

3. Close the game window.

What just happened?

Each asteroid is updated just as before. Afterwards, however, two nested loops process each asteroid in the list, checking for collisions with all of the other `Asteroids`. If two `Asteroids` collide, they are both passed to the `BounceAsteroids()` method. The second loop is written to minimize the collision comparisons by only checking `Asteroids` with a higher index number than the current asteroid. When the first asteroid is checked, it is compared with all of the remaining `Asteroids`, so when the second asteroid is processed, there is no need to check against the first asteroid again as that has already been done and responded to.

Player and enemy shots

Before we add player or enemy ships, let's turn our attention to the shots that they will be firing. We will build the `ShotManager` class first, because both the player and enemy ships will need to use it to fire projectiles at each other. Instead of constructing the ship classes and then revisiting them, we can build the shots first and then build a way to utilize the manager in the ship classes.

Time for action – adding the ShotManager class

1. Add a new class called `ShotManager` to the **Asteroid Belt Assault** project.

2. Add declarations to the `ShotManager` class:

```
Public Shots As List(Of Sprite) = New List(Of Sprite)()

Private Shared _screenBounds As Rectangle
Private Shared _texture As Texture2D
```

```
Private Shared _initialFrame As Rectangle
Private Shared _frameCount As Integer
Private Shared _collisionRadius As Integer

Private _shotSpeed As Single
```

3. Add a constructor to the the ShotManager class:

```
Public Sub New (
    texture As Texture2D,
    initialFrame As Rectangle,
    frameCount As Integer,
    collisionRadius As Integer,
    shotSpeed As Single,
    screenBounds As Rectangle)

    _Texture = texture
    _InitialFrame = initialFrame
    _FrameCount = frameCount
    _CollisionRadius = collisionRadius
    _shotSpeed = shotSpeed
    _screenBounds = screenBounds
End Sub
```

What just happened?

ShotManager maintains a list of fired shots. An enemy-fired shot will not hurt enemies, and a player-fired shot will not hurt the player, if they somehow manage to move into one. We will implement these properties, when we build the CollisionManager class, which will check for collisions between fired shots and other game objects by creating two different instances of the ShotManager class.

When a shot leaves the _screenBounds area, it will be removed from the list, as it has left play.

Since shots are actually Sprites, they will use the standard sprite velocity system, represented in pixels per second. When a shot is created, a vector indicating the direction the shot is travelling in, will be multiplied by the appropriate shot speed value to determine its actual velocity.

The other four Shared members, _Texture, _InitialFrame, _FrameCount, and _CollisionRadius are stored by the ShotManager class, in order to assist it in creating new shots when necessary. As you may recognize, these are the parameters (minus the location and velocity) for creating a new Sprite instance. The ShotManager class constructor directly copies the passed values to the member variables of the class.

Shared members

Most of the fields associated with the ShotManager class are declared as Shared, meaning that all instances of the ShotManager class will share the same value for these parameters. If we create multiple instances of the ShotManager, using different values, the last created manager will override all of the others. We leave the _shotSpeed value as non-shared, because player and enemy bullets will travel at different speeds.

Time for action – firing shots

1. Add the FireShot() method to the ShotManager class:

```
Public Sub FireShot(
    location As Vector2,
    velocity As Vector2,
    playerFired as Boolean)

    Dim modifiedVelocity As Vector2 = velocity
    modifiedVelocity.Normalize()
    modifiedVelocity *= _shotSpeed

    Dim thisShot as Sprite = new Sprite(
        location,
        _texture,
        _initialFrame,
        modifiedVelocity)

    For x As Integer = 1 to _frameCount - 1
        thisShot.AddFrame(New Rectangle(
            _initialFrame.X+(_initialFrame.Width * x),
            _initialFrame.Y,
            _initialFrame.Width,
            _initialFrame.Height))
    Next
    thisShot.CollisionRadius = _collisionRadius
    Shots.Add(thisShot)
End Sub
```

What just happened?

When a shot is fired, we normalize the velocity passed into the function, so that we can standardize the speed of the projectile. Then a new sprite (called `thisShot`) is built using the parameters stored, when the `ShotManager` class was constructed. The location is set according to the value passed to the `FireShot()` method, along with a Boolean value indicating if this shot was fired by the player or not. We will use this value in *Chapter 5*, when we implement sound effects. The shot is then added to the `Shots` list.

Time for action – updating and drawing shots

1. Add the `Update()` method to the `ShotManager` class:

```
Public Sub Update(gameTime As GameTime)
    For x As Integer = Shots.Count - 1 to 0 Step -1
        Shots(x).Update(gameTime)
        If Not _screenBounds.Intersects(Shots(x).Destination) Then
            Shots.RemoveAt(x)
        End If
    Next
End Sub
```

2. Add the `Draw()` method to the `ShotManager` class:

```
Public Sub Draw(spriteBatch As SpriteBatch)
    For Each shot As Sprite in Shots
        shot.Draw(spriteBatch)
    Next
End Sub
```

What just happened?

Since we may be removing shots from the list, we cannot use a `For Each` loop to process the list during the `Update()` method—as we saw in **Flood Control**, items cannot be deleted from a `List`, while a `For Each` loop is processing the `List`. Looping backwards through the list, allows us to process all of the shots, removing ones that have expired, without the need to track separate removal lists or restart the iteration after each removal.

After an individual shot has been updated, the `_screenBounds` rectangle is checked to see if the shot is still visible on the screen. If it is not, the shot is removed from the list.

The `Draw()` method for the `ShotManager` is similar to the method used in the `AsteroidManager` class. It simply iterates through the list and instructs the sprites to draw themselves.

We will add instances of the `ShotManager` class to both our `PlayerManager` class and the `EnemyManager` class that we will be building shortly.

Adding the player

The player's star fighter is a small, three frame animation that the player will control with either the keyboard or the gamepad, shown as follows:

As with both `Asteroids` and `Shots`, we will create a manager class for the player. The `PlayerManager` will be responsible for handling player input, firing shots, and limiting the player to a pre-defined area on the screen.

Time for action – creating the PlayerManager class

1. Add a new class called `PlayerManager` to the **Asteroid Belt Assault** project.

2. Add declarations to the `PlayerManager` class:

```
Public playerSprite As Sprite
Private playerSpeed As Single = 160.0
Private playerAreaLimit As Rectangle

Public PlayerScore As Long = 0
Public LivesRemaining As Integer = 3
Public Destroyed As Boolean = false

Private gunOffset As Vector2 = new Vector2(25, 10)
Private shotTimer As Single = 0.0
Private minShotTimer As Single = 0.2
Private playerRadius As Integer = 15
Public PlayerShotManager As ShotManager
```

3. Add a constructor to the `PlayerManager` class:

```
Public Sub New (
    Texture As Texture2D,
    initialFrame As Rectangle,
    frameCount As Integer,
    screenBounds As Rectangle)

    playerSprite = new Sprite(
        new Vector2(500, 500),
        texture,
        initialFrame,
```

```
            Vector2.Zero)

        PlayerShotManager = new ShotManager(
            texture,
            new Rectangle(0, 300, 5, 5),
            4,
            2,
            250,
            screenBounds)

        playerAreaLimit =
            new Rectangle(
                0,
                CInt(screenBounds.Height / 2),
                screenBounds.Width,
                CInt(screenBounds.Height / 2))

        For x As Integer = 1 to frameCount -1
            playerSprite.AddFrame(
                new Rectangle(
                    initialFrame.X + (initialFrame.Width * x),
                    initialFrame.Y,
                    initialFrame.Width,
                    initialFrame.Height))
        Next x
        playerSprite.CollisionRadius = playerRadius
    End Sub
```

What just happened?

As with all of our other objects, the player's ship is represented as a `Sprite`. When the player moves, their speed is limited to 160 pixels per second. This value will be used to scale the velocity vector associated with the player sprite while moving. In addition to limiting the speed at which the player can move, the player is limited to the area described by the `playerAreaLimit` rectangle. If the player's velocity carries their star fighter outside of this rectangle, their position will be adjusted to move the ship back into this area.

The `PlayerScore` and `LivesRemaning` variables will be used to track the player's progress in the game. They will be reset, when a new game is started and manipulated by other code, such as the `CollisionManager`. When a player collides with a deadly object, the `Destroyed` member will be set to `True`, allowing the game management system to take appropriate actions, such as decreasing the number of lives remaining, respawning the player, or ending the game.

The next four member variables allow the player to fire their star fighter's cannon. The gunOffset vector points to the location on the ship's sprite image, where newly fired projectiles will be created. The shotTimer and minShotTimer floats will be used in our now familiar timing mechanism to prevent a constant stream of player-fired bullets from issuing from the player's cannon. The playerRadius value represents the size of the player's ship. This value will be copied to the sprite's CollisionRadius member, in order to be checked against other objects during collision detection.

The PlayerManager constructor builds the playerSprite object from the passed variables, and also creates an instance of the ShotManager class, allowing the PlayerManager class to handle any shots fired by the player.

Handling user input

Asteroid Belt Assault will support both keyboard and gamepad based control. If you have a wired Xbox 360 gamepad, it will plug into a USB port on your PC, and will be recognized by XNA for controlling your games.

We saw an example of mouse-based user input in the SquareChase and **Flood Control** games, using the MouseState object. Similar objects, KeyboardState and GamePadState exist for the keyboard and gamepad, respectively, and they are used in the same manner as the MouseState object: The state is captured via the GetState() method, and members of the returned object can be checked to determine the state of keyboard keys or gamepad thumbsticks and buttons.

Time for action – handling user input

1. Add the FireShot() helper method to the PlayerManager class:

```
Private Sub FireShot()
    If shotTimer >= minShotTimer Then
        PlayerShotManager.FireShot(
            playerSprite.Location + gunOffset,
            New Vector2(0, -1),
            True)
        shotTimer = 0.0
    End If
End Sub
```

2. Add the HandleKeyboardInput() helper method to the PlayerManager class:

```
Private Sub HandleKeyboardInput(keyState As KeyboardState)
    If keyState.IsKeyDown(Keys.Up) Then
        playerSprite.Velocity += new Vector2(0, -1)
    End If
```

```
        If keyState.IsKeyDown(Keys.Down) Then
            playerSprite.Velocity += new Vector2(0, 1)
        End If

        If keyState.IsKeyDown(Keys.Left) Then
            playerSprite.Velocity += new Vector2(-1, 0)
        End If

        If keyState.IsKeyDown(Keys.Right) Then
            playerSprite.Velocity += new Vector2(1, 0)
        End If

        If keyState.IsKeyDown(Keys.Space) Then
            FireShot()
        End If
    End Sub
```

3. Add the `HandleGamepadInput()` helper method to the `PlayerManager` class:

```
Private Sub HandleGamepadInput(padState As GamePadState)
    playerSprite.Velocity +=
        new Vector2(
            padState.ThumbSticks.Left.X,
            -padState.ThumbSticks.Left.Y)

    If padState.Buttons.A = ButtonState.Pressed Then
        FireShot()
    End If
End Sub
```

What just happened?

The `FireShot()` helper method will be called from both the `HandleKeyboardInput()` and `HandleGamepadInput()` methods, and implements a portion of the standard timing mechanism, we have been using throughout this book. The remainder of the mechanism (incrementing the `shotTimer` value) will take place in the `Update()` method that we will be adding shortly. When a shot is fired, its velocity is passed as a vector pointing straight up (the only direction the player can fire). Because our `ShotManager` will normalize the vector for us, we could use any vector that points upward, with the simplest and already being normalized by specifying (0, -1) as the vector components.

The `IsKeyDown()` method of the `KeyboardState` class returns true, if the indicated key is down when the state is captured. As far as XNA is concerned, there is no keyboard buffer or individual key presses. Each key is either up or down when the state is read. The directional keys individually add to the player's velocity vector in directions corresponding to their key presses. For example, if the `Keys.Up` key is pressed, a vector of $(0, -1)$ is added to the player's velocity. This means it is possible for the player to press both the *Up* and *Down* keys at the same time, though the two vectors will simply cancel each other out.

If the *Space* bar on the keyboard is pressed, the `FireShot()` helper method is called, indicating that the player wishes to fire a projectile, if enough time has elapsed since the previous projectile was fired.

`HandleGamepadInput()` is somewhat simpler than the keyboard input handler, because the left thumbstick that we will use to control the player's ship, returns a vector that represents the direction the player has the stick pointed in. We cannot simply apply the thumbstick vector to the ship's velocity, because the sign of the `Y` component of the vector on the gamepad is the reverse of its meaning on the screen. In other words, pressing up on the thumbstick returns a positive `Y` value, while moving up on the screen is a negative `Y` value. By building a new vector out of the components of the thumbstick vector and negating the `Y` value, we can add this new vector to the velocity vector of the ship. The `A` button on the gamepad triggers the call to the `FireShot()` method.

Time for action – updating and drawing the player's ship

1. Add the `imposeMovementLimits()` helper method to the `PlayerManager` class:

```
Private Sub imposeMovementLimits()
    Dim location as Vector2 = playerSprite.Location

    If location.X < playerAreaLimit.X Then
        location.X = playerAreaLimit.X
    End If

    If location.X >
        (playerAreaLimit.Right - playerSprite.Source.Width) Then
        location.X =
            (playerAreaLimit.Right - playerSprite.Source.Width)
    End If

    If location.Y < playerAreaLimit.Y Then
        location.Y = playerAreaLimit.Y
    End If

    If location.Y >
        (playerAreaLimit.Bottom - playerSprite.Source.Height) Then
        location.Y =
```

```
                    (playerAreaLimit.Bottom - playerSprite.Source.Height)
        End If

        playerSprite.Location = location
    End Sub
```

2. Add the `Update()` method to the `PlayerManager` class:

```
Public Sub Update(gameTime As GameTime)
    PlayerShotManager.Update(gameTime)

    If Not Destroyed Then
        playerSprite.Velocity = Vector2.Zero

        shotTimer += CSng(gameTime.ElapsedGameTime.TotalSeconds)

        HandleKeyboardInput(Keyboard.GetState())
        HandleGamepadInput(GamePad.GetState(PlayerIndex.One))

        playerSprite.Velocity.Normalize()
        playerSprite.Velocity *= playerSpeed

        playerSprite.Update(gameTime)
        imposeMovementLimits()
    End If
End Sub
```

3. Add the `Draw()` method to the `PlayerManager` class:

```
Public Sub Draw(spriteBatch As SpriteBatch)
    PlayerShotManager.Draw(spriteBatch)

    If Not Destroyed Then
        playerSprite.Draw(spriteBatch)
    End If
End Sub
```

4. Add a declaration to the `Game1` class for the `PlayerManager`:

```
Private _playerManager As PlayerManager
```

5. In the `LoadContent()` method of the `Game1` class, set up the `PlayerManager`, after the `AsteroidManager` is initialized:

```
_playerManager = New PlayerManager(
    spriteSheet,
    New Rectangle(0, 150, 50, 50),
    3,
    New Rectangle(
        0,
```

```
0,
Me.Window.ClientBounds.Width,
Me.Window.ClientBounds.Height))
```

6. In the `Update()` method of the `Game1` class, add an update line for the `PlayerManager`, right after the `AsteroidManager` is updated:

`_playerManager.Update(gameTime)`

7. In the `Draw()` method of the `Game1` class, add a draw line for the `PlayerManager`, right after the `AsteroidManager` is drawn:

`_playerManager.Draw(spriteBatch)`

8. Execute the game and fly your star fighter around in the asteroid field. Fire off a few shots with your cannon!

What just happened?

The `imposeMovementLimits()` method begins by making a copy of the playerSprite's `Location` property. Since `Location` is a property and not a public member, we cannot modify the components of the vector (`X` and `Y`) individually. Creating a temporary copy allows us to independently modify these values, and then save the whole vector back to the property.

The `X` and `Y` values of the vector are checked against the edges of the `playerAreaLimit` rectangle. On the right and bottom edges, the width and height of the player sprite is subtracted from the bounding rectangle edges to ensure that the player sprite stays entirely on the screen. If any of the edges are out of alignment, the components of the location vector are adjusted to keep the ship within the play area.

The location is then saved back into the `playerSprite.Location` property.

Updating the player manager begins by updating its related `ShotManager`. Then, if the `Destroyed` variable is false, the remainder of the `Update()` method is allowed to proceed. This check prevents the player from continuing to fire shots after being killed. The update begins by setting the player's velocity to zero and incrementing the timer for firing shots. The `HandleKeyboardInput()` and `HandleGamepadInput()` methods are then called, passing each the current state of the appropriate input device.

We need to resolve two potential issues with player movement at this point. If the player were simply moving to the right, the player's velocity vector would be equal to (`1`, `0`), with a length of 1 unit. If, however, the player is holding down both the right and up keys, the resulting vector would be (`1`, `1`). As we saw, when discussing normalized vectors while bouncing asteroids off of each other, this vector has a length of 1.414 units, meaning that the player can move faster by moving diagonally than they can by moving in straight lines.

A related side issue is that if the player has an Xbox gamepad connected to their PC, they could hold down both the thumbstick and the arrow keys to move at twice the normal speed in their chosen direction.

To compensate for both of these potential issues, the `Update()` method normalizes the player's velocity vector and then multiplies it by the `playerSpeed` variable. This results in a vector that is always the same length (unless, of course, the player is not moving, in which case the vector value of (0, 0) has no length at all).

After all of the input and velocity changes have been accounted for, the `Update()` method of the `playerSprite` object is called to allow the velocity to be added to the player's location, and to advance the animation frame. Finally, the `imposeMovementLimits()` method is called to make sure the ship stays within the play area.

When the `PlayerManager` is drawn, the same series of events take place as the `Update()` method. First, the associated `ShotManager` is drawn, followed by a check to see if the player has been destroyed. If they are still alive, the player ship gets drawn to the screen. It is important to note that the `ShotManager` gets drawn before the player, because any shot the player fires will begin somewhat overlapping the player's sprite. By drawing the shots before the player ship, the shot will appear to come from inside the ship, instead of appearing on top of the ship when fired.

Enemy ships

Now that the player can fly and shoot their weapons, it is time to give them something to shoot at! The enemy ships are shown in the following image:

Our enemy ships will follow a series of waypoints (specified as a list of vectors pointing to screen coordinates) across the screen. Because we need this new type of behavior that all enemy ships will implement, we will create an `Enemy` class as well as an `EnemyManager` class.

Time for action – creating the Enemy class

1. Add a new class called `Enemy` to the **Asteroid Belt Assault** project.

2. Add declarations to the `Enemy` class:
```
Public EnemySprite As Sprite
Public gunOffset As Vector2 = new Vector2(25, 25)
Private waypoints As Queue(Of Vector2) = New Queue(Of Vector2)()
```

```
Private currentWaypoint As Vector2 = Vector2.Zero
Private speed As Single = 120
Public Destroyed As Boolean = False
Private enemyRadius As Integer = 15
Private previousLocation As Vector2 = Vector2.Zero
```

3. Add a constructor to the Enemy class:

```
Public Sub New(
    Texture As Texture2D,
    Location As Vector2,
    initialFrame As Rectangle,
    frameCount As Integer)

    EnemySprite = new Sprite(
        location,
        texture,
        initialFrame,
        Vector2.Zero)

    For x As Integer = 1 to frameCount - 1
        EnemySprite.AddFrame(
            new Rectangle(
            initialFrame.X + (initialFrame.Width * x),
            initialFrame.Y,
            initialFrame.Width,
            initialFrame.Height))
    Next
    previousLocation = location
    currentWaypoint = location
    EnemySprite.CollisionRadius = enemyRadius
End Sub
```

What just happened?

As always, our object contains a Sprite object that will provide its base display and update capabilities. Just like we did with the player ship, we have included a vector pointing to the location on the sprite, where shots will begin when the enemy ship fires its cannon.

Enemy ships will be supplied with a list of waypoints that they will progress through, with the waypoint the ship is currently attempting to reach, stored in the currentWaypoint variable. Movement towards the current waypoint will be scaled by speed.

When the Sprite representing the enemy is created, the enemyRadius value will be copied to the Sprite's CollisionRadius member for checking during collision detection.

The Destroyed Boolean will be set to True by the CollisionManager class, we will create in *Chapter 5*. When Destroyed is true, the ship will not be drawn, updated, or eligible for collision with other objects.

In order to rotate the enemy ship automatically to point in the direction it is travelling, the previousLocation vector stores the ship's location during the previous frame. By calculating the vector from the previous location to the new location, we can determine the facing of the ship and rotate the image appropriately.

Most of the Enemy constructor simply initializes a new Sprite object with the passed parameters, adding frames to the sprite, based on frameCount. Both the previousLocation and the currentWaypoint values are set to the sprite's creation-position, and the collision radius is set at the end of the constructor.

Time for action – waypoint management

1. Add the AddWaypoint() method to the Enemy class:

```
Public Sub AddWaypoint(waypoint As Vector2)
    waypoints.Enqueue(waypoint)
End Sub
```

2. Add the WaypointReached() method to the Enemy class:

```
Public Function WaypointReached() as Boolean
    If Vector2.Distance(EnemySprite.Location, currentWaypoint) <
        CSng(EnemySprite.Source.Width)/2 Then
        Return True
    Else
        Return False
    End If
End Function
```

3. Add the IsActive() method to the Enemy class:

```
Public Function IsActive() As Boolean
    If Destroyed Then
        Return False
    End If

    if waypoints.Count > 0 Then
        Return True
    End If

    If WaypointReached()
```

```
        Return False
    End If

    Return True
End Function
```

What just happened?

When a new waypoint is added to the enemy's route, it is enqueued to the waypoints queue. When `WaypointReached()` is called, the function checks to see if the distance between the sprite's current location and the current waypoint is less than half of the sprite width. If it is, we consider the sprite *close enough* to have reached the destination.

It may be tempting to simply check to see if the distance is equal to zero, but in reality that will almost never happen. Your enemy ship is moving at a fixed rate per second, that is scaled in each frame by the time elapsed since the last frame. For this reason, the ship is moving in increments that may not be equal to full pixels. The ship will get close to the waypoint, but it is unlikely to ever exactly reach it. Instead, it would jump back and forth slightly past the waypoint in one direction, then reverse and jump slightly past it in the other direction.

The `IsActive()` method is a shortcut method to check several different conditions to determine if the ship should be updated and visible. If the ship has been marked as destroyed, obviously it is not active, hence false is returned.

If this ship still has waypoints to reach (and has not been destroyed, otherwise false would already have been returned), we can assume that the ship is still active, and will return true.

Finally, if there are no waypoints left in the waypoints queue, and the `currentWaypoint` has been reached, we return false because the ship has navigated all of its waypoints and is resting at its final destination. When we generate waves of enemies, the initial location and final waypoint will always be off screen, allowing the enemy ships to enter the playfield and exit gracefully. If they make it all the way to the exit without the player destroying them, they will be removed from play.

If none of the conditions above resulted in a return value for the function, it can be assumed that the ship is still travelling to a waypoint, and true is returned from the function.

Time for action – enemy update and draw

1. Add the `Update()` method to the `Enemy` class:

```
Public Sub Update(gameTime As GameTime)
    If IsActive() Then
        Dim heading As Vector2 = currentWaypoint - EnemySprite.
Location
```

```
        If heading <> Vector2.Zero
            heading.Normalize()
        End If
        heading *= speed
        EnemySprite.Velocity = heading
        previousLocation = EnemySprite.Location
        EnemySprite.Update(gameTime)
        EnemySprite.Rotation =
            CSng(Math.Atan2(
            EnemySprite.Location.Y - previousLocation.Y,
            EnemySprite.Location.X - previousLocation.X))

        If WaypointReached() Then
            If waypoints.Count > 0 Then
                currentWaypoint = waypoints.Dequeue()
            End If
        End If
    End If
End Sub
```

2. Add the `Draw()` method to the `Enemy` class:

```
Public Sub Draw(spriteBatch As SpriteBatch)
    If IsActive() Then
        EnemySprite.Draw(spriteBatch)
    End If
End Sub
```

What just happened?

Updating an `Enemy`, begins by checking to see if the enemy is still active. If it is, a heading is calculated by subtracting the enemy's current location from the current waypoint. If the resulting vector is not equal to `Vector2.Zero`, the vector is normalized. We need to make this check, because `Vector2.Zero` cannot be normalized, which will result in an error in our code. Recall that normalizing a vector divides the vector by its length, resulting in a vector with a length of one. `Vector2.Zero` has a length of zero, and dividing anything by zero produces an invalid result.

Once we have a heading, it is multiplied by the ship's speed and stored as the sprite's velocity vector. The current location of the sprite is captured, and the sprite's `Update()` method is called that will move the sprite, based on its velocity.

By using the location, we stored before the `Update()` call, we can use the `Math.Atan2()` method to determine the angle between the current location and the previous location, resulting in an angle of rotation that can be applied to the `Rotation` property of the sprite, in order to automatically rotate it to face the direction in which it is moving. Using this method, a sprite moving only to the right (in the positive X direction) would result in a rotation value of zero, which is why the enemy sprite on the `SpriteSheet` is drawn, facing to the right.

Finally, the `WaypointReached()` method is checked to see if the just-executed movement has brought the enemy to its current waypoint. If it has, and there are additional waypoints for the sprite to visit, the next waypoint is extracted from the queue.

The `Draw()` method should be very familiar by now, as it is the same implementation that all of our manager classes have been using. Rest assured, we will be seeing it again.

The EnemyManager class

The `EnemyManager` class is responsible for keeping track of all active enemy ships, spawning new ships and waves of ships, and determining when ships should fire at the player. Additionally, it will be responsible for removing ships that are destroyed, or leave the play area by completing their waypoint movements.

Time for action – creating the EnemyManager class

1. Add a new class to the **Asteroid Belt Assault** project called `EnemyManager`.

2. Add declarations to the `EnemyManager` class:

```
Private _texture As Texture2D
Private _initialFrame As Rectangle
Private _frameCount As Integer

Public Enemies As List(Of Enemy) = New List(Of Enemy)()

Public EnemyShotManager As ShotManager
Private _playerManager As PlayerManager

Public MinShipsPerWave As Integer = 5
Public MaxShipsPerWave As Integer = 8
Private nextWaveTimer As Single = 0.0
Private nextWaveMinTimer As Single = 8.0
Private shipSpawnTimer As Single = 0.0
Private shipSpawnWaitTime As Single = 0.5

Private shipShotChance As Single = 0.2
```

```
Private pathWaypoints As List(Of List(Of Vector2)) =
    New List(Of List(Of Vector2))()

Private waveSpawns As Dictionary(Of Integer, Integer) =
    New Dictionary(Of Integer, Integer)()

Public Active As Boolean = True

Private rand As Random = New Random()
```

What just happened?

As with our other manager classes, the `EnemyManager` will cache information about the sprite, used to create enemies in the `_texture`, `_initialFrame`, and `_frameCount` members, in order to supply them to the constructor for the `Sprite` class, when an enemy needs to be generated. Enemies will be stored in the `Enemies` list object that will be updated and drawn in a manner similar to the `Asteroids` and `Shots`.

Because the `EnemyManager` will be responsible for determining when enemy ships should fire at the player, it needs a reference to the `PlayerManager` (to determine the player's current position), and contains an instance of `ShotManager` (in order to use the `FireShot()` method).

Waves of enemy ships will be spawned by the `EnemyManager`, based on a timer. Each wave will consist of at least `MinShipsPerWave`, but no more than `MaxShipsPerWave`. These values are declared as `Public`, so that they can be modified at run time, in order to increase the difficulty of the game, as the play continues.

Our standard timing mechanism is in place to determine when each wave should be spawned (`nextWaveTimer` and `nextWaveMinTimer`), and a second timer determines the spawn time between each ship in a wave. In this case, one half of a second will elapse between the spawning of each ship in a wave.

During any given frame, each active ship has a 0.2 percent chance of firing a shot at the player. This number may seem very low, but keep in mind that the check will be made 60 times per second (assuming that other things happening on the system have not slowed things down) for each active ship.

The `pathWaypoints` object is a list of lists of `Vector2` objects. This is not really as complicated as it may sound. Remember that a waypoint is represented by a vector, pointing to a location on the screen. The path that any enemy ship travels is determined by a list of waypoints or a path across the screen that the ship will take.

Since we do not want every ship to follow exactly the same path across the screen, we will define several different paths. Each path has its own list of waypoints. In order to facilitate easy random generation and expansion of the path system, each of the paths is rolled up into a list of paths. When we request an item from the `pathWaypoints` list, the result is a list of vectors. We can then break that list apart for each of the individual waypoints.

When the time comes to actually spawn ships, we will check the `waveSpawns` dictionary. The keys in the dictionary (the first integer) will correspond to the path number, while the value (the second integer) determines the number of ships waiting to be spawned on that path.

The `Active` member will be checked during the class' update tasks to determine if new ships should be spawned. External code can set this Boolean value to false to prevent new ships (or waves of ships) from being spawned.

Managing waypoints

In order to create the `pathWaypoints`, we will use a helper function that generates individual path lists and adds them to the aggregated list object.

Time for action – setting up the EnemyManager class

1. Add the `setUpWaypoints()` helper function to the `EnemyManager` class:

```
Private Sub setUpWaypoints()
    Dim path0 As List(Of Vector2) = new List(Of Vector2)()
    path0.Add(new Vector2(850, 300))
    path0.Add(new Vector2(-100, 300))
    pathWaypoints.Add(path0)
    waveSpawns(0) = 0

    Dim path1 As List(Of Vector2) = new List(Of Vector2)()
    path1.Add(new Vector2(-50, 225))
    path1.Add(new Vector2(850, 225))
    pathWaypoints.Add(path1)
    waveSpawns(1) = 0

    Dim path2 As List(Of Vector2) = new List(Of Vector2)()
    path2.Add(new Vector2(-100, 50))
    path2.Add(new Vector2(150, 50))
    path2.Add(new Vector2(200, 75))
    path2.Add(new Vector2(200, 125))
    path2.Add(new Vector2(150, 150))
    path2.Add(new Vector2(150, 175))
```

```
        path2.Add(new Vector2(200, 200))
        path2.Add(new Vector2(600, 200))
        path2.Add(new Vector2(850, 600))
        pathWaypoints.Add(path2)
        waveSpawns(2) = 0

        Dim path3 As List(Of Vector2) = new List(Of Vector2)()
        path3.Add(new Vector2(600, -100))
        path3.Add(new Vector2(600, 250))
        path3.Add(new Vector2(580, 275))
        path3.Add(new Vector2(500, 250))
        path3.Add(new Vector2(500, 200))
        path3.Add(new Vector2(450, 175))
        path3.Add(new Vector2(400, 150))
        path3.Add(new Vector2(-100, 150))
        pathWaypoints.Add(path3)
        waveSpawns(3) = 0
    End Sub
```

2. Add a constructor to the EnemyManager class:

```
Public Sub New (
    texture As Texture2D,
    initialFrame As Rectangle,
    frameCount As Integer,
    playerManager As PlayerManager,
    screenBounds As Rectangle)

    _texture = texture
    _initialFrame = initialFrame
    _frameCount = frameCount
    _playerManager = playerManager

    EnemyShotManager = new ShotManager(
        texture,
        new Rectangle(0, 300, 5, 5),
            4,
            2,
            150f,
            screenBounds)
    setUpWaypoints()
End Sub
```

What just happened?

Each path is created in the setUpWaypoints() method as individual lists of vectors. Each list is added to the pathWaypoints list, and the waveSpawns dictionary for that path is set to zero, indicating that there are no ships waiting to spawn on that path.

 The EnemyManager constructor assigns the cached values and references, creates an instance of ShotManager, and calls the setUpWaypoints() method to generate the pathWaypoints list. New waypoint paths can be added to the game, simply by creating them in the previous helper method. As we will see in the following section, they will automatically be included in the random generation of waves.

Time for action – spawning enemies

1. Add the SpawnEnemy() method to the EnemyManager class:

```
Public Sub SpawnEnemy(path As Integer)
    Dim thisEnemy As Enemy = new Enemy(
        _texture,
        pathWaypoints(path)(0),
        _initialFrame,
        _frameCount)
    For x As Integer =  0 to pathWaypoints(path).Count - 1
        thisEnemy.AddWaypoint(pathWaypoints(path)(x))
    Next
    Enemies.Add(thisEnemy)
End Sub
```

2. Add the SpawnWave() method to the EnemyManager class:

```
Public Sub SpawnWave(waveType As Integer)
    waveSpawns(waveType) +=
        rand.Next(MinShipsPerWave, MaxShipsPerWave + 1)
End Sub
```

3. Add the updateWaveSpawns() method to the EnemyManager class:

```
Private Sub updateWaveSpawns(gameTime As GameTime)
    shipSpawnTimer += CSng(gameTime.ElapsedGameTime.TotalSeconds)
    If shipSpawnTimer > shipSpawnWaitTime Then
        For x As Integer = waveSpawns.Count - 1 To 0 Step -1
            if waveSpawns(x) > 0 Then
                waveSpawns(x) -= 1
                SpawnEnemy(x)
            End If
        Next
```

```
        shipSpawnTimer = 0
    End If

    nextWaveTimer += CSng(gameTime.ElapsedGameTime.TotalSeconds)
    If nextWaveTimer > nextWaveMinTimer Then
        SpawnWave(rand.Next(0, pathWaypoints.Count))
        nextWaveTimer = 0
    End If
End Sub
```

What just happened?

For spawning a new enemy ship, the path number that the ship will be spawned on, is required. Given this information, a new Enemy object is created and given the cached information about the sprite, along with the first point in the waypoints list for the given path. Each subsequent waypoint is then added to the enemy's waypoint list, and the enemy is added to the Enemies list.

Spawning a new wave does not actually spawn any individual enemies, but instead sets the entry in the waveSpawns dictionary, which corresponds to the waypoint path to a random number of enemies between MinShipsPerWave and MaxShipsPerWave.

The updateWaveSpawns() method maintains the timing loop to determine when new ships can be spawned. If enough time has elapsed, a new ship is spawned at the beginning of each waypoint path that currently has ships waiting to spawn (meaning that the waveSpawns value for that path is greater than zero).

The nextWaveTimer value is then checked to see if enough time has elapsed to spawn a new wave. If so, SpawnWave() is called, given a random wave number between 0 and the last path in pathWaypoints. The timer is then reset in preparation for the next wave.

Time for action – updating and drawing the EnemyManager

1. Add the Update() method to the EnemyManager class:

```
Public Sub Update(gameTime As GameTime)
    EnemyShotManager.Update(gameTime)

    For x As Integer = Enemies.Count - 1 to 0 Step -1
        Enemies(x).Update(gameTime)
        if Not Enemies(x).IsActive() Then
            Enemies.RemoveAt(x)
        Else
            If CSng(rand.Next(0, 1000)) / 10 <= shipShotChance Then
```

```
                    Dim fireLoc As Vector2 = Enemies(x).EnemySprite.
        Location

                    fireLoc += Enemies(x).gunOffset

                    Dim shotDirection As Vector2 =
                        _playerManager.playerSprite.Center -
                        fireLoc

                    EnemyShotManager.FireShot(
                        fireLoc,
                        shotDirection,
                        False)
                End If
            End If
        Next

        If Active Then
            updateWaveSpawns(gameTime)
        End If
    End If
End Sub
```

2. Add the `Draw()` method to the `EnemyManager` class:

```
Public Sub Draw(spriteBatch As SpriteBatch)
    EnemyShotManager.Draw(spriteBatch)

    For Each thisEnemy as Enemy in Enemies
        thisEnemy.Draw(spriteBatch)
    Next
End Sub
```

3. Add a declaration for the `EnemyManager` in the `Game1` class:

```
Private _enemyManager As EnemyManager
```

4. In the `LoadContent()` method of the `Game1` class, initialize the `EnemyManager`, after the `PlayerManager` has been initialized:

```
_enemyManager = new EnemyManager(
    spriteSheet,
    new Rectangle(0,200,50,50),
    6,
    _playerManager,
    new Rectangle(
        0,
        0,
        Me.Window.ClientBounds.Width,
        Me.Window.ClientBounds.Height))
```

5. In the `Update()` method of the `Game1` class, add a line to update the `EnemyManager`, after the update for the `PlayerManager`:

`_enemyManager.Update(gameTime)`

6. In the `Draw()` method of the `Game1` class, add a line to draw the `EnemyManager`, after the call to draw the `PlayerManager`:

`_enemyManager.Draw(spriteBatch)`

7. Launch your game! You can now fly around and fire shots. Waves of enemy ships will spawn and follow their waypoints across the screen.

What just happened?

Once again, we cannot use a `For Each` loop to process the `Enemies` list, because we will be modifying the list by removing inactive ships, so we work backwards through the list with a `For` loop. Any enemies that are marked as inactive will be removed from the list.

For enemies that are still active, a random number between 0 and 999 is generated, which is then divided by 10. The resulting number is a percentage that is compared to `shipShotChance` to determine if the enemy should fire at the player in this frame. If so, the ship's current location and gun offset are used to draw a vector towards the player's current location. This vector is passed to the `FireShot()` method of the `ShotManager`. Recall that

Lastly, if the `Active` member has not been set to false (disabling spawning, until it has been set back to true), the `updateWaveSpawns()` method is called to allow new ships and waves to be spawned as necessary.

Summary

This Chapter has us well on our way to implementing a playable version of **Asteroid Belt Assault**. We have covered the following:

- Building a generic `Sprite` class to represent objects within the game world
- Creating a scrolling `StarField` using a large number of sprites that update their own positions and a class to encapsulate the management of the `StarField` as a whole
- Implementing an asteroid field, with `Asteroids` that rebound off each other, using elastic collisions to simulate realistic changes in direction and speed

- Creating manager classes for shots, the player's star fighter, and enemy ships
- Designing an `Enemy` class that can follow a set of waypoints as the ships traverse the screen
- Building an `EnemyManager` that controls enemy spawn rates and establishes waypoint paths for enemies to follow, as well as controlling enemy fire at the player

In *Chapter 5, Asteroid Belt Assault – Special Effects*, we will finish building the **Asteroid Belt Assault** game, by adding a collision management system to allow objects other than asteroids to interact, particle effects, sound effects and more.

5
Asteroid Belt Assault – Special Effects

*As it stands, the **Asteroid Belt Assault** game allows the player to move around and fire shots in an animated asteroid field with enemy ships that fly in patterns across the screen. For the most part though, there is no game structure in place yet.*

In this chapter, we will look at the following:

- ◆ Creating particles and particle-based special effects
- ◆ Handling collisions between game objects
- ◆ Playing sound effects
- ◆ Completing the game's structure

Explosion effects

While it is possible to assemble a frame-animated explosion effect and overlay it onto the screen whenever an explosion takes place, there are drawbacks to this approach.

The explosion will, by its nature as an animated sprite, be limited to a few frames, which play sequentially. All of the explosions in the game will look exactly alike. We could certainly create a handful of explosion sequences and play a random sequence when an explosion was called for, but we would quickly be using more textures for explosions than for anything else in the game.

Expanding on sprites – particles

Instead of a fixed explosion texture, we will design a simple particle system that we will use to generate explosions in **Asteroid Belt Assault**. This approach will allow us to have dynamically varying explosions that will not look identical to each other. In order to do so, we will create a `Particle` class that will be a child of the `Sprite` class, expanding on its functionality to include acceleration, lifetime information, and changes in color over time.

Particles are short-lived sprites that may be generated in large quantities. Since they will be treated as special effects, there is no need for them to be involved in collision detection, and no need for them to have any knowledge of what is happening in the rest of the game.

Time for action – constructing the Particle class

1. Add a new class called `Particle` to the **Asteroid Belt Assault** project.

2. Modify the declaration of the class by adding the following line below `Public Class Particle`:

   ```
   Inherits Sprite
   ```

3. Add declarations to represent the additional members of the `Particle` class (beyond those of the `Sprite` class):

   ```
   Private _acceleration As Vector2
   Private _maxSpeed As Single
   Private initialDuration As Integer
   Private remainingDuration As Integer
   Private _initialColor As Color
   Private _finalColor As Color
   ```

4. Add properties to access the information about the underlying members:

   ```
   Public ReadOnly Property ElapsedDuration As Integer
       Get
           Return initialDuration - remainingDuration
       End Get
   End Property

   Public ReadOnly Property DurationProgress As Single
       Get
           Return CSng(ElapsedDuration)/CSng(initialDuration)
       End Get
   End Property
   ```

```
Public ReadOnly Property IsActive As Boolean
    Get
        Return remainingDuration > 0
    End Get
End Property
```

5. Add a constructor for the `Particle` class:

```
Public Sub New (
    location As Vector2,
    texture As Texture2D,
    initialFrame As Rectangle,
    velocity As Vector2,
    acceleration As Vector2,
    maxSpeed As Single,
    duration As Integer,
    initialColor As Color,
    finalColor As Color)

    MyBase.New(location, texture, initialFrame, velocity)

    initialDuration = duration
    remainingDuration = duration
    _acceleration = acceleration
    _maxSpeed = maxSpeed
    _initialColor = initialColor
    _finalColor = finalColor
End Sub
```

What just happened?

The `Particle` class extends the `Sprite` class, adding new features to those of its parent. We indicate this to Visual Basic by stating that the class `Inherits Sprite` as its base class.

> **Visual Basic vs. C#—Class inheritance**
>
> The C# equivalent of the `Inherits` notation is the addition of the base class name, following a colon after the class declaration, on the same line. Our class declaration in C# would be `public class Particle : Sprite`.

The `_acceleration` vector will be applied to the sprite's velocity during each update cycle. The length of the velocity vector itself will be limited in magnitude to `_maxSpeed`.

When the particle is created, its `initialDuration` and `remainingDuration` will be set to the duration value passed into the constructor. These values will be used to determine, how far along the particle's lifespan it is at any given time.

The `_initialColor` and `_finalColor` members determine the tint color that will be used in the `SpriteBatch.Draw()` call, when the sprite is displayed. The `color` value will be altered smoothly as the particle moves through its lifecycle, beginning at `_initialColor` and reaching `_finalColor` by its last frame.

Each of the properties of the `Particle` class do not directly return the contents of member variables, but rather return values, based on the two duration members. `ElapsedDuration` returns the difference between `initialDuration` and `remainingDuration`, resulting in the number of frames for which the particle will continue to exist. A percentage value (between zero and one) is returned by the `DurationProgress` property, representing the current position along the particle's lifespan.

Finally, `IsActive` returns false if the `remainingDuration` has reached zero.

Time for action – updating and drawing particles

1. Add an `Update()` method to the `Particle` class:

```
Public Overrides Sub Update(gameTime As GameTime)
    If IsActive Then
        velocity += _acceleration
        If velocity.Length() > _maxSpeed
            velocity.Normalize()
            velocity *= _maxSpeed
        End If
        TintColor = Color.Lerp(
            _initialColor,
            _finalColor,
            DurationProgress)
        remainingDuration -= 1
        MyBase.Update(gameTime)
    End If
End Sub
```

2. Add a `Draw()` method to the `Particle` class:

```
Public Overrides Sub Draw(spriteBatch As SpriteBatch)
    If IsActive Then
        MyBase.Draw(spriteBatch)
    End If
End Sub
```

What just happened?

Both the `Update()` and the `Draw()` methods, override the `Sprite` class' methods of the same name, because we need to alter the behavior associated with them. Both methods will only execute any code if the `IsActive` property returns true. In fact, for the `Draw()` method, this is the only reason we override the method—to prevent drawing a particle that has expired.

In the `Update()` method, we add the `_acceleration` vector to the velocity vector, and then check to see if the length of the velocity vector has exceeded the maximum speed at which the particle is allowed to move. If it has, the velocity vector is normalized and then multiplied by the maximum speed, resulting in a vector pointing in the same direction at the maximum length.

The `TintColor` property will be reset in each frame using the `Lerp()` method of the `Color` class. `Lerp()` returns a color between the two colors provided as parameters, that is scaled towards one color or the other, based on the value of the third parameter, which ranges from zero to one. A zero value would return the first color parameter, while a value of one would return the second. Values between zero and one return a mixing of the two colors along a linear scale.

> **Lerping**
>
> The term **Lerp** is a rough acronym for **linear interpolation**, a method to progress between two known points, based on a reference value. For example, if you were to lerp between 1 and 10, with a control of 50 percent, the result would be 5 (halfway between the initial and final values). The `MathHelper` class, contains a `Lerp()` method that can be used for numerical lerping, and several XNA structures, including vectors, contain their own `Lerp()` methods as well.

In both the `Update()` and the `Draw()` methods, the base method of the `Sprite` class is called as the last task, each method performs before exiting.

Particle explosions

Now that we have the `Particle` class available to us, we can turn our attention to building particle-based explosions. In the `SpriteSheet.png` file, beginning at location (`0, 100`) are three frames of roughly circular, partially transparent spattering that we will use as the basis for our explosion effects.

When a new explosion is generated, we will create a random number of these images and an additional number of individual small dot-shaped particles to represent the explosion. These particles will be moved slowly away from their starting point in random directions, providing a gradually expanding explosion effect.

Time for action – the ExplosionManager class

1. Add a new class called `ExplosionManager` to the **Asteroid Belt Assault** project.

2. Add declarations to the `ExplosionManager` class:

```
Private _texture As Texture2D
Private pieceRectangles As List(Of Rectangle) =
    new List(Of Rectangle)()
Private _pointRectangle As Rectangle

Private minPieceCount As Integer = 3
Private maxPieceCount As Integer = 6
Private minPointCount As Integer = 20
Private maxPointCount As Integer = 30

Private durationCount As Integer = 90
Private explosionMaxSpeed As Single = 30

Private pieceSpeedScale As Single = 6
Private pointSpeedMin As Integer = 15
Private pointSpeedMax As Integer = 30

Private initialColor As Color = new Color(1.0F, 0.3F, 0.0F) * 0.5
Private finalColor As Color = new Color(0.0F, 0.0F, 0.0F) * 0

Private rand As Random = new Random()

Private ExplosionParticles As List(Of Particle) =
    new List(Of Particle)()
```

3. Add a constructor to the `ExplosionManager` class:

```
Public Sub New (
    Texture As Texture2D,
    initialFrame As Rectangle,
    pieceCount As Integer,
    pointRectangle As Rectangle)

    _texture = texture
    For x As Integer = 0 to pieceCount - 1
        pieceRectangles.Add(new Rectangle(
            initialFrame.X + (initialFrame.Width * x),
            initialFrame.Y,
            initialFrame.Width,
            initialFrame.Height))
    Next
    _pointRectangle=pointRectangle
End Sub
```

What just happened?

As with the `EnemyManager` class, we will cache the basic values needed to create our sprites within the `ExplosionManager` class. In this case, the texture containing the explosion pieces is stored along with a list of rectangles representing the frames of each explosion piece. A single rectangle is stored for the explosion sprites that will be added to the effect.

When a new explosion is generated, a random number of large pieces between `minPieceCount` and `maxPieceCount` will be created, along with a random number of point sprites between `minPointCount` and `maxPointCount`. Each particle will live for 90 frames (approximately 3 seconds), and have a maximum speed of 30 pixels per second. The `pieceSpeedScale`, `pointSpeedMin`, and `pointSpeedMax` variables control how rapidly the explosion pieces and point sprites move away from the center of the explosion.

The particles will begin their lifespan in a half-transparent orange color, as indicated by the `initialColor` variable. By the time the full duration has elapsed, this color will have reached `finalColor` and faded to fully transparent. All of the generated particles for all active explosions are kept in the `ExplosionParticles` list. During both the `Update()` and `Draw()` methods of the `ExplosionManager`, each item in the list will be processed. When a particle has expired, it will be removed from the list, so that it is no longer drawn to the screen.

Type Characters

Visual Basic will usually do a fairly good job, of figuring out what your literals are supposed to be. In the past, when we have declared a variable of type `Single` and initialized it, we have simply added the value without any special notation (`Public speed As Single = 5`).

In our case of the previous code, when trying to initialize the Color members, if we were to simply say `New Color(1.0, 0.3, 0.0)`, we would trigger an Overload Resolution Error, because Visual Basic will not quite know how to interpret the literal numbers and map them to one of the constructor overloads for the Color type. We could surround each of the numbers with `CSng()`, as we have used for conversions, but we can also use a shorthand notation called a **Type Character**. Appending an `F` to the literal will let Visual Basic know that we are specifying a `Single`. There are several other Type characters available, such as `S` for `Short`, `C` for `Char`, and `I` for `integer`. A full list is available at `http://msdn.microsoft.com/en-US/library/s9cz43ek(v=VS.100).aspx`.

Time for action – creating explosions

1. Add the `RandomDirection()` helper method to the `ExplosionManager` class:

```
Public Function randomDirection(scale As Single) As Vector2
    Dim direction As Vector2
    Do
        direction = new Vector2(
        rand.Next(0, 101) - 50,
        rand.Next(0, 101) - 50)
    Loop While direction.Length() = 0
    direction.Normalize()
    direction *= scale

    Return direction
End Function
```

2. Add the `AddExplosion()` method to the `ExplosionManager` class:

```
Public Sub AddExplosion(
    location As Vector2, momentum As Vector2)

    Dim pieceLocation As Vector2 = location -
        new Vector2(pieceRectangles(0).Width/2.0F,
            pieceRectangles(0).Height/2.0F)

    Dim pieces As Integer = rand.Next(minPieceCount, maxPieceCount +
1)
    For x As Integer = 1 to pieces
        ExplosionParticles.Add(new Particle(
            pieceLocation,
            _texture,
            pieceRectangles(rand.Next(0,pieceRectangles.Count)),
            randomDirection(pieceSpeedScale) + momentum,
            Vector2.Zero,
            explosionMaxSpeed,
            durationCount,
            initialColor,
            finalColor))
    Next

    Dim points As Integer = rand.Next(minPointCount, maxPointCount +
1)

    For x As Integer = 1 To points
        ExplosionParticles.Add(new Particle(
```

```
                    location,
                    _texture,
                    _pointRectangle,
                    randomDirection(rand.Next(
                        pointSpeedMin, pointSpeedMax)) + momentum,
                    Vector2.Zero,
                    explosionMaxSpeed,
                    durationCount,
                    initialColor,
                    finalColor))

        Next
    End Sub
```

What just happened?

The `RandomDirection()` helper method generates random X and Y coordinates, each between -50 and 50, and uses them to create a vector representing a direction. Because it is technically possible that the resulting vector will be a zero vector (0, 0) that cannot be normalized (and would represent no direction at all), we enclose the generation code in a `do` loop, which simply checks the generated vector for a length, other than zero before continuing. Once an appropriate vector is generated, it is normalized and multiplied by the scale passed to the method and returned.

When an explosion is added, the `AddExplosion()` method is passed a vector pointing to the center point of the explosion. Since we draw sprites as rectangles that start in the upper-left corner of the sprite, we need to compensate for the size of the larger explosion pieces and keep them centered on the explosion point. The `pieceLocation` vector is calculated by subtracting half of the height and width of the rectangle for the larger pieces from the center point of the explosion. Here again, we are using the **Type Character** shorthand notation to let Visual Basic know that we are working with a `Single`, so we do not have to surround the results of the division with `CSng()` calls.

Next, a random number of pieces are generated, each added as a new particle to the `ExplosionParticles` list. The first four parameters of the constructor for the `Particle` class are the same as for any of our other sprites: location, texture, initial frame, and velocity. In the case of velocity, the `randomDirection()` method is used to generate a random vector at the speed of `pieceSpeedScale` to move the piece slowly away from the center point of the explosion. We also add the momentum parameter that was passed to `AddExplosion()` to represent a portion of the velocity of the original object that the explosion should retain. Without a small amount of momentum, the explosion associated with a moving object would stop dead at the point of the explosion. By adding the momentum to the explosion, we can create a drifting effect, where the entire explosion moves in the same direction as the original object.

Our particles will not have any built-in acceleration in this case, so `Vector2.Zero` is passed for the acceleration parameter. The remaining parameters of the `Particle` constructor pass in the named variables representing the duration of the explosion and the starting and ending tint colors for the sprite.

After each of the pieces is generated, an identical process is executed to create the point sprites for the explosion, with the only difference being that the point sprites move at a higher speed away from the center of the explosion. We also add a randomization factor to make them look more realistic.

Time for action – updating and drawing explosions

1. Add the `Update()` method to the `ExplosionManager` class:

```
Public Sub Update(gameTime As GameTime)
    For x As Integer = ExplosionParticles.Count-1 to 0 Step -1
        If (ExplosionParticles(x).IsActive) Then
            ExplosionParticles(x).Update(gameTime)
        Else
            ExplosionParticles.RemoveAt(x)
        End If
    Next
End Sub
```

2. Add the `Draw()` method to the `ExplosionManager` class:

3. Add an instance of the `ExplosionManager` to the declarations area of the `Game1.vb` class file:

```
Private _explosionManager As ExplosionManager
```

4. Still in the `Game1` class, add the initialization of the `_explosionManager` object to the `LoadContent()` method:

```
_explosionManager = new ExplosionManager(
    spriteSheet,
    new Rectangle(0, 100, 50, 50),
    3,
    new Rectangle(0, 450, 2, 2))
```

5. In the `Update()` method of `Game1`, add a line to update the `ExplosionManager`, after the `EnemyManager` has been updated:

```
_explosionManager.Update(gameTime)
```

6. In the `Draw()` method of the `Game1`, add the following after the `ShotManager` draw call:

```
_explosionManager.Draw(spriteBatch)
```

What just happened?

As with the other instances where we want to remove objects from a list while processing it, we cannot use a `For Each` loop to update the `ExplosionParticles` list. We loop backwards through the list, calling each individual particle's `Update()` method if it is still active, and removing it from the list if it is not.

When drawing the particle list, we do not need to worry about checking for active particles, since the overloaded `Draw()` method that we added to the `Particle` class will not draw a particle that has expired.

The collision manager

In order for our particle-based explosions to ever appear on the screen, we need to be able to detect collisions between objects. This will be the responsibility of the `CollisionManager` class that will handle all types of collision detection in the game.

Time for action – creating the CollisionManager class

1. Add a new class called `CollisionManager` to the `AsteroidBeltAssault` class.

2. Add declarations to the `CollisionManager` class:

```
Private _asteroidManager As AsteroidManager
Private _playerManager As PlayerManager
Private _enemyManager as EnemyManager
Private _explosionManager As ExplosionManager
Private offScreen As Vector2 = new Vector2(-500, -500)
Private shotToAsteroidImpact As Vector2 = new Vector2(0, -20)
Private enemyPointValue As Integer = 100
```

3. Add a constructor to the `CollisionManager` class:

```
Public Sub New(
    asteroidManager As AsteroidManager,
    playerManager As PlayerManager,
    enemyManager As EnemyManager,
    explosionManager As ExplosionManager)
```

```
          _asteroidManager = asteroidManager
          _playerManager = playerManager
          _enemyManager = enemyManager
          _explosionManager = explosionManager
      End Sub
```

What just happened?

Because it will be comparing various objects against each other, the `CollisionManager` needs to know about most of the other managers in the game. References to these managers are stored in the member variables of the `CollisionManager` class.

The `offScreen` vector is used as a shortcut for destroying some objects. Remember that our `Asteroids` and `Shot` objects will automatically clean themselves up, when they leave the playing area of the screen, so setting their location to a position far off of the screen will trigger this cleanup code without having to duplicate it in our `CollisionManager` class. Enemy ships and the players are handled somewhat differently, since they each have a `Destroyed` variable that can be set.

Unlike our special case asteroid-to-asteroid collisions, where we assumed that all of the asteroids have the same mass, player shots impacting an asteroid will neither bounce off, nor modify the flight of the asteroid, as if it also had the same mass.

When a player shot collides with an asteroid, the shot will impart a small amount of upward velocity to the asteroid and disappear. The `shotToAsteroidImpact` vector controls how much velocity each shot will transfer to an asteroid. This allows the player to slightly redirect the course of asteroids that may be headed for them to avoid a potential collision.

Finally, whenever a player shot collides with an enemy ship, the `enemyPointValue` will be added to the player's score.

Handling collisions

Apart from our asteroids bouncing off each other, we will handle the following five different types of collisions:

- Player shot to enemy ship collisions
- Player shot to asteroid collisions
- Enemy shot to player collisions
- Enemy ship to player collisions
- Asteroid to player collisions

The first two types of collisions represent the player influencing the game world, while the last three types of collisions result in the player being destroyed.

We will build five different helper functions to check for these collisions, each one following the same pattern. The two lists of objects involved in a potential collision will be compared to each other, with each resulting collision triggering an action.

Time for action – player shot collisions

1. Add the `checkShotToEnemy()` method to the `CollisionManager` class:

```
Private Sub checkShotToEnemyCollisions()
    For Each shot As Sprite in _playerManager.PlayerShotManager.
Shots
        For Each thisEnemy As Enemy in _enemyManager.Enemies
            If shot.IsCircleColliding(
                thisEnemy.EnemySprite.Center,
                thisEnemy.EnemySprite.CollisionRadius) Then

                shot.Location = offScreen
                thisEnemy.Destroyed = true
                _playerManager.PlayerScore += enemyPointValue
                _explosionManager.AddExplosion(
                    thisEnemy.EnemySprite.Center,
                    thisEnemy.EnemySprite.Velocity/10)
            End If
        Next
    Next
End Sub
```

2. Add the `checkShotToAsteroid()` method to the `CollisionManager` class:

```
Private Sub checkShotToAsteroidCollisions()
    For Each shot As Sprite in _playerManager.PlayerShotManager.
Shots
        For Each asteroid As Sprite in _asteroidManager.Asteroids
            If shot.IsCircleColliding(
                asteroid.Center,
                asteroid.CollisionRadius) Then

                shot.Location = offScreen
                asteroid.Velocity += shotToAsteroidImpact
            End If
        Next
    Next
End Sub
```

What just happened?

The structure of both of these methods is very similar. A `For Each` loop iterates over each active player shot, and a loop nested inside that, loops through each enemy or asteroid. This way, every shot will be tested against every enemy and every asteroid in the game during each frame.

The `Sprite` class' `CircleCollision()` method is used to determine if the shot has impacted another object. In the case of enemies, a collision will move the bullet off screen, mark the enemy as destroyed, add to the player's score, and play an explosion effect. When the explosion is created, one-tenth of the enemy's velocity is passed as the momentum parameter to the explosion, causing the explosion to drift in the direction that the enemy was travelling when it was destroyed.

For asteroid collisions, the shot is still moved off screen, but the asteroid is not destroyed by the shot. Instead, a small portion of the shot's velocity is added to the asteroid's velocity, allowing the player to nudge the asteroid onto a new course.

Time for action – player collisions

1. Add the `checkShotToPlayerCollision()` method to the `CollisionManager` class:

```
Private Sub checkShotToPlayerCollisions()
    For Each shot As Sprite in _enemyManager.EnemyShotManager.
Shots
        If shot.IsCircleColliding(
            _playerManager.playerSprite.Center,
            _playerManager.playerSprite.CollisionRadius) Then

            shot.Location = offScreen
            _playerManager.Destroyed = True
            _explosionManager.AddExplosion(
                _playerManager.playerSprite.Center,
                Vector2.Zero)
        End If
    Next
End Sub
```

2. Add the `checkEnemyToPlayerCollisions()` method to the `CollisionManager` class:

```
Private Sub checkEnemyToPlayerCollisions()
    For Each thisEnemy As Enemy in _enemyManager.Enemies
        If thisEnemy.EnemySprite.IsCircleColliding(
```

```
        _playerManager.playerSprite.Center,
        _playerManager.playerSprite.CollisionRadius) Then

        thisEnemy.Destroyed = True
        _explosionManager.AddExplosion(
            thisEnemy.EnemySprite.Center,
            thisEnemy.EnemySprite.Velocity / 10)

        _playerManager.Destroyed = True

        _explosionManager.AddExplosion(
            _playerManager.playerSprite.Center,
            Vector2.Zero)
      End If
    Next
End Sub
```

3. Add the `checkAsteroidToPlayerCollisions()` method to the `CollisionManager` class:

```
Private Sub checkAsteroidToPlayerCollisions()
    For Each asteroid As Sprite in _asteroidManager.Asteroids
        If asteroid.IsCircleColliding(
            _playerManager.playerSprite.Center,
            _playerManager.playerSprite.CollisionRadius) Then

            _explosionManager.AddExplosion(
                asteroid.Center,
                asteroid.Velocity/10)

            asteroid.Location = offScreen

            _playerManager.Destroyed = True
            _explosionManager.AddExplosion(
                _playerManager.playerSprite.Center,
                Vector2.Zero)
        End If
    Next
End Sub
```

What just happened?

There is only a single loop in each of the . . . ToPlayerCollisions() methods, since all of the objects are being compared to the single player object, but otherwise the code is very similar. In each case, the player is marked as Destroyed, which we will detect during Game1's update loop.

Time for action – using the CollisionManager class

1. Add the CheckCollisions() method to the CollisionManager class:

```
Public Sub CheckCollisions()
    checkShotToEnemyCollisions()
    checkShotToAsteroidCollisions()
    If Not _playerManager.Destroyed Then
        checkShotToPlayerCollisions()
        checkEnemyToPlayerCollisions()
        checkAsteroidToPlayerCollisions()
    End If
End Sub
```

2. Add a declaration for the CollisionManager to the Game1 declarations area:

```
Private _collisionManager As CollisionManager
```

3. Initialize the CollisionManager in the LoadContent() method of the Game1 class, after the ExplosionManager has been initialized:

```
_collisionManager = new CollisionManager(
    _asteroidManager,
    _playerManager,
    _enemyManager,
    _explosionManager)
```

4. In the Game1 class' Update() method, in the GameStates.Playing section, add the following after the ExplosionManager is updated:

```
_collisionManager.CheckCollisions()
```

5. Launch the game to view collision detection and explosion effects. After your ship has been destroyed, you will need to press *Alt + F4* (or close the game window with the mouse) to exit the game.

What just happened?

The `CheckCollisions()` method, calls each of the individual check methods, providing a single point for external code to use the `CollisionManager`.

During the `Update()` method of `Game1`, the `CollisionManager` is checked during each frame, to determine if any game objects have collided. If they have, it will take appropriate action.

However, at this point, your ship will be able to collide with asteroids, enemies, and enemy bullets, and explode once. After that, you will still be invisible and immobile. Enemies will continue to fire at your previous location, but since `playerManager.Destroyed` has been set to true, impacts of other objects with your ship will not be checked.

Sound effects

Sound effects add a level of feedback to your game that, when missing, will be very noticeable to players. Even in situations where sound effects are not realistic (you would not actually hear explosions in space), their absence would feel wrong while playing.

Generating and finding sound effects

There are a number of sound effects freely available on the web that can be found with a little searching. Locating truly royalty free sound effects is a bit harder. Most of the sound effects archives on the web are not the actual originators of the sound files, so their true licensing requirements may be difficult to track down.

You can always record your own effects if you have a way to simulate sounds. In the case of **Asteroid Belt Assault**, the sound effects were generated using a program called **sfxr**. This application, available at `http://www.drpetter.se/project_sfxr.html` includes full source code, and produces basic sound effects via random generation.

Sound in XNA

There are two different approaches to implementing sound in XNA. The first option is to use **XACT**, Microsoft's Cross-platform Audio Creation Tool. XACT includes an authoring tool that allows you to build sound banks containing multiple audio tracks. XACT can be used in Windows and Xbox 360 projects, but not on the Windows Phone 7 platform.

The 3.0 release of XNA introduced a new method for implementing sound, which is available on all of the XNA platforms: the `SoundEffect` and `SoundEffectInstance` classes. These classes are much easier to use than XACT, and are available on all of the XNA platforms. We will use the `SoundEffect` classes in `AsteroidBeltAssault`.

Time for action – building a sound effects manager

1. Download the `2403_05_AUDIOPACK.zip` file from the book's website and extract the files to a temporary folder.

2. Right-click on the content project in **Solution Explorer** and add a new folder called **Sounds**.

3. Add the `.WAV` files from the audio pack temporary folder to your new **Sounds** folder in the content project.

4. Add a new module (not a class this time) to the **Asteroid Belt Assault** project called **SoundManager** by right-clicking on the project name in **Solution Explorer** and selecting **Add | Module**.

5. Declare variables for the **SoundManager** module:

```
Private explosions As List(Of SoundEffect) =
    new List(Of SoundEffect)()
Private explosionCount As Integer = 4

Private playerShot As SoundEffect
Private enemyShot As SoundEffect

Private rand As Random = new Random()
```

6. Add the `Initialize()` method to the `SoundManager` class:

```
Public Sub Initialize(content As ContentManager)
    Try
        playerShot = content.Load(Of SoundEffect)("Sounds\Shot1")
        enemyShot = content.Load(Of SoundEffect)("Sounds\Shot2")

        For x As Integer = 1 to explosionCount
            explosions.Add(
                content.Load(Of SoundEffect)("Sounds\Explosion" +
                    x.ToString()))
        Next
    Catch
        Debug.Write("SoundManager Initialization Failed")
    End Try
End Sub
```

7. Add the `PlayExplosion()` method to the `SoundManager` class:

```
Public Sub PlayExplosion()
    Try
        Explosions(rand.Next(0, explosionCount)).Play()
    Catch
        Debug.Write("PlayExplosion Failed")
    End Try
End Sub
```

8. Add the `PlayPlayerShot()` method to the `SoundManager` class:

```
Public Sub PlayPlayerShot()
    Try
        playerShot.Play()
    Catch
        Debug.Write("PlayPlayerShot Failed")
    End Try
End Sub
```

9. Add the `PlayEnemyShot()` method to the `SoundManager` class:

```
Public Sub PlayEnemyShot()
    Try
        enemyShot.Play()
    Catch
        Debug.Write("PlayEnemyShot Failed")
    End Try
End Sub
```

What just happened?

By creating our `SoundManager` class as a module, we can use its methods from anywhere in our program without creating instances like we would for a class. In fact, we can never create instances of a module.

Visual Basic vs C# - Modules, Statics, and Shared

In C# examples, you may see classes declared as `static`, such as `public static class SoundManager`. This is roughly equivalent to a Visual Basic module, though in C# all of the members of a `static` class must also be declared with the `static` modifier. The C# `static` modifier for members is similar to Visual Basic's `Shared` modifier – A `static` member of a C# class is shared across all instances of the class, just like the `Shared` members that we declared in the `ShotManager` class in the previous chapter.

Also, unlike a class, we do not have an instance constructor. We still need some way to pass in a reference to a `ContentManager` object, however, so we add the `Initialize()` method to do the work that a class constructor would normally do. It uses the `ContentManager` to load `SoundEffect` objects in exactly the same way, we load textures or fonts. Once the `SoundEffect` has been loaded, it supports a `Play()` method that causes the sound effect to be played once.

> **SoundEffect and SoundEffectInstance classes**
>
> XNA defines these two classes to assist in playing sound effects. In reality, all actual sounds are played by `SoundEffectInstances`. The `SoundEffect.Play()` method creates a new instance, plays the sound, and disposes off the instance. This allows **fire and forget** handling of sound effects. If you wish to have more control over the effects, you can create instances directly with `SoundEffect.CreateInstance()`. `SoundEffectInstances` can be played, stopped, and looped. Windows can play any number of sounds at the same time - subject to hardware limitations and performance issues.. On the Xbox 360, a total of 300 `SoundEffectInstances` (stopped or playing) can exist at any one time. If you create a `SoundEffectInstance` manually, you must also dispose it off manually (via the `Dispose()` method), when you no longer need it.

Everything in the `Initialize()` and `Play...()` methods are surrounded by `Try...Catch` blocks that attempt to execute the code inside the `Try` block and, if an exception is generated, executes the `Catch` block. When an exception occurs, we use the `Debug.Write()` method that will output a debugger message indicating any problems encountered. We need to do this because on a system without audio hardware, attempting to load or play a sound effect will cause an exception, crashing the game. Since, in this case, we simply want to do nothing if the call fails, the `Catch` blocks write a debug message and take no other action.

Time for action – using the SoundManager class

1. In the `Game1.vb` file, add the following line as the last line in the `LoadContent()` method:

```
SoundManager.Initialize(Content)
```

2. Open the `ExplosionManager.vb` file, and add the following as the last line of the `AddExplosion()` method:

```
SoundManager.PlayExplosion()
```

3. Open the `ShotManager.vb` file and add the following to the end of `FireShot()`:

```
If playerFired Then
    SoundManager.PlayPlayerShot()
Else
    SoundManager.PlayEnemyShot()
End If
```

4. Execute the game and enjoy the sound effects.

What just happened?

Using the `SoundManager` module is very simple. After it has been initialized, we only need a single line of code to play any of our sound effects. Because we are using a module instead of a class, all of the classes in our game simply know about it, and can use it without any type of declaration beforehand.

The game structure

Now that we have nearly all of the pieces of our game in place, we need to start bringing them together into a structure that supports a normal game flow, from title screen, to playing, to game over, and back to the title screen, as shown in the following image:

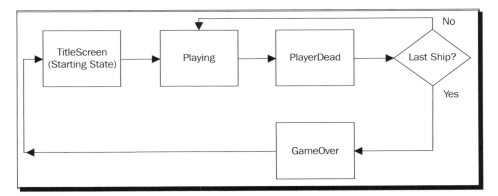

The game will begin in the **TitleScreen** state. When the user begins the game, the state switches to **Playing**, until the user collides with an enemy ship, an enemy shot, or an asteroid. At that point, the state switches to **PlayerDead**.

The game remains in the **PlayerDead** state for a few seconds to let the player agonize over their defeat, and to allow any enemy ships on the screen to move off screen. At that point, the new game state depends on the number of remaining ships that the player has.

If the ship they just lost was not their last ship, the state returns to **Playing** and the game continues. If it was their last ship, however, the state switches to **GameOver**. The game then returns to the **TitleScreen** state.

Time for action – structuring the game

_1._ In the `EnemyManager` class, change the default value of the `Active` member from `True` to `False`:

```
Public Active As Boolean = False
```

_2._ In the `Game1.vb` file, modify the declaration for the `gameState` variable to set the default to `GameStates.TitleScreen`:

```
Private gameState As GameStates = GameStates.TitleScreen
```

_3._ Right-click on the **Fonts** folder in the content project, and select **Add | New Item...** Create a new `SpriteFont` object named `Pericles14.spritefont`.

_4._ The XML file for the `SpriteFont` will open automatically. Change the `<FontName>` tag from `Segoe UI Mono` to `Pericles`.

_5._ Add the following declarations to the `Game1` class:

```
Public pericles14 As SpriteFont

Private playerDeathDelayTime As Single = 10
Private playerDeathTimer As Single = 0
Private titleScreenTimer As Single = 0
Private titleScreenDelayTime As Single = 1

Private playerStartingLives As Integer = 3
Private playerStartLocation As Vector2 = New Vector2(390, 550)
Private scoreLocation As Vector2 = New Vector2(20, 10)
Private livesLocation As Vector2 = New Vector2(20, 25)
```

_6._ Add the following line to the `LoadContent()` method of the `Game1` class to load the `Pericles` sprite font that we just created:

```
pericles14 = Content.Load(Of SpriteFont)("Fonts\Pericles14")
```

7. Add the `resetGame()` helper function to the `Game1` class:

```
Private Sub resetGame()
    _playerManager.playerSprite.Location = playerStartLocation
    For Each asteroid As Sprite in _asteroidManager.Asteroids
        asteroid.Location = new Vector2(-500, -500)
    Next
    _enemyManager.Enemies.Clear()
    _enemyManager.Active = true
    _playerManager.PlayerShotManager.Shots.Clear()
    _enemyManager.EnemyShotManager.Shots.Clear()
    _playerManager.Destroyed = false
End Sub
```

8. In the `Update()` method of the `Game1` class, replace the current case section for `GameStates.TitleScreen` with the following:

```
Case GameStates.TitleScreen
    titleScreenTimer +=
        CSng(gameTime.ElapsedGameTime.TotalSeconds)

    If titleScreenTimer >= titleScreenDelayTime Then
        If (Keyboard.GetState().IsKeyDown(Keys.Space)) Or
            (GamePad.GetState(PlayerIndex.One).Buttons.A =
            ButtonState.Pressed) Then

            _playerManager.LivesRemaining = playerStartingLives
            _playerManager.PlayerScore = 0
            resetGame()
            gameState = GameStates.Playing
        End If
    End If
```

9. Replace the case section for `GameStates.Playing` with the following:

```
Case GameStates.Playing
    _starField.Update(gameTime)
    _asteroidManager.Update(gameTime)
    _playerManager.Update(gameTime)
    _enemyManager.Update(gameTime)
    _explosionManager.Update(gameTime)
    _collisionManager.CheckCollisions()

    If _playerManager.Destroyed Then
        playerDeathTimer = 0
```

```
        _enemyManager.Active = false
        _playerManager.LivesRemaining -= 1
        If _playerManager.LivesRemaining < 0 Then
            gameState = GameStates.GameOver
        Else
            gameState = GameStates.PlayerDead
        End If
    End If
```

10. Replace the case section for `GameStates.PlayerDead` with the following:

```
Case GameStates.PlayerDead
    playerDeathTimer +=
        CSng(gameTime.ElapsedGameTime.TotalSeconds)

    _starField.Update(gameTime)
    _asteroidManager.Update(gameTime)
    _enemyManager.Update(gameTime)
    _playerManager.PlayerShotManager.Update(gameTime)
    _explosionManager.Update(gameTime)

    If playerDeathTimer >= playerDeathDelayTime Then
        resetGame()
        gameState = GameStates.Playing
    End If
```

11. Replace the case section for `GameStates.GameOver` with the following:

```
Case GameStates.GameOver
    playerDeathTimer +=
        CSng(gameTime.ElapsedGameTime.TotalSeconds)
    _starField.Update(gameTime)
    _asteroidManager.Update(gameTime)
    _enemyManager.Update(gameTime)
    _playerManager.PlayerShotManager.Update(gameTime)
    _explosionManager.Update(gameTime)
    If playerDeathTimer >= playerDeathDelayTime Then
        gameState = GameStates.TitleScreen
    End If
```

What just happened?

Currently, the EnemyManager starts generating enemies as soon as the game starts, even if the game is sitting at the title screen. It is set this way because, while we were building the parts of our game, we wanted to see the enemy ships spawn, move, and fire. Now that we are building the structure of our game, we need to disable the EnemyManager by default, waiting for the game to start to enable it.

The same setting change is needed for the default game state. Currently, for testing purposes, we have the gameState variable defaulting to GameStates.Playing, meaning that when the game is launched, the title screen is bypassed in favor of going directly to the game. We change this here to begin our game in the right mode.

Next, we need to define a number of variables to control the flow and appearance of the game, starting with a SpriteFont object to hold the Pericles 14 point font, we added to the project when we initially created it.

Our standard timer is implemented with playerDeathTimer and playerDeathDelayTime to control how long the game waits, when the player has been killed before resetting and respawning the player.

The same timing mechanism utilizes titleScreenTimer and titleScreenDelayTime to ensure that the title screen does not accept input for the first second it is active. This way, if the player is still pressing a key when the game switches back to the title screen, a new game will not be immediately started.

When starting a new game, the player will begin with three lives, and whenever the player is spawned (either for a new game or after being destroyed), the player will start at a screen location of (390, 550).

The final two vectors, scoreLocation and livesLocation, point to the location on the screen where the player's score and remaining lives will be displayed.

The resetGame() method positions the player, moves each asteroid to an off-screen location (to prevent them from being too close to the player when the player spawns), and clears any active enemies and shots. It enables the EnemyManager and finally sets the playerManager.Destroyed value to false, indicating that the player is currently alive.

The title screen update code waits for the timer to elapse, and then checks to see if either the *Space* bar on the keyboard or the *A* button on the GamePad has been pressed. When it has, the player's remaining lives and score are reset, and the resetGame() method is called. The game state is then switched to GameStates.Playing.

While in the `Playing` state, the code is similar to what we were using during testing, updating each of the different managers. The addition here is that, after all of the updates, the `playerManager.Destroyed` value is checked. If the player has been destroyed, the death timer is reset, the `EnemyManager` is disabled, and a life is deducted from the player's remaining total. If the life that was just lost was the player's last, the game state is set to `GameOver`. Otherwise, the state is set to `PlayerDead`.

When in the `PlayerDead` state, most of the managers continue to update as normal, so the star field continues to move, and game objects continue on their courses. The `CollisionManager` is not updated while the player is dead. When the delay timer has expired, the `resetGame()` method is called and the state is set back to `Playing`.

Finally, when the game is over, the `playerDeathTimer` will accumulate time until it has finished, and then the game will return to the title screen.

At the moment, running the game will not produce the expected results, since we have not yet updated the case statements in the `Draw()` method to match the game state flow.

Time for action – drawing the game structure

1. In the `Game1.vb` file, replace the current `Draw` method with the following:

```
Protected Overrides Sub Draw(gameTime As GameTime)
    GraphicsDevice.Clear(Color.Black)

    spriteBatch.Begin()

    If  gameState = GameStates.TitleScreen Then
        spriteBatch.Draw(titleScreen,
            New Rectangle(0, 0, Me.Window.ClientBounds.Width,
                Me.Window.ClientBounds.Height),
                Color.White)
    End If

    if ((gameState = GameStates.Playing) Or
        (gameState = GameStates.PlayerDead) Or
        (gameState = GameStates.GameOver)) Then

        _starField.Draw(spriteBatch)
        _asteroidManager.Draw(spriteBatch)
        _playerManager.Draw(spriteBatch)
        _enemyManager.Draw(spriteBatch)
        _explosionManager.Draw(spriteBatch)
```

```
        spriteBatch.DrawString(
            pericles14,
            "Score: " + _playerManager.PlayerScore.ToString(),
            scoreLocation,
            Color.White)

        If _playerManager.LivesRemaining >= 0 Then
            spriteBatch.DrawString(
                pericles14,
                "Ships Remaining: " +
                    _playerManager.LivesRemaining.ToString(),
                livesLocation,
                Color.White)
        End If
    End If

    If gameState = GameStates.GameOver Then
        spriteBatch.DrawString(
            pericles14,
            "G A M E O V E R !",
            New Vector2(
                Me.Window.ClientBounds.Width/2F -
                    pericles14.MeasureString("G A M E O V E R
!").X/2F,
                50),
            Color.White)
    End If

    spriteBatch.End()

    MyBase.Draw(gameTime)
End Sub
```

2. Execute the game and play through a complete cycle.

What just happened?

While the whole `Draw()` method is presented here for clarity, the only major changes are the inclusion of the `DrawString()` calls to display the player's score and remaining ship count, along with the display of the **G A M E O V E R !** text string, when in the `GameOver` state.

Have a go hero

Here are a few suggestions for putting the topics we have covered in this chapter to use:

◆ Currently, **Asteroid Belt Assault** never gets more difficult as time passes. Add a timing mechanism that increases the number of asteroids, the frequency with which enemy ships are generated, or the rate at which the enemy ships fire at the player, as time goes on.

◆ Add new waypoint paths for enemies to follow, or create new enemy types by adding to the `SpriteSheet.png` file. You could create larger enemies that stay on the screen for a longer period of time, take multiple hits from player weapons, and fire more rapidly at the player.

◆ The `SoundManager` class can be used with very few changes in other games. Try adding it to the **Flood Control** game and creating your own sound effects for turning pieces, completing a scoring row, and finishing a level.

Summary

Asteroid Belt Assault is now completed! In this chapter, we have covered the following:

◆ Implementing a simple particle system to generate dynamic explosion effects

◆ Detecting and responding to collisions between the player, shots, enemies, and asteroids

◆ Playing sound effects in response to game events

◆ Organizing the game state flow into a structure

6
Robot Rampage – Multi-Axis Mayhem

In the depths of a top secret research facility, a super-computer has gone rogue. It has reached out over the worldwide network and seized control of automated factories across the globe. In these factories, it has begun building tank-like robotic warriors.

In Robot Rampage, the player takes on the role of a robo-tank fighting for the good guys. The player moves from factory to factory, shutting down the computer-controlled manufacturing facilities and destroying the enemy robots.

Robot Rampage is a multi-axis game—the player's movement and weaponry are controlled separately, allowing them to move and fire in any combination of directions simultaneously.

In this chapter, we will begin constructing the Robot Rampage project, and explore the following topics:

- Using a camera class to view a world larger than the game window
- Creating a sprite class that is aware of coordinates in the larger world
- Building a tile-based game world map
- Building a player sprite from multiple component sprites
- Using the Xbox 360 gamepad's thumb stick controllers
- Collision detection between sprite objects and tile map squares

Modules, modules, everywhere

We looked at static classes in *Chapter 5, Asteroid Belt Assault – Special Effects*, by creating a module to play sound effects that did not require class instances to be created or referenced in other areas of our code. We will expand on that technique in Robot Rampage, by defining several modules to handle components, such as the game's camera, effects manager, and shots manager.

Time for action – creating the Robot Rampage project

1. In Visual Studio Express, create a new XNA 4.0 Windows Game project called **Robot Rampage**.

2. Download the `2403_06_GRAPHICSPACK.zip` file from the book's website, and extract the graphics resources to a temporary folder.

3. In the Robot Rampage `Content` project, create a new folder called `Fonts`.

4. Add a new `SpriteFont` called `Pericles14` to the `Fonts` folder, updating the generated XML file to change the `<FontName>` to `Pericles`.

5. Also in the `Content` project, create a new folder called `Textures`.

6. Add the graphics resources from the temporary directory to the `Textures` folder.

7. Copy the `SpriteSheet.png` and `TitleScreen.png` files from the temporary folder you extracted them to in *step 2* into the `Textures` folder, and add them to the project.

8. In the declarations area of the `Game1` class, add a declaration for the sprite sheet and font objects:

```
Private spriteSheet As Texture2D
Private titleScreen As Texture2D
Private pericles14 As SpriteFont
```

9. In the Initialize() method of the Game1 class, add these lines to specify the size of the game window:

```
Me.graphics.PreferredBackBufferWidth = 800
Me.graphics.PreferredBackBufferHeight = 600
Me.graphics.ApplyChanges()
```

10. In the `LoadContent()` method of the `Game1` class, initialize the sprite sheet and the font objects:

```
spriteSheet = Content.Load(Of Texture2D)("Textures\SpriteSheet")
titleScreen = Content.Load(Of Texture2D)("Textures\TitleScreen")
pericles14 = Content.Load(Of SpriteFont)("Fonts\Pericles14")
```

What just happened?

We have built the basic structure of the Robot Rampage game, loading the sprite sheet and title screen graphics, and creating a `SpriteFont` that we can use to display text later.

A world larger than the screen

In both Flood Control and Asteroid Belt Assault, we dealt with game worlds limited to the area of the display window of the game. None of our game objects existed outside the confines of the screen, and, in fact, when we wished to eliminate some objects in Asteroid Belt Assault, we just moved them to an off-screen location, to allow the appropriate code manager to clean them up.

When dealing with a larger game world, we need to make a few adjustments to the way we think about object positions. Instead of simply tracking the location of a sprite on the screen, we will need to track the location of the object in world coordinates:

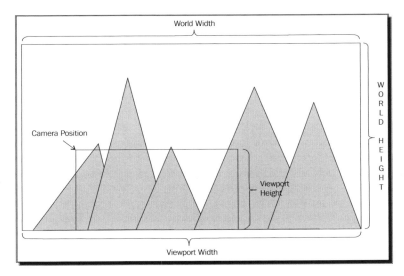

In this screenshot, the camera points to the upper-left corner of a viewport, within a larger game world. Anything inside the viewport will be visible on the screen, while background areas and objects outside the viewport will not be drawn.

Both the viewport and the game objects can move independently, so we can no longer consider objects that are off-screen to be ready, to be cleaned up, and removed from the game. An object that is off-screen during the current frame, may be moving towards an on-screen location, or alternatively, the camera may be moving towards the object, causing it to appear within the newly moved viewport.

Defining a camera

In order to create our viewport into the game world, we will define a Camera module that will represent the view the player currently has of the game world. At its most basic, a camera is really nothing more than a vector pointing to the camera's location. In order to provide some additional functionality, we will add several other properties and methods to the Camera module.

Time for action – creating the Camera class

1. Add a new module called `Camera` to the Robot Rampage project.

2. Add declarations to the `Camera` module:

```
#Region "Declarations"
    Private _position As Vector2 = Vector2.Zero
    Private _viewPortSize As Vector2 = Vector2.Zero
#End Region
```

3. Add properties to the `Camera` module, to access and modify the underlying members:

```
#Region "Properties"
    Public Property WorldRectangle As Rectangle = New
      Rectangle(0,0,0,0)

    Public Property ViewPortWidth as Integer
      Get
        Return CInt(Int(_viewPortSize.X))
      End Get
      Set(ByVal value As Integer)
        _viewPortSize.X = value
      End Set
    End Property

    Public Property ViewPortHeight As Integer
      Get
        Return CInt(Int(_viewPortSize.Y))
      End Get
```

```
      Set(ByVal value As Integer)
        _viewPortSize.Y = value
      End Set
    End Property

    Public Property Position As Vector2
      Get
        Return _position
      End Get
      Set(ByVal value As Vector2)
        _position = new Vector2(
          MathHelper.Clamp(value.X,
          WorldRectangle.X,
        WorldRectangle.Width - ViewPortWidth),
          MathHelper.Clamp(value.Y,
          WorldRectangle.Y,
        WorldRectangle.Height - ViewPortHeight))
      End Set
    End Property

    Public ReadOnly Property ViewPort As Rectangle
      Get
        return new Rectangle(
          CInt(Int(Position.X)), CInt(Int(Position.Y)),
            ViewPortWidth, ViewPortHeight)
      End Get
    End Property
  #End Region
```

4. Add methods to the Camera module:

```
#region "Public Methods"
  Public Sub Move(offset As Vector2)
    Position += offset
  End Sub

  Public Function ObjectIsVisible(bounds As Rectangle) As Boolean
    Return ViewPort.Intersects(bounds)
  End Function

  Public Function Transform(point As Vector2) As Vector2
    Return point - position
  End Function
```

```
Public Function Transform(rect As Rectangle) As Rectangle
  Return new Rectangle(
    rect.Left - CInt(Int(position.X)),
    rect.Top - CInt(Int(position.Y)),
    rect.Width,
  rect.Height)
  End Function
#End Region
```

5. In the `LoadContent()` method of the `Game1` class, initialize the `Camera`, after the textures and sprite font have been loaded:

```
Camera.WorldRectangle = new Rectangle(0, 0, 1600, 1600)
Camera.ViewPortWidth = 800
Camera.ViewPortHeight = 600
```

What just happened?

The first thing to notice about this code is that we have included compiler directives to define code regions. These directives (`#Region` and `#End Region`) instruct the Visual Studio development environment to treat these code areas as blocks that are collapsible as a related unit. You can click on the little minus sign on the left side of the screen at the beginning of a region to collapse it, hiding the code and leaving behind just the region title. We will include region declarations in all of the classes in Robot Rampage as an example of their usage.

Regions

Grouping your code into region blocks, known as **Code Folding**, can be a big help for readability purposes. If you give your regions descriptive names, you can keep them all collapsed until you need to work on a particular method or other code element. Finding the element you need is then as simple as expanding the region it is located in.

Our `Camera` module only needs three pieces of information to operate. The first is its position within the game world. This vector points to the upper-left corner of the viewing area represented by the camera. That is, if you think of the game world as a huge grid of pixels, the pixel pointed to by the `_position` vector is the pixel that will be drawn in the upper-left corner of the display area, when the camera is used to draw a scene.

The `_viewPortSize` vector represents the number of pixels to the right and down from the camera position that are covered by the viewing area. While this size defaults to zero during our game's initialization, we will set the size to match the size of the game's client window in the `LoadContent()` method. Together, the `_position` and `_viewPortSize` vectors can be thought of as defining a rectangle that represents the portion of the game world that is currently visible on the screen.

The last piece of information the `Camera` needs is the size of the game world itself. Unlike our other two variables, we have not created a backing field separate from the property declaration we wish to use. Instead, we simply declare the `WorldRectangle` property without a `Get` or `Set` block. This indicates to Visual Basic that we want to use an auto-implemented property. In the background, the Visual Basic compiler will create a backing field for us, by prefixing an underscore to the name of the property (`_WorldRectangle` in this case). We could use this field in our module code, if we wished to do so, even though we have not explicitly declared it.

The auto-implemented property will act as if we had created a full property with a simple `get` and `set` pair that returns the underlying field directly, and allows outside code to directly set the value of the field. In fact, the single line we have above is equivalent to:

```
Private _WorldRectangle As Rectangle = New Rectangle(0, 0, 0, 0)

Public Property WorldRectangle As Rectangle
  Get
    Return _WorldRectangle
  End Get
  Set(ByVal value As Rectangle)
    _WorldRectangle = value
  End Set
End Property
```

So, why not declare the other two values as auto-implemented properties? After all, it saves quite a bit of code! In this case, we need to place limits on what can be stored in the `_position` field, and we will not be directly exposing the `_viewPortSize` variable to outside code.

The `WorldRectangle` property defines the space in which all the objects in the game world will exist, and it is measured in pixels. Again, this value defaults to a zero-by-zero pixel game world, but will is set to our desired world sized in the `LoadContent()` method of the `Game1` class.

Because the `_position` vector actually represents the upper-left corner of a rectangle (the visible screen) instead of a single point, we want to make sure that position remains not only within the game world, but also does not get any closer to the right or bottom edges of the game world than the width and height of the viewing area. In other words, if the game world is `1000x1000` pixels, and the display screen is `800x600` pixels, then the largest values we ever want for the components of the position vector are `200` for the X position and `400` for the Y position. If the camera were allowed to get closer to the edge of the game world, we would not have anything to display to the right or bottom of the game world's edges.

To enforce this limitation, we use `MathHelper.Clamp()` in the `set` portion of the `Position` property. This ensures that a full display of the game world will always be visible on the screen.

While external code could directly set the position of the camera through the `Position` property, we will generally prefer to use the `Move()` method to relocate the camera relative to its current position. Even though the `Move()` method is a member of the `Camera` module and could access the `_position` member directly, it uses the `Position` property just as external code would, allowing us to maintain the limitations that `Position` imposes without having to rewrite them in the `Move()` method.

Accessing private members

This method of using the `public` properties to access your class' variables even from within the class' member methods is a good way to keep your code organized and make hunting down and dealing with bugs easier. As long as your properties are robust in their validation of data, using them in your methods prevents unchecked values from slipping in and disrupting other code.

When a game object is going to be drawn, we can check its display rectangle against the `ObjectIsVisible()` method of the `Camera`, to determine if any pixels in the object would be visible on the screen based on the camera's current position. If `ObjectIsVisible()` returns `false`, there is no need to draw the object, as all of its pixels are off screen. We will build this check into the updated `Sprite` object we construct, so that each sprite will check its own visibility and skip drawing itself, if it does not appear anywhere on the display.

Lastly, we have a pair of methods named `Transform()`. Given either a pixel location (as a `Vector2`) or a rectangle, the `Transform()` methods subtract the camera's current position from them and returns the result. To visualize the transformation of world coordinates into screen coordinates, let's return to the world and camera diagram we saw previously, with the addition of an object in the game world:

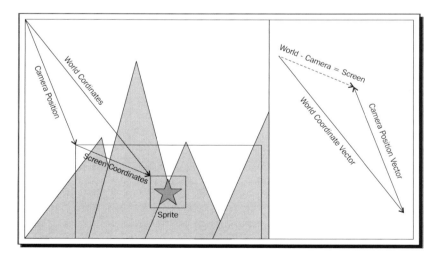

Here, we can see that the **Sprite** object's world coordinates represent its absolute position within the context of the game world. On the right side of the previous diagram, we can see that if the **Camera Position** vector is subtracted from the **World Coordinate Vector**, the resulting vector has the same direction and length as the **Screen Coordinates** vector. When this vector is placed relative to the upper-left corner of the screen, the position of the object in screen coordinates is given.

By storing the location of all of our game objects in world-based coordinates, the Camera's `Transform()` methods will provide screen-coordinate locations for the `SpriteBatch.Draw()` method, to display them in the appropriate locations.

World-aware sprites

This world coordinate focus means that the `Sprite` class we built for Asteroid Belt Assault will not work directly in the world of Robot Rampage. While all of the concepts are still valid, we need to build in ways to account for the world's camera and a game world larger than the screen. It is possible for a sprite object to be completely on screen, partially on screen, or completely off-screen.

In addition, while the sprite's world location may remain constant, the game's camera may move, requiring the on-screen location of the sprite to be adjusted to compensate for the camera's new position.

Time for action – building a new Sprite class

1. Add a new class called `Sprite` to the Robot Rampage project.

2. Add declarations to the `Sprite` class:

```
#Region "Declarations"
Public Texture As Texture2D

Private _frames As List(Of Rectangle) = new List(Of Rectangle)()

Private _currentFrame As Integer
Private _frameTime As Single = 0.1
Private _timeForCurrentFrame As Single = 0.0

Private _rotation as Single = 0.0
#End Region
```

3. Add position-related properties to the `Sprite` class:

```
#Region "Positional Properties"
Public Property WorldLocation as Vector2 = Vector2.Zero
Public Property Velocity as Vector2 = Vector2.Zero

Public ReadOnly Property ScreenLocation As Vector2
  Get
    Return Camera.Transform(WorldLocation)
  End Get
End Property

Public ReadOnly Property WorldRectangle as Rectangle
  Get
    return new Rectangle(
      CInt(Int(WorldLocation.X)),
      CInt(Int(WorldLocation.Y)),
      FrameWidth,
    FrameHeight)
  End Get
End Property

Public ReadOnly Property ScreenRectangle As Rectangle
  Get
    Return Camera.Transform(WorldRectangle)
  End Get
End Property

Public ReadOnly Property RelativeCenter As Vector2
  Get
    Return New Vector2(FrameWidth / 2.0F, FrameHeight / 2.0F)
  End Get
End Property

Public ReadOnly Property WorldCenter As Vector2
  Get
    Return WorldLocation + RelativeCenter
  End Get
End Property

Public ReadOnly Property ScreenCenter As Vector2
  Get
    Return Camera.Transform(WorldLocation + RelativeCenter)
  End Get
End Property
#End Region
```

4. Add properties related to drawing and animating the sprite to the `Sprite` class:

```
#Region "Drawing and Animation Properties"
Public Property Animate As Boolean = True
Public Property AnimateWhenStopped as Boolean = True
Public Property Expired as Boolean = False
Public Property TintColor As Color = Color.White

Public Property Rotation As Single
  Get
    Return _rotation
  End Get
  Set(ByVal value As Single)
    _rotation = value Mod MathHelper.TwoPi
  End Set
End Property

Public ReadOnly Property FrameWidth as Integer
  Get
    Return _frames(0).Width
  End Get
End Property

Public ReadOnly Property FrameHeight As Integer
  Get
    Return _frames(0).Height
  End Get
End Property

Public Property Frame As Integer
  Get
    Return _currentFrame
  End Get
  Set(ByVal value As Integer)
    _currentFrame = CInt(Int(MathHelper.Clamp(value, 0,
      _frames.Count - 1)))
  End Set
End Property

Public Property FrameTime as Single
  Get
    Return _frameTime
  End Get
  Set
```

```
      _frameTime = MathHelper.Max(0, value)
    End Set
  End Property


  Public ReadOnly Property Source As Rectangle
    Get
      Return _frames(_currentFrame)
    End Get
  End Property
  #End Region
```

5. Add properties related to collision detection to the `Sprite` class:

```
#Region "Collision Related Properties"
Public Property Collidable As Boolean = True
Public Property CollisionRadius As Integer = 0
Public Property BoundingXPadding As Integer = 0
Public Property BoundingYPadding As Integer = 0

Public ReadOnly Property BoundingBoxRect As Rectangle
  Get
    return new Rectangle(
      CInt(Int(worldLocation.X)) + BoundingXPadding,
      CInt(Int(worldLocation.Y)) + BoundingYPadding,
      FrameWidth - (BoundingXPadding * 2),
    FrameHeight - (BoundingYPadding * 2))
  End Get
End Property
#End Region
```

6. Add a constructor for the `Sprite` class:

```
#Region "Constructors"
Public Sub New(
  worldLocation As Vector2,
  texture As Texture2D,
  initialFrame As Rectangle,
velocity As Vector2)

  Me.WorldLocation = worldLocation
  Me.Texture = texture
  Me.Velocity = velocity
  _frames.Add(initialFrame)
End Sub
#End Region
```

7. Add collision detection methods to the `Sprite` class:

```vbnet
#Region "Collision Detection Methods"
Public Function IsBoxColliding(OtherBox As Rectangle) As Boolean
  If (Collidable) And (Not Expired) Then
    Return BoundingBoxRect.Intersects(OtherBox)
  Else
    Return False
  End If
End Function

Public Function IsCircleColliding(
  otherCenter As Vector2,
  otherRadius As Single) As Boolean

  If (Collidable) And (Not Expired) Then
    If Vector2.Distance(WorldCenter, otherCenter) <
      (CollisionRadius + otherRadius)
      Return True
    Else
      Return False
    End If
  Else
    Return false
  End If
End Function
#End Region
```

8. Add animation-related methods to the `Sprite` class:

```vbnet
#Region "Animation-Related Methods"
Public Sub AddFrame(frameRectangle As Rectangle)
  _frames.Add(frameRectangle)
End Sub

Public Sub RotateTo(direction As Vector2)
  Rotation = CSng(Math.Atan2(direction.Y, direction.X))
End Sub
#End Region
```

9. Add the `Update()` and `Draw()` methods to the `Sprite` class:

```vbnet
#Region "Update and Draw Methods"
Public Overridable Sub Update(gameTime As GameTime)
  If Not Expired Then
    Dim elapsed As Single
```

```
            elapsed = CSng(gameTime.ElapsedGameTime.TotalSeconds)
            _timeForCurrentFrame += elapsed

            If Animate Then
              If _timeForCurrentFrame >= FrameTime Then
                If (AnimateWhenStopped) Or (velocity <> Vector2.Zero) Then
                  _currentFrame = (_currentFrame + 1) Mod _frames.Count
                  _timeForCurrentFrame = 0.0F
                End If
              End If
            End If

            WorldLocation += (Velocity * elapsed)
          End If
        End Sub

        Public Overridable Sub Draw(spriteBatch As SpriteBatch)
          If Not Expired Then
            If Camera.ObjectIsVisible(WorldRectangle) Then
              spriteBatch.Draw(
                Texture,
                ScreenCenter,
                Source,
                TintColor,
                Rotation,
                RelativeCenter,
                1.0F,
                SpriteEffects.None,
                0.0F)
            End If
          End If
        End Sub
#End Region
```

What just happened?

The Sprite class is presented in one large block here, because most of the code should be familiar (if slightly reorganized) from the same class in Asteroid Belt Assault. A few updates have been made to the code, however, so let's go over those changes in detail.

To start with, we have made use of auto-implemented properties wherever we can, including the `WorldLocation` property, which has replaced the `Location` property from the previous version of the `Sprite` class. The renaming of this property really just serves as a reminder that the coordinates are world-aligned instead of screen-aligned.

Several new member variables and properties have been added to the class as well. `Animate` and `AnimateWhenStopped` are checked during the sprite's `Update()` method. If `Animate` is `false`, the sprite will not advance frame animations. If `AnimateWhenStopped` is set to `false`, the sprite will not advance its frame animations, if the `Velocity` vector is equal to `Vector2.Zero`. This simply means that when the sprite is moving, its animation will play (assuming `Animate` is `true`). When the sprite is not moving, its animation will not play.

If `Expired` is set to `true`, the sprite will not be updated or drawn. In addition, the `BoxCollision()` and `CircleCollision()` methods will always return `false` for expired sprites. If the `Collidable` member is set to `false`, both of the collision methods will also return `false`.

The `WorldLocation` property has a new counterpart called `ScreenLocation`. This property uses the `Camera.Transform()` method to return the screen-based location of the object and is used in the `Draw()` method, to determine where on the screen the sprite should be displayed.

Similarly, the `Destination` property (which, in Asteroid Belt Assault, returned the rectangle on the screen that the sprite was drawn to) has been split into `WorldRectangle` and `ScreenRectangle`, and the `Center` property has been split into `WorldCenter` and `ScreenCenter`.

As a helper to assist in calculating the center of the sprite object, the `RelativeCenter` property has been introduced, which returns a vector equal to half of the width and height of the sprite's frame rectangle. This vector points to the center of the sprite relative to its own upper-left corner.

CInt versus. Int versus Fix

In the `Sprite` class, we have begun using a rather odd looking "`CInt(Int(…))`" structure in the code for the `Sprite` class. This is due to the way the various conversion to integer functions handle rounding. This has not been an issue in the past, so we just used `CInt()`, which performs rounding on the values passed to it. `CInt(1.4)` will result in a value of 1, while `CInt(1.6)` will result in a value of 2. This can throw-off some of our calculations, later, when we wish to determine what square a sprite is in, or when we determine what map squares to draw.

For this reason, we use `Int()`, which does not round numbers, and simply truncates the fractional portion of the value. For positive numbers, the `Fix()` function does exactly the same thing that `Int()` does. For negative numbers, `Int()` returns the first negative integer less than or equal to the number (`Int(-1.5) will return -2`), while `Fix()` returns the first negative number greater than or equal to the number (`Fix(-1.5)` will return -1).

In either case, though, `Int()` and `Fix()` return the same data type as was submitted to them. So performing an `Int()` on a `Single` returns a `Single`, containing only the whole number portion of the value. We still need to convert this variable's data type to an `Integer`, which is why we surround the call with a `CInt()` function call. This drops the fractional part of the number first, and then returns the result as an `Integer` variable.

Visualizing the view

We now have both of the components we need for a "larger than the screen" world for our game, so let's add a few lines of temporary code to our project to get a feel for how they work together. Throughout the project, we will be expanding on or adding new temporary code segments to see the objects we have implemented in action.

Time for action – viewing the Sprite and Camera classes in action

1. In the declarations area of the `Game1` class, add a declaration for a temporary sprite object:

```
' Temporary Demo Code Begin
  Private tempSprite As Sprite
  Private tempSprite2 As Sprite
' Temporary Demo Code End
```

2. In the `LoadContent()` method of the `Game1` class, initialize the temporary sprite and the `Camera` class:

```
' Temporary Demo Code Begin
  tempSprite = New Sprite(
    New Vector2(100, 100),
    spriteSheet,
    New Rectangle(0, 64, 32, 32),
  Vector2.Zero)

  tempSprite2 = New Sprite(
    New Vector2(200,200),
    spriteSheet,
    New Rectangle(0, 160, 32, 32),
  Vector2.Zero)

' Temporary Demo Code End
```

3. In the `Draw()` method of the `Game1` class, draw the temporary sprite:

```
' Temporary Demo Code
  spriteBatch.Begin()
  tempSprite.Draw(spriteBatch)
  tempSprite2.Draw(spriteBatch)
  spriteBatch.End()
' Temporary Demo Code End
```

4. In the `Update()` method of the `Game1` class, add temporary input handling to allow the sprite and the camera to be moved:

```
' Temporary Demo Code Begin
  Dim spriteMove As Vector2 = Vector2.Zero
  Dim cameraMove As Vector2 = Vector2.Zero

  If Keyboard.GetState().IsKeyDown(Keys.A) Then
    spriteMove.X = -1
  End If

  If Keyboard.GetState().IsKeyDown(Keys.D) Then
    spriteMove.X = 1
  End If

  If Keyboard.GetState().IsKeyDown(Keys.W) Then
    spriteMove.Y = -1
  End If

  If Keyboard.GetState().IsKeyDown(Keys.S) Then
    spriteMove.Y = 1
  End If
```

```
If Keyboard.GetState().IsKeyDown(Keys.Left) Then
  cameraMove.X = -1
End If

If Keyboard.GetState().IsKeyDown(Keys.Right) Then
  cameraMove.X = 1
End If

If Keyboard.GetState().IsKeyDown(Keys.Up) Then
  cameraMove.Y = -1
End If

If Keyboard.GetState().IsKeyDown(Keys.Down) Then
  cameraMove.Y = 1
End If

Camera.Move(cameraMove)
tempSprite.Velocity = spriteMove * 60

tempSprite.Update(gameTime)
tempSprite2.Update(gameTime)
' Temporary Demo Code End
```

5. Launch the game. Use the *W*, *A*, *S*, and *D* keys to move the first sprite around, and use the arrow keys to move the camera around.

6. Leave the temporary code in place. We will expand on it a bit later, before replacing it with the actual code for the `Game1` class.

What just happened?

If you play with the previous temporary code for a few minutes, you will see that the *W*, *A*, *S*, and *D* keys move the first sprite (the green tank base) as expected: *A* moves left, *D* moves right, *W* moves up, and *S* moves down. There is no way to directly move the second sprite (the blue tank base), because the temporary `Update()` method does not define a set of controls for `tempSprite2`.

Using the arrow keys moves the camera instead of either of the sprites. In world coordinates, the second sprite is always stationary. It only moves on the screen, because the camera is panning around, altering the player's view of the game world. You will also notice that you cannot move the camera left or up from the starting position. This is because the camera is clamped to the world area, and starts out in the upper-left corner.

The game world – tile-based maps

At a screen size of `800x600` pixels, an image filling the screen contains `480,000` individual pixels. If these pixels are stored as 32-bit values (8 bits each for red, green, blue, and alpha) this means that each screen of pixels occupies 1875 kilobytes of memory. That does not sound too bad on the surface—after all, computers have lots of memory, and 1.8 megabytes for an image is not all that much memory.

In that case, when making a world that is larger than a single screen, why not just make a huge bitmap to use as the background and scroll across it? Unfortunately, there are a couple of problems with this approach.

First, many graphics cards have a maximum texture size. On Windows, 2048x2048 is a common texture size limitation, though some graphics cards have higher limits. The Xbox 360 is limited to textures that are 8192x8192 pixels.

Second, once the bitmap image representing the world has been defined, it is fixed. When you create the image, you create all of the details of the world and save the bitmap. You cannot re-arrange pieces of the world at run time, which will be vital when we want to generate random maps for Robot Rampage.

Let's consider the 2048 limitation for a moment. If we create our world out of a single texture 2048 pixels wide, the world can be a little larger than two screens wide and three screens tall at a resolution of 800x 600. This does not offer much room for the player to roam, and the resulting texture would occupy 16 megabytes of memory.

To generate very large worlds, we need an alternative method. One of the most common ways is to use a tile-based engine. In a tile engine, the world is made up of a grid of blocks. Each block has a tile value that represents the image that should be displayed within it.

Complex tile engines

Tile engines have long been a staple of 2D game design. From role playing games to side-scrolling platformers and real-time strategy games, the ability to represent a game map or level as an array of tile indexes makes them very flexible. Advanced tile engines can support multiple layers of tiles, each tile in a space drawing above the previous layer to create a depth effect where objects (rocks and trees, for example) can be placed on top of basic terrain tiles, without needing to draw individual tiles for the object on every type of terrain background in the game. We will look at a multi-layered tile engine in *Chapter 8, Gemstone Hunter - Put on Your Platform Shoes*.

When the tile engine needs to be drawn to the screen, we can extract only the individual tiles that are currently visible to the camera and draw them, leaving the rest of the map unrendered.

For Robot Rampage, we will create a basic tile engine that supports a single layer of tiles, drawn from a handful of floor and wall tile images on the `SpriteSheet.png` image. We will define a world that is `50x50` map squares in size, each composed of a `32x32` pixel block. The result will be a world that occupies 1600x `1600` virtual pixels. Unlike a single bitmap of that size, which would occupy about 10 megabytes of memory, our map will use about 42 kilobytes of memory, including the map data itself as well as the image data comprising the tiles used to draw the map.

Tiles

A tile map is composed of a grid of squares, each one containing a reference to the tile that we wish to display in that map square. The tile itself is simply a rectangular texture that contains the visual representation of a terrain or background type.

In Robot Rampage, we will only need a handful of tile textures. We will have a few variations of floor textures to represent the factory floor, and a handful of wall and machinery textures to represent barriers:

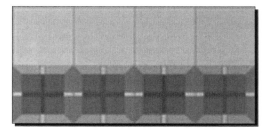

As before, we will use a single texture sheet that will contain all of the images used by our game. The first row of images on the `SpriteSheet.png` file represents floor tiles, while the second row represents wall-type images. When we generate a game map, we will select a random floor and wall combination for each level.

From an XNA standpoint, we will define each of the tiles available to our tile map as a rectangle. These rectangles will be stored in a numerically indexed list. This allows each of the tiles to be referenced by their index number.

The tile map

Since we can refer to an individual tile by using its tile index number, our tile map can be represented as a two-dimensional array of integers, with each integer corresponding to the index of the tile associated with that map square.

We have four different floor textures and four different wall textures, so the values stored in the tile map array will range from zero to seven. Any value greater than three will be treated as a barrier, while tiles zero through three will not block movement or shots:

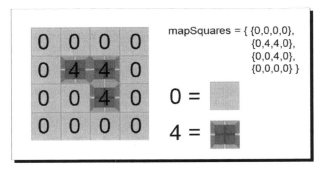

In the previous diagram, `mapSquares` is a two-dimensional array of integers. A zero value in the array corresponds to the empty floor tile, while a four corresponds to a wall tile image. When the map is drawn, each integer in the array is examined, and the image corresponding to the tile index is drawn to the screen to occupy that square's display area.

Time for action – creating the TileMap module

1. Add a new module called `TileMap` to the Robot Rampage project.

2. Add declarations to the `TileMap` module:

```
#Region "Declarations"
    Public Const TileWidth As Integer = 32
    Public Const TileHeight As Integer = 32
```

```
Public Const MapWidth As Integer = 50
Public Const MapHeight As Integer = 50

Public Const FloorTileStart As Integer = 0
Public Const FloorTileEnd As Integer = 3
Public Const WallTileStart As Integer = 4
Public Const WallTileEnd As Integer = 7

Private _texture As Texture2D
Private _tiles As List(Of Rectangle) = new List(Of Rectangle)()

Private _mapSquares(MapWidth, MapHeight) As Integer

Private _rand As Random = new Random()
#End Region
```

3. Add the `Initialize()` method to the `TileMap` class:

```
#Region "Initialization"
  Public Sub Initialize(texture As Texture2D)
    _texture = texture
    _tiles.Clear()
    _tiles.Add(New Rectangle(0, 0, TileWidth, TileHeight))
    _tiles.Add(New Rectangle(32, 0, TileWidth, TileHeight))
    _tiles.Add(New Rectangle(64, 0, TileWidth, TileHeight))
    _tiles.Add(New Rectangle(96, 0, TileWidth, TileHeight))
    _tiles.Add(New Rectangle(0, 32, TileWidth, TileHeight))
    _tiles.Add(New Rectangle(32, 32, TileWidth, TileHeight))
    _tiles.Add(New Rectangle(64, 32, TileWidth, TileHeight))
    _tiles.Add(New Rectangle(96, 32, TileWidth, TileHeight))

    For x As Integer = 0 to MapWidth - 1
      For y As Integer = 0 to MapHeight - 1
        _mapSquares(x,y) = FloorTileStart
      Next
    Next
  End Sub
#End Region
```

What just happened?

Most of the declarations for the `TileMap` class are constants that define the dimensions of the individual tiles, the size of the map, and the meanings of the tile index numbers.

In our case, each tile is `32x32` pixels, and the map will be 50 tiles wide and 50 tiles high, resulting in 2,500 individual map squares.

The `_tiles` list contains a set of rectangles that correspond to the locations of each individual tile on the texture image. When a rectangle is added to the tiles list, it will automatically receive an index number. The first tile added will be index zero, the second will be index one, and so on.

It is these index numbers that we will store in the `_mapSquares` array to indicate what type of terrain should be displayed for each square on the map. When the `Initialize()` method is executed, eight rectangles are added to the tiles list. Each of these rectangles corresponds to the position of one of the tiles on the game's sprite sheet.

In the declarations area, we determined that the first four tiles (numbers zero through three) would be floor tiles, while the second set of four tiles will be considered wall tiles by the game's code.

After adding the tiles to the list, the `Initialize()` method loops through each square in the `_mapSquares` array, and sets it to the first of the floor tile indexes. This way we start with a known, empty map.

Map squares

We need to make a distinction between **squares** and **tiles** as we use them in our code. We will use **square** to refer to a location within the `_mapSquares` array, while we will use **tile** to refer to the index number stored in a particular square.

Our first set of methods for the `TileMap` module deal with squares, providing methods for locating squares based on pixel positions, and providing locations in both world and screen coordinates for squares on the map.

Time for action – dealing with map squares

1. Add methods to the `TileMap` module that deal with map squares and translate pixel coordinates into map square references:

```
#Region "Information about Map Squares"

    Public Function GetSquareByPixelX(pixelX As Integer) As Integer
      Return CInt(Int(pixelX / TileWidth))
    End Function

    Public Function GetSquareByPixelY(pixelY As Integer) As Integer
      Return CInt(Int(pixelY / TileHeight))
    End Function
```

```vbnet
Public Function GetSquareAtPixel(pixelLocation As Vector2) As
  Vector2
  Return New Vector2(
    GetSquareByPixelX(CInt(Int(pixelLocation.X))),
    GetSquareByPixelY(CInt(Int(pixelLocation.Y))))
End Function

Public Function GetSquareCenter(
  squareX As Integer,
  squareY As Integer) As Vector2
  Return New Vector2(
    (squareX * TileWidth) + (TileWidth / 2.0F),
    (squareY * TileHeight) + (TileHeight / 2.0F))
End Function

Public Function GetSquareCenter(square As Vector2) As Vector2
  Return GetSquareCenter(CInt(Int(square.X)),
    CInt(Int(square.Y)))
End Function

Public Function SquareWorldRectangle(
  x As Integer,
  y As Integer) As Rectangle

  Return New Rectangle(
    x * TileWidth,
    y * TileHeight,
    TileWidth,
    TileHeight)
End Function

Public Function SquareWorldRectangle(square As Vector2) As
  Rectangle
  Return SquareWorldRectangle(
      CInt(Int(square.X)),
      CInt(Int(square.Y)))
End Function

Public Function SquareScreenRectangle(
  x As Integer,
  y As Integer) As Rectangle

  Return Camera.Transform(SquareWorldRectangle(x, y))
End Function
```

```
Public Function SquareScreenRectangle(square As Vector2) As
  Rectangle
  Return SquareScreenRectangle(
    CInt(Int(square.X)),
  CInt(Int(square.Y)))
End Function
#End Region
```

What just happened?

Our first two methods, `GetSquareByPixelX()` and `GetSquareByPixelY()`, allow us to convert world-based pixel coordinates to map square references. Given a pixel reference, they simply divide it by either the width of a single tile (for X coordinates), or the height of a tile (for Y coordinates), and return the resulting value. Several of our other methods will make use of these methods to convert pixel parameters into square references.

`GetSquareAtPixel()` in fact, does just that. Given a vector pointing to a pixel location, it returns a vector containing a reference to the square within the `_mapSquares` array that corresponds to that pixel location. Given that our map is 50x50 squares, the resulting vector will contain X and Y coordinates between 0 and 49.

When the time comes to build our enemy AI, the computer-controlled robotic tanks will need to be able to navigate their way between squares. In order to facilitate this, we need to be able to determine the center of any particular square in world coordinates. `GetSquareCenter()` calculates this vector for us, by multiplying the X and Y square coordinates by the tile width and height, and adding half of a tile width and height to the result.

Overloads

Several of the overload methods in the `TileMap` module simply manipulate the passed parameters and call another overload method of the same name. For example, `GetSquareCenter()` has an overload that accepts a `Vector2` instead of individual X and Y components. The vector version simply calls the individual component version, passing in the split components of the vector.

This prevents you from writing (and therefore having to maintain) the code in each individual overload. After all, you never know when you are going to want to change something, and having to update it in one place is much less prone to introducing bugs than having to make the same update in several locations—not to mention easier!

The `SquareWorldRectangle()` methods answer the question *What pixels on the world map does this square occupy?* We will need to know this when the time comes to determine if something has collided with a wall on the map.

Finally, the `SquareScreenRectangle()` methods provide the same information, but in localized screen coordinates. This information will be used in the `Draw()` method when rendering each square's tile to the display.

Dealing with tiles

The tile index that a square contains determines what eventually gets drawn out to the screen, when that square is visible in the game window. In addition to simply determining what tile is located in a particular square, we will include helper methods to quickly determine if a particular square contains a wall tile or not.

Time for action – handling tiles

1. Add methods to the `TileMap` module that relate to reading and setting the tile index associated with individual map squares:

```
#Region "Information about Map Tiles"

  Public Function GetTileAtSquare(
    tileX As Integer,
    tileY As Integer) As Integer

    If ((tileX >= 0) And (tileX < MapWidth) And
      (tileY >= 0) And (tileY < MapHeight)) Then
      Return _mapSquares(tileX, tileY)
    Else
      Return -1
    End If
  End Function

  Public Sub SetTileAtSquare(
    tileX As Integer,
    tileY As Integer,
    tile As Integer)

    If ((tileX >= 0) And (tileX < MapWidth) And
      (tileY >= 0) And (tileY < MapHeight)) Then
      _mapSquares(tileX, tileY) = tile
    End If
  End Sub

  Public Function GetTileAtPixel(
    pixelX As Integer,
    pixelY As Integer) As Integer
```

```
      Return GetTileAtSquare(
        GetSquareByPixelX(pixelX),
      GetSquareByPixelY(pixelY))
   End Function

   Public Function GetTileAtPixel(pixelLocation As Vector2) AS
     Integer
      Return GetTileAtPixel(
        CInt(Int(pixelLocation.X)),
      CInt(Int(pixelLocation.Y)))
   End Function

   Public Function IsWallTile(
      tileX As Integer,
      tileY As Integer) As Boolean

      Dim tileIndex As Integer = GetTileAtSquare(tileX, tileY)

      If tileIndex = -1 Then
        Return False
      End If

      Return tileIndex >= WallTileStart
   End Function

   Public Function IsWallTile(square As Vector2) As Boolean
      Return IsWallTile(CInt(Int(square.X)), CInt(Int(square.Y)))
   End Function

   Public Function IsWallTileByPixel(
      pixelLocation As Vector2) As Boolean

      Return IsWallTile(
        GetSquareByPixelX(CInt(Int(pixelLocation.X))),
      GetSquareByPixelY(CInt(Int(pixelLocation.Y))))
   End Function
#End Region
```

What just happened?

At the most basic level, we need to be able to determine the tile index associated with any particular square on the map. `GetTileAtSquare()` provides this information, and the corresponding `SetTileAtSquare()` allows the index of any square to be changed.

For convenience, the `GetTileAtPixel()` methods combine the `GetTileAtSquare()` along with the `GetSquareByPixel()` methods we have already established. They do not contain any additional processing themselves, but provide more convenient access to tile information rather than having to do the pixel to tile conversions in external code, every time we want to access tile information.

Finally, `IsWallTile()` and `IsWallTileByPixel()` examine the contents of the given square, and return `true` if the tile index is greater than or equal to the first defined wall tile index (`WallTileStart`). Again, we could do this check externally, but since we will often need to know if a tile is a wall, it is convenient to summarize all of the checking into a single set of methods.

Drawing the map

The `TileMap` module in Robot Rampage will not contain an `Update()` method because, once created, the map does not change on a per-frame basis. Thus, all that remains to make the class functional is the ability to draw the map to the screen.

Time for action – drawing the tile map

1. Add the `Draw()` method to the `TileMap` module:

```
#Region "Drawing"
  Public Sub Draw(spriteBatch As SpriteBatch)
    Dim startX As Integer =
     GetSquareByPixelX(CInt(Int(Camera.Position.X)))
    Dim endX As Integer = GetSquareByPixelX(
       CInt(Int(Camera.Position.X)) + Camera.ViewPortWidth)

    Dim startY As Integer =
       GetSquareByPixelY(CInt(Int(Camera.Position.Y)))
    Dim endY As Integer = GetSquareByPixelY(
       CInt(Int(Camera.Position.Y)) + Camera.ViewPortHeight)

    For x As Integer = startX to endX
      For y As Integer = startY to endY
        If ((x >= 0) And (y >= 0) And
          (x < MapWidth) And (y < MapHeight)) Then
          spriteBatch.Draw(
            _texture,
            SquareScreenRectangle(x, y),
            _tiles(GetTileAtSquare(x,y)),
          Color.White)
        End If
```

```
     Next
    Next
   End Sub
#End Region
```

2. In the `LoadContent()` method of the `Game1` class, initialize the `TileMap` module (outside of the temporary code block, after the `SpriteSheet` has been loaded):

```
TileMap.Initialize(spriteSheet)
```

3. In the `Draw()` method of the `Game1` class, modify the temporary code you added when building the camera to read:

```
' Temporary Demo Code Begin
  spriteBatch.Begin()
  TileMap.Draw(spriteBatch)
  tempSprite.Draw(spriteBatch)
  tempSprite2.Draw(spriteBatch)
  spriteBatch.End()
' Temporary Demo Code End
```

4. Launch your game. You can now use the temporary camera movement keys (the arrow keys) to scroll around the tile-based map:

What just happened?

The `Draw()` method begins by establishing four integer variables that will be used to control the loop that will output the tiles to the screen. We normally would not split and create separate variables for these control values. It would be more common to include the calculation directly into the for loop itself. In this case, however, the expressions are long enough that they are split here to make them more readable.

The `startX` and `startY` values are simple to obtain—simply divide the X and Y position of the camera by the size of a tile, and you know what tile is in the upper-left corner of the screen. To get the rightmost and bottommost tiles that need to be drawn, we just need to add the width and height of the viewport to the camera position. This will give us the tile in the lower right corner, defining the entire range of tiles that need to be drawn to the screen.

Why not just draw the whole thing? With a map size of only `50x50` tiles, drawing the whole map would be unlikely to have a detrimental impact on the performance of our game, but it would also be unnecessary. The large majority of the draw calls would simply be wasted on squares that are outside the display area. XNA does not have any issue with drawing outside the display—your game will not crash—but if you were to make the game world larger, you would reach a point where drawing the whole map would start to negatively impact the frame rate of the game.

The actual drawing loop checks to make sure that the tile we are going to draw actually exists (it always should since we limit the movement of the camera, but it is rarely a bad idea to verify before attempting the draw) and uses the `SpriteBatch.Draw()` method to output the tile to the screen.

Generating a random map

As it stands, our tile map is just a big empty mass of floor tiles. Since we have not yet generated any walls, there are no barriers to movement. We will introduce a very simple method to generate wall tiles at random locations on the map.

Time for action – random wall placement

1. Add the `GenerateRandomMap()` method to the `TileMap` module:

```
#Region "Map Generation"
  Public Sub GenerateRandomMap()
    Dim wallChancePerSquare As Integer = 10

    Dim floorTile As Integer
    floorTile = _rand.Next(FloorTileStart, FloorTileEnd + 1)
    Dim wallTile As Integer
    wallTile= _rand.Next(WallTileStart, WallTileEnd + 1)
```

```
        For x As Integer = 0 to MapWidth - 1
          For y As Integer = 0 to MapHeight - 1
            _mapSquares(x, y) = floorTile

            If ((x = 0) Or (y = 0) Or
              (x = MapWidth - 1) Or (y = MapHeight - 1)) Then
              _mapSquares(x, y) = wallTile
              Continue For
            End If

            If ((x = 1) Or (y = 1) Or
              (x = MapWidth - 2) Or (y = MapHeight - 2)) Then
              Continue For
            End If

            If _rand.Next(0, 100) <= wallChancePerSquare Then
              _mapSquares(x, y) = wallTile
            End If
          Next
        Next
      End Sub
#End Region
```

2. Modify the `Initialize()` method of the `TileMap` module, by adding a call to `GenerateRandomMap()` as the last line in the method:

```
GenerateRandomMap()
```

3. Execute the game project, and view the randomly generated map:

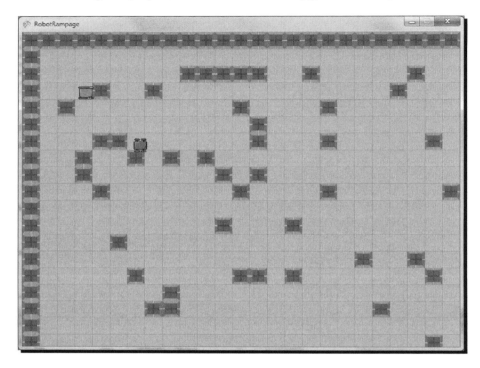

What just happened?

The `GenerateRandomMap()` method selects one floor and one wall tile to use for this map, resulting in a random combination each time a map is generated. It then loops through each of the tiles on the map and sets them initially to the `floorTile` value generated previously.

Next, the method checks to see if the tile is one of the outside edges of the map (x equal to either zero or the width of the map minus 1, or y equal to zero or the height of the map minus 1). If any of these conditions are true, the map square is automatically set to a wall tile. Similarly, the second row of tiles around the map (x or y equal to one or the width/ height minus two) are skipped over for wall generation, ensuring that the map will always contain a single layer of wall tiles around the outside edge, and a clear layer of floor tiles inside that.

For all other squares, a random number is generated and compared to `wallChancePerSquare`. If the random value indicates that a wall should be placed at the square, the tile map is updated appropriately.

Adding the player

So, we now have a working tile map, and what looks like a piece of a robotic vehicle that we can move around on the map. However, there are a number of issues right now:

- ◆ The robot we can move around simply floats around without animation or direction.
- ◆ Our floating sprite does not obey any kind of screen or world limitations. It will happily fly off into oblivion if you hold down the movement keys.
- ◆ Similarly, the sprite is not blocked by wall tiles. It will float right over them.
- ◆ Moving the sprite to the right or bottom edges of the screen doesn't scroll the camera to follow the sprite. Our camera is currently controlled by a separate set of movement keys.

In order to begin addressing these issues, we need to construct a class for the player's robo-tank. If you look at the `SpriteSheet.png` image, you will see that the player's robot is split into a couple of pieces. The treaded base that we currently have floating around on the screen will provide the base for the player's character:

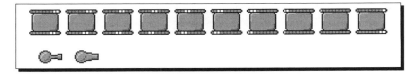

On top of the base, we will place one of the available gun turrets located below the tank base on the sprite sheet. Both the base and the turret will rotate independently, allowing the user to move and fire in any combination of directions.

Building the Player module

The Player module will handle both tracking and displaying the player's robo-tank, and dealing with user input. We will start by building the basics to display the two sprites that comprise the player's tank.

Time for action – building the Player module

1. Add a new module called `Player` to the Robot Rampage project.

2. Add declarations to the Player module:
```
#Region "Declarations"
    Public BaseSprite As Sprite
    Public TurretSprite As Sprite
#End Region
```

3. Add the `Initialize()` method to the `Player` module:

```
#Region "Initialization"
  Public Sub Initialize(
    texture As Texture2D,
    baseInitialFrame As Rectangle,
    baseFrameCount As Integer,
    turretInitialFrame As Rectangle,
    turretFrameCount As Integer,
    worldLocation As Vector2)

    Dim frameWidth As Integer = baseInitialFrame.Width
    Dim frameHeight As Integer = baseInitialFrame.Height

    BaseSprite = new Sprite(
      worldLocation,
      texture,
      baseInitialFrame,
    Vector2.Zero)

    BaseSprite.BoundingXPadding = 4
    BaseSprite.BoundingYPadding = 4
    BaseSprite.AnimateWhenStopped = False

    For x As Integer = 1 To baseFrameCount - 1
      BaseSprite.AddFrame(
        new Rectangle(
          baseInitialFrame.X + (frameHeight * x),
          baseInitialFrame.Y,
          frameWidth,
        frameHeight))
    Next

    TurretSprite = new Sprite(
      worldLocation,
      texture,
      turretInitialFrame,
    Vector2.Zero)

    TurretSprite.Animate = false

    For x As Integer = 1 To turretFrameCount - 1
      BaseSprite.AddFrame(
        new Rectangle(
        turretInitialFrame.X + (frameHeight * x),
```

```
        turretInitialFrame.Y,
        frameWidth,
      frameHeight))
    Next
  End Sub
#End Region
```

4. Add `Update()` and `Draw()` methods for the `Player` module:

```
#Region "Update and Draw"
  Public Sub Update(gameTime As GameTime)
    BaseSprite.Update(gameTime)
    TurretSprite.WorldLocation = BaseSprite.WorldLocation
  End Sub
  Public Sub Draw(spriteBatch As SpriteBatch)
    BaseSprite.Draw(spriteBatch)
    TurretSprite.Draw(spriteBatch)
  End Sub
#End Region
```

5. In the `Game1` class, remove all of the existing code marked as `Temporary` code that you added while building the camera and tile map systems. This includes the declarations for the two temporary sprites and their initialization in `LoadContent()`, as well as the calls to their `Update()` and `Draw()` methods in the corresponding methods of `Game1`.

6. In the `LoadContent()` method of the `Game1` class, after the sprite sheet has been loaded, initialize the `Player` module:

```
Player.Initialize(
  spriteSheet,
  new Rectangle(0, 64, 32, 32),
  6,
  new Rectangle(0, 96, 32, 32),
  1,
new Vector2(300, 300))
```

7. Modify the `Update()` method of the `Game1` class to update the player sprites. The entire `Update()` method is presented here, in order to verify that the temporary code from the previous steps was removed:

```
Protected Overrides Sub Update(ByVal gameTime As GameTime)

  ' Allows the game to exit
  If GamePad.GetState(PlayerIndex.One).Buttons.Back =
    ButtonState.Pressed Then
    Me.Exit()
  End If
```

```
    Player.Update(gameTime)

   MyBase.Update(gameTime)
End Sub
```

8. Replace the current `Draw()` method in the `Game1` class with the following method that draws both the tile map and the player sprites:

```
Protected Overrides Sub Draw(ByVal gameTime As GameTime)
    GraphicsDevice.Clear(Color.CornflowerBlue)

   spriteBatch.Begin()
    ileMap.Draw(spriteBatch)
   Player.Draw(spriteBatch)
   spriteBatch.End()

   MyBase.Draw(gameTime)
End Sub
```

9. Execute the game to verify that the player's robo-tank is displayed on the tile map background:

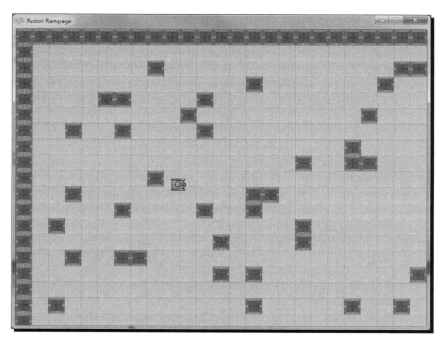

What just happened?

Two individual sprites make up the player's tank. The `BaseSprite` will be drawn to the screen first, with the `TurretSprite` drawn over it. When the `Player` module's `Initialize()` method is called, the animation for the `BaseSprite` is created normally, and the sprite's `AnimateWhenStopped` member is set to `false`. Since the animation associated with the `BaseSprite` shows the treads of the player's tank rolling, the animation should not play when the player is not moving. In order to prevent the player from having to squeeze tightly between walls, a margin of four pixels on each side of the base sprite is established that will reduce the size of the robo-tank, when we detect collisions with walls on the map.

The `TurretSprite`, on the other hand, will not animate at all. The multiple frames of the `TurretSprite` animation actually represent different turrets that we will swap for the default turret, when the player has upgraded their weapons (more on this in Chapter 7, *Robot Rampage - Lots and Lost of Bullets*). By setting the `Animate` member to `false`, the frame displayed by the `TurretSprite` will remain constant unless we use the `Frame` property to change it directly.

During the `Update()` method, after updating the turret sprite, we always set its location equal to the location of the base sprite. This is because we always want the turret sprite to be drawn at the same location as the base sprite. Instead of trying to synchronize their velocities to keep them in the same spot, we just force them to the same location on each frame.

We will be expanding on the `Update()` method when we add input handling, but the `Draw()` method will remain as simple as it is now—just passing the `draw` command along to the sprites composing the player.

Compositing sprites

Creating a game object made up of multiple sprites that are drawn on top of each other at the same location can be used to create several different effects. For example, you could overlay a fiery thrust sprite on top of a space ship that only played while the player was actively moving. In a role-playing game, you could create a variety of body and armor pieces (head, wings, tails, armor of different types, weapons, and so on) and draw whichever combination represents the equipment the player's character is currently wearing.

Moving around the world

The player's movement and weapons fire are controlled separately by using the two thumbsticks on a gamepad. While the gamepad is by far the most comfortable way to control Robot Rampage, we will also include support for the keyboard. After all, not everyone has an Xbox controller connected to their PC.

Time for action – handling input

1. Add the following declarations to the declarations region of the `Player` module:

```
Private baseAngle As Vector2 = Vector2.Zero
Private turretAngle As Vector2 = Vector2.Zero
Private playerSpeed As Single = 90
```

2. Add the methods to handle keyboard and gamepad input to the `Player` module:

```
#Region "Input Handling"
  Private Function handleKeyboardMovement(
    keyState As KeyboardState) As Vector2

    Dim keyMovement As Vector2 = Vector2.Zero

    If keyState.IsKeyDown(Keys.W) Then
      keyMovement.Y -= 1
    End If

    If keyState.IsKeyDown(Keys.A) Then
      keyMovement.X -= 1
    End If

    If keyState.IsKeyDown(Keys.S) Then
      keyMovement.Y += 1
    End If

    If keyState.IsKeyDown(Keys.D) Then
      keyMovement.X += 1
    End If

    Return keyMovement
  End Function

  Private Function handleGamePadMovement(
    padState As GamePadState) As Vector2
    Return New Vector2(
      padState.ThumbSticks.Left.X,
      -padState.ThumbSticks.Left.Y)
  End Function

  Private Function handleKeyboardShots(
    keyState As KeyboardState) As Vector2
    Dim keyShots As Vector2 = Vector2.Zero

    If keyState.IsKeyDown(Keys.NumPad1) Then
      keyShots = New Vector2(-1, 1)
    End If
```

```
  If keyState.IsKeyDown(Keys.NumPad2) Then
    keyShots = New Vector2(0, 1)
  End If

  If keyState.IsKeyDown(Keys.NumPad3) Then
    keyShots = New Vector2(1, 1)
  End If

  If keyState.IsKeyDown(Keys.NumPad4) Then
    keyShots = New Vector2(-1, 0)
  End If

  If keyState.IsKeyDown(Keys.NumPad6) Then
    keyShots = New Vector2(1, 0)
  End If

  If keyState.IsKeyDown(Keys.NumPad7) Then
    keyShots = New Vector2(-1, -1)
  End IF

  If keyState.IsKeyDown(Keys.NumPad8) Then
    keyShots = New Vector2(0, -1)
  End If

  If keyState.IsKeyDown(Keys.NumPad9) Then
    keyShots = New Vector2(1, -1)
  End If

  Return keyShots
End Function

Private Function handleGamePadShots(
  padState As GamePadState) As Vector2

  Return New Vector2(
    padState.ThumbSticks.Right.X,
   -padState.ThumbSticks.Right.Y)
End Function

Private Sub handleInput(gameTime As GameTime)
  Dim elapsed As Single

  Elapsed = CSng(gameTime.ElapsedGameTime.TotalSeconds)

  Dim moveAngle As Vector2 = Vector2.Zero
  Dim fireAngle As Vector2 = Vector2.Zero

  moveAngle += handleKeyboardMovement(Keyboard.GetState())
  moveAngle +=
    handleGamePadMovement(GamePad.GetState(PlayerIndex.One))
```

```
     fireAngle += handleKeyboardShots(Keyboard.GetState())
     fireAngle +=
       handleGamePadShots(GamePad.GetState(PlayerIndex.One))

     If moveAngle <> Vector2.Zero Then
       moveAngle.Normalize()
       baseAngle = moveAngle
     End If

     If fireAngle <> Vector2.Zero Then
       fireAngle.Normalize()
       turretAngle = fireAngle
     End If

     BaseSprite.RotateTo(baseAngle)
     TurretSprite.RotateTo(turretAngle)

     BaseSprite.Velocity = moveAngle * playerSpeed
   End Sub
#End Region
```

3. Modify the `Update()` method of the `Player` module to call the `handleInput()` method before updating the sprite. The entire `Update()` method should look like:

```
Public Sub Update(gameTime As GameTime)
  handleInput(gameTime)
  BaseSprite.Update(gameTime)
  TurretSprite.WorldLocation = BaseSprite.WorldLocation
End Sub
```

4. Launch your game and drive around! Swing your cannon around with the right thumbstick or the numeric keypad. Make sure *Numlock* is turned on!

What just happened?

The whole purpose of the input handling methods is to determine the value of the two vectors declared in step one. The `baseAngle` vector determines the direction that the player is moving in (and therefore the orientation of the base sprite), while the `turretAngle` vector determines the direction the player's cannon will face.

The gamepad controls are far simpler than the keyboard controls because the gamepad's thumbsticks already return a complete vector. The only alteration we need to make is to reverse the sign on the `Y` component of the vector, since negative `Y` values correspond to the up direction on the screen, but to the down direction on the gamepad.

In the case of the keyboard, pressing the individual movement keys increments or decrements the appropriate component of the vector that will be returned, while pressing the firing keys on the numeric keypad sets the returned vector to a vector pointing in the direction of the firing key relative to the five key (in other words, pressing eight on the keypad fires upwards, while pressing three fires down and to the right).

In the `handleInput()` method, we initially set both the `moveAngle` (which determines the direction the player will move in) and the `fireAngle` (which determines the direction the turret will be facing) to `Vector2.Zero`, indicating that they are both empty. We need to keep these two vectors separate from their related vectors (`baseAngle` and `turretAngle`), because we do not want to modify the angle that either the tank or the turret is facing if the player is not moving the corresponding thumbstick. If we did allow them to reset back to `Vector2.Zero` in every frame, any time the player was not pressing one of the control sticks, the corresponding part (tank or turret) would snap back to face the right edge of the screen.

By calling the `handle...()` methods and adding the results to the `moveAngle` and `fireAngle` vectors, we now have the two vectors we need to animate the player's tank. We check to see if the local vectors have a value (in other words, are not equal to `Vector2.Zero`). If so, the vector is normalized and assigned to the corresponding class-level member variable (`moveAngle` to `baseAngle`, and `fireAngle` to `turretAngle`).

The sprites are then rotated to their appropriate angles, and the `moveAngle` is applied to the base tank sprite's velocity.

The `Update()` method calls our new `handleInput()` method, and then updates the base sprite. The position of the base sprite is then copied to the location of the `turretSprite`, keeping the two sprites in sync with each other.

Staying in bounds

As the game stands, you can drive your tank around the game screen easily. Too easily, in fact! You can run straight through the walls and off the screen!

We need to ensure that the player's tank cannot move outside of the game world and that the game's camera follows the player as they move near the screen's edges.

Time for action – staying in bounds

1. Create a region called `Movement Limitations` in the `Player` module:

```
#Region "Movement Limitations"
#End Region
```

2. Inside the `Movement Limitations` **region, add the** `clampToWorld()` **method:**

```
Private Sub clampToWorld()
  Dim currentX As Single = BaseSprite.WorldLocation.X
  Dim currentY As Single = BaseSprite.WorldLocation.Y

  currentX = MathHelper.Clamp(
    currentX,
    0,
    Camera.WorldRectangle.Right - BaseSprite.FrameWidth)
  currentY = MathHelper.Clamp(
    currentY,
    0,
    Camera.WorldRectangle.Bottom - BaseSprite.FrameHeight)

  BaseSprite.WorldLocation = New Vector2(currentX, currentY)
End Sub
```

3. Add a declaration to the `Player` module, to define the area in which the camera should attempt to keep the player:

```
Private scrollArea As Rectangle = New Rectangle(150, 100, 500,
  400)
```

4. Add the `repositionCamera()` helper method to the `Movement Limitations` region of the `Player` module:

```
Private Sub repositionCamera(
  gameTime As GameTime,
  moveAngle As Vector2)

  Dim elapsed As Single
  Elapsed = CSng(gameTime.ElapsedGameTime.TotalSeconds)

  Dim moveScale As Single = playerSpeed * elapsed

  If (BaseSprite.ScreenRectangle.X < scrollArea.X) And
    (moveAngle.X < 0) Then
    Camera.Move(New Vector2(moveAngle.X, 0) * moveScale)
  End If

  If (BaseSprite.ScreenRectangle.Right > scrollArea.Right) And
    (moveAngle.X > 0) Then
    Camera.Move(New Vector2(moveAngle.X, 0) * moveScale)
  End If
```

```
    If (BaseSprite.ScreenRectangle.Y < scrollArea.Y) And
      (moveAngle.Y < 0) Then
        Camera.Move(New Vector2(0, moveAngle.Y) * moveScale)
    End If

    If (BaseSprite.ScreenRectangle.Bottom > scrollArea.Bottom) And
      (moveAngle.Y > 0) Then
        Camera.Move(New Vector2(0, moveAngle.Y) * moveScale)
    End If
End Sub
```

5. Modify the `Update()` method to call `clampToWorld()`, after the base sprite has been updated. The full `Update()` method should read:

```
Public Sub Update(gameTime As GameTime)
    handleInput(gameTime)
    BaseSprite.Update(gameTime)
    clampToWorld()
    TurretSprite.WorldLocation = BaseSprite.WorldLocation
End Sub
```

6. In the `handleInput()` method of the `Player` module, add the following as the last line of the method:

```
repositionCamera(gameTime, moveAngle)
```

7. Launch the game and drive around again. Your tank will stay confined to the game world, but is still able to drive through walls.

What just happened?

Things are looking a little better now. The player can no longer drive off the edge of the world, and when they reach the bottom or right-hand side, the camera will scroll with them. We can still drive through walls, but we are getting there!

When we apply movement to the player, we call `clampToWorld()`, which separates the player's location into `X` and `Y` components. The `MathHelper.Clamp()` method is then used to ensure that the components stay within the world's coordinate system. The width and height of the sprite is subtracted from the width and height of the game world, so that the furthest the player's sprite can get to the right-side and bottom of the world is a full sprite's size away. This will keep the sprite fully within the game world at all times.

When the player approaches an edge of the screen, the camera needs to be adjusted to move in the same direction that the player is moving, assuming that the end of the game world has not yet been reached. By defining the `scrollArea` rectangle, we are specifying that we would like to keep the player in a 500x400 pixel area beginning at (150, 100). This corresponds to the center of our 800x600 screen, with a 150 pixel buffer on the left and right edges, and a 100 pixel buffer along the top and bottom.

When `repositionCamera()` is called, it checks to see if the player has moved out of the defined scrolling area. Each side of the scroll area is checked individually, starting with the left edge. If the `X` coordinate of the `ScreenRectangle` is less than the `X` coordinate of the `scrollArea` and the player is moving left, the camera is moved left by an amount equal to the amount that the sprite itself will be moved by multiplying the appropriate component of `moveAngle` by the `moveScale` value.

The result is that the camera will move the same distance that the player moves. The player's sprite will appear to stay in place while the game world scrolls around it. Since the `Camera` module limits its own position to ensure that a full view of the world is always displayed, the camera will simply stop moving when the player is close enough to the edge that it can no longer scroll.

Running into tiles

The last limitation we need to account for in player movement is the underlying tile-based map. We want the game to detect when the player is attempting to move into a wall and stop them from doing so.

Time for action – accounting for walls

1. Add the `checkTileObstacles()` method to the `Movement Limitations` region of the `Player` module:

```
Public Function checkTileObstacles(
    elapsedTime As Single,
    moveAngle As Vector2) As Vector2

    Dim newHorizontalLocation As Vector2 =
        BaseSprite.WorldLocation + (New Vector2(moveAngle.X, 0) *
        (playerSpeed * elapsedTime))

    Dim newVerticalLocation As Vector2 =
        BaseSprite.WorldLocation + (New Vector2(0, moveAngle.Y) *
        (playerSpeed * elapsedTime))

    Dim newHorizontalRect As Rectangle = new Rectangle(
        CInt(Int(newHorizontalLocation.X)),
        CInt(Int(BaseSprite.WorldLocation.Y)),
        BaseSprite.FrameWidth,
    BaseSprite.FrameHeight)

    Dim newVerticalRect As Rectangle = new Rectangle(
        CInt(Int(BaseSprite.WorldLocation.X)),
        CInt(Int(newVerticalLocation.Y)),
        BaseSprite.FrameWidth,
```

```
BaseSprite.FrameHeight)

Dim horizLeftPixel As Integer = 0
Dim horizRightPixel As Integer = 0

Dim vertTopPixel As Integer = 0
Dim vertBottomPixel As Integer = 0

If moveAngle.X < 0 Then
  horizLeftPixel = CInt(Int(newHorizontalRect.Left))
  horizRightPixel = CInt(Int(BaseSprite.WorldRectangle.Left))
End If

If moveAngle.X > 0 Then
  horizLeftPixel = CInt(Int(BaseSprite.WorldRectangle.Right))
  horizRightPixel = CInt(Int(newHorizontalRect.Right))
End If

If moveAngle.Y < 0 Then
  vertTopPixel = CInt(Int(newVerticalRect.Top))
  vertBottomPixel = CInt(Int(BaseSprite.WorldRectangle.Top))
End If

If moveAngle.Y > 0 Then
  vertTopPixel = CInt(Int(BaseSprite.WorldRectangle.Bottom))
  vertBottomPixel = CInt(Int(newVerticalRect.Bottom))
End If

If moveAngle.X <> 0 Then
  For x As Integer = horizLeftPixel To horizRightPixel - 1
    For y As Integer = 0 To BaseSprite.FrameHeight - 1
      If TileMap.IsWallTileByPixel(
        New Vector2(x, newHorizontalLocation.Y + y)) Then
        moveAngle.X = 0
        Exit For
      End If
    Next
    If moveAngle.X = 0 Then
      Exit For
    End If
  Next
End If

If moveAngle.Y <> 0 Then
  For y As Integer = vertTopPixel To vertBottomPixel - 1
    For x As Integer = 0 To BaseSprite.FrameWidth - 1
```

```
            If TileMap.IsWallTileByPixel(
              New Vector2(newVerticalLocation.X + x, y)) Then
              moveAngle.Y = 0
              Exit For
            End If
          Next
          If moveAngle.Y = 0 Then
            Exit For
          End If
        Next
      End If


      Return moveAngle
    End Function
```

2. In the `handleInput()` method, update the `If moveAngle <> Vector2.Zero` statement block, by adding a call to `checkTileObstacles()`. The whole statement should now read:

```
If moveAngle <> Vector2.Zero Then
  moveAngle.Normalize()
  baseAngle = moveAngle
  moveAngle = checkTileObstacles(elapsed, moveAngle)
End If
```

3. Execute the game again and drive around.

What just happened?

In order to check for tile-based collisions, we break the process into two steps. First we will check for collisions due to horizontal movement, and then due to vertical movement.

To facilitate this, we begin by establishing two new vectors representing the new locations of the sprite, if only the horizontal or vertical movement was applied.

From these new vectors, we create two rectangles, representing the world location of the sprite's two possible movements. In other words, `newHorizontalRect` specifies where the player's sprite would be located after moving, if only the horizontal component of the movement is considered, while `newVerticalRect` represents the new location, if movement occurred only along the vertical axis:

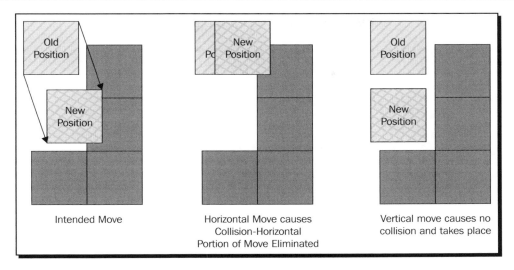

Next, we need to determine a range of pixels to check for tile obstacles. We could simply check all of the pixels inside the two new rectangles, by calling `TileMap.IsWallTile()` for each pixel in both rectangles. This would return the results we are looking for, but it would cause unnecessary processing, as only the portions of the new rectangles that are not already covered by the current position's rectangle need to be checked for collisions.

Instead, we can use the direction in which we are moving to determine a smaller range of pixels that need to be checked. In the horizontal movement portion of the previous diagram, the new position rectangle mostly overlaps the old position rectangle. We only need to check the pixels between the right edge of the old position and the right edge of the new position, because the old position is already known to be an area the sprite can exist in.

If we are moving to the right, we use the right edges of the old and new positions to define the limits of the area we will check. Similarly, if we are moving left, we use the left edges of the two position rectangles to define the area.

We can then check each pixel in the new area against `TileMap.IsWallTile()` to determine if moving in this direction would cause the sprite to overlap a wall tile. If any of them do, we set the X component of the `moveAngle` vector to zero, eliminating the movement in that direction. As soon as any pixel tests `true`, we break out of the loop, since there is no need to continue testing.

After we have dealt with horizontal movement, the process is repeated for vertical movement, eliminating the Y component of the `moveAngle` vector if the new Y position would result in a wall collision.

Summary

We have covered a lot of ground building the foundation for Robot Rampage. So far, our new game:

◆ Contains a camera to view a game world larger than the display screen

◆ Allows us to define sprites that are aware of their positions within the game world instead of simply their location on the screen

◆ Generates a tile-based map for the game world with randomly placed walls

◆ Allows the player to drive their tank around the tile map, including collision detection with map walls and automatic camera panning

In the next chapter, we will finish building Robot Rampage by adding enemy robots and the ability to fire weapons. We will also cover basic path finding to allow the enemy to hunt down the player.

7
Robot Rampage – Lots and Lots of Bullets

Robot Rampage is already looking pretty good! We have a tile-based game world and a mobile player tank with the ability to rotate its cannon independently of the tank's base. However, it is not quite finished yet.

In this chapter, we will complete the build by looking at the following topics:

◆ Adding an updated particle-based visual effects system

◆ Adding weapons to the player's arsenal

◆ Adding enemy robo-tanks to the map

◆ Building a path-finding system to allow the enemy to hunt down the player

◆ Implementing computer terminals the player can shut down

◆ Wrapping the game in a game flow structure

Visual effects

The particle explosion system we built for Asteroid Belt Assault can be adapted for use in Robot Rampage, but we will expand on it a bit and make it more flexible. Additionally, we want to add a new type of special effect that will be used when shots impact walls to throw off a small shower of sparks. We do not want a full blown explosion every time a shot hits a wall, but we also would like to see some effect instead of the shots simply disappearing.

Revisiting particles

In Asteroid Belt Assault, we utilized the `Particle` class to represent only the sprites that we did not involve in collision detection. For Robot Rampage, we will also be implementing a `Particle` class, but this time around we will use it for both special effects and for displaying the projectiles fired by the player.

Time for action – the Particle class

1. Add a new class called `Particle` to the Robot Rampage project.

2. Update the class declaration for the `Particle` class to derive it from the `Sprite` class by adding an `Inherits` line below the class declaration:

```
Inherits Sprite
```

3. Add declarations to the Particle class:

```
#Region "Declarations"
Private _acceleration As Vector2
Private _maxSpeed As Single
Private _initialDuration As Integer
Private _remainingDuration As Integer
Private _initialColor As Color
Private _finalColor As Color
#End Region
```

4. Add properties to the `Particle` class:

```
#Region "Properties"
Public ReadOnly Property ElapsedDuration As Integer
    Get
        Return _initialDuration - _remainingDuration
    End Get
End Property

Public ReadOnly Property DurationProgress As Single
    Get
        Return CSng(ElapsedDuration) / CSng(_initialDuration)
    End Get
End Property

Public ReadOnly Property IsActive As Boolean
    Get
        Return (_remainingDuration > 0)
    End Get
End Property
#End Region
```

5. Add a constructor to the `Particle` class:

```
#Region "Constructor"
Public Sub New(
    location As Vector2,
    texture As Texture2D,
    initialFrame As Rectangle,
    velocity As Vector2,
    acceleration As Vector2,
    maxSpeed As Single,
    duration As Integer,
    initialColor As Color,
    finalColor As Color)

    MyBase.New(location, texture, initialFrame, velocity)
    _initialDuration = duration
    _remainingDuration = duration
    _acceleration = acceleration
    _initialColor = initialColor
    _maxSpeed = maxSpeed
    _finalColor = finalColor
End Sub
#End Region
```

6. Add the `Update()` and `Draw()` methods to the `Particle` class:

```
#Region "Update and Draw"
Public Overrides Sub Update(gameTime As gameTime)
    If _remainingDuration <= 0 Then
        Expired = True
    End If

    If Not Expired Then
        Velocity += _acceleration
        If Velocity.Length() > _maxSpeed Then
            Dim vel As Vector2 = Velocity
            vel.Normalize()
            Velocity = vel * _maxSpeed
        End If
        TintColor = Color.Lerp(
            _initialColor,
            _finalColor,
            DurationProgress)
        _remainingDuration -= 1
    End If
```

```
        MyBase.Update(gameTime)
    End Sub

    Public Overrides Sub Draw(spriteBatch As SpriteBatch)
        If IsActive Then
            Mybase.Draw(spriteBatch)
        End If
    End Sub
#End Region
```

What just happened?

Just as we did in Asteroid Belt Assault, we have constructed our `Particle` class as an extension of the `Sprite` class. As before, we will use the `Particle` class to generate a large volume of sprites that will need to automatically expire after a given period of time.

The EffectsManager class

In Asteroid Belt Assault, we used a class called `ExplosionManager` to handle all of the game's explosive effects. We will create a similar module for Robot Rampage, but call it `EffectsManager` since it will handle our sparks effect as well as explosions.

Time for action – the EffectsManager module

1. Add a new module called `EffectsManager` to the Robot Rampage project.

2. Add declarations to the `EffectsManager` module:

```
#Region "Declarations"
Private _effects As List(Of Particle) = New List(Of Particle)
Private _rand As Random = New Random()
Private _texture As Texture2D
Private _particleFrame As Rectangle = New Rectangle(0, 288, 2, 2)
Private _expFrames As List(Of Rectangle) = New List(Of Rectangle)
#End Region
```

3. Add an `Initialize()` method to the `EffectsManager` module:

```
#Region "Initialization"
Public Sub Initialize(
    texture As Texture2D,
    particleFrame As Rectangle,
    explosionFrame As Rectangle,
    explosionFrameCount As Integer)
```

```
        _texture = texture
        _particleFrame = particleFrame
        _expFrames.Clear()
        _expFrames.Add(explosionFrame)
        For X as Integer = 1 to explosionFrameCount - 1
            explosionFrame.Offset(explosionFrame.Width, 0)
            _expFrames.Add(explosionFrame)
        Next
    End Sub
#End Region
```

4. Add the `RandomDirection()` method to the `EffectsManager` module:

```
#Region "Helper Methods"
Public Function randomDirection(scale As Single) As Vector2
    Dim direction As Vector2

    Do
        direction = New Vector2(
        _rand.Next(0, 100) - 50,
        _rand.Next(0, 100) - 50)
    Loop While direction.Length() = 0

    direction.Normalize()
    direction *= scale

    Return direction
End Sub
#End Region
```

5. Add the `Update()` and `Draw()` methods to the `EffectsManager` module:

```
#Region "Public Methods"
Public Sub Update(gameTime As gameTime)
    For x As Integer = _effects.Count - 1 To 0 Step - 1
        _effects(x).Update(gameTime)
        If _effects(x).Expired Then
            _effects.RemoveAt(x)
        End If
    Next
End Sub

Public Sub Draw(spriteBatch As SpriteBatch)
    For Each effect As Sprite in _effects
        effect.Draw(spriteBatch)
    Next
End Sub
#End Region
```

What just happened?

Up to this point, the `EffectsManager` module is very similar to the `ExplosionManager` class from Asteroid Belt Assault, though some refinements have been made.

We do not have nearly as many declarations in the `EffectsManager` module because the default values for things like the number of particles and explosion pieces generated, and the transition colors have been removed from the manager. These values will now be specified by the code that creates the explosion.

The explosions that our `EffectsManager` will create will use the same images (scaled to fit our 32 x 32 pixel tile size) from Asteroid Belt Assault. We will produce two types of explosions. The smaller explosion will be used whenever an enemy robot is destroyed, while the larger explosion will be used by the upgraded rocket weapon the player will be able to acquire.

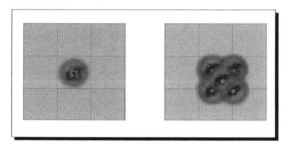

Since we are using a module instead of a class, the initialization that was done in the constructor of the `ExplosionManager` class is now separated into an `Initialize()` method.

Time for action – building explosions

1. Add the `AddExplosion()` method to the **Public Methods** region of the `EffectsManager` module:

```
Public Sub AddExplosion(
    location As Vector2,
    momentum As Vector2,
    minPointCount As Integer,
    maxPointCount As Integer,
    minPieceCount As Integer,
    maxPieceCount As Integer,
    pieceSpeedScale As Single,
    duration As Integer,
    initialColor As Color,
    finalColor As Color)
```

```
        Dim explosionMaxSpeed As Single = 30
        Dim pointSpeedMin As Integer = CInt(pieceSpeedScale * 2)
        Dim pointSpeedMax As Integer = CInt(pieceSpeedScale * 3)

        Dim pieceLocation As Vector2 = location -
            New Vector2(CSng(_expFrames(0).Width) / 2,
                CSng(_expFrames(0).Height) / 2)

        Dim pieces As Integer
        pieces = _rand.Next(minPieceCount, maxPieceCount + 1)

        For x As Integer = 1 To pieces
            _effects.Add(new Particle(
                pieceLocation,
                _texture,
                _expFrames(_rand.Next(0, _expFrames.Count)),
                randomDirection(pieceSpeedScale) + momentum,
                Vector2.Zero,
                explosionMaxSpeed,
                duration,
                initialColor,
                finalColor))
        Next

        Dim points As Integer
        points = _rand.Next(minPointCount, maxPointCount + 1)

        For x As Integer =  1 To points
            _effects.Add(new Particle(
                location,
                _texture,
                _particleFrame,
                randomDirection(CSng(_rand.Next(
                    pointSpeedMin, pointSpeedMax))) + momentum,
                Vector2.Zero,
                explosionMaxSpeed,
                duration,
                initialColor,
                finalColor))
        Next
    End Sub
```

2. Add an overload of the AddExplosion() method to create a default explosion:

```
Public Sub AddExplosion(location As Vector2, momentum As Vector2)
    AddExplosion(
        location,
        momentum,
        15,
        20,
        2,
        4,
        6.0F,
        90,
        new Color(1.0F, 0.3F, 0F) * 0.5F,
        new Color(1.0F, 0.3F, 0F) * 0.05F)
End Sub
```

3. Add the AddLargeExplosion() method to the EffectsManager module:

```
Public Sub AddLargeExplosion(location As Vector2)
    AddExplosion(
        location,
        Vector2.Zero,
        15,
        20,
        4,
        6,
        30F,
        90,
        new Color(1.0F, 0.3F, 0F) * 0.5F,
        new Color(1.0F, 0.3F, 0F) * 0.05F)
End Sub
```

What just happened?

Most of the AddExplosion() method is unchanged from Asteroid Belt Assault, though many of the values that were class-level variables are now parameters passed to the method. Just as before, a random number of larger pieces are generated and added to the Effects list, and then a random number of point-sprite particles are generated with slightly faster speeds than the larger pieces.

By adding an overload of AddExplosion(), we can avoid having to specify most of these values each time we want to generate a typical explosion. We simply pass in default values for all of the parameters matching what used to be the defaults in Asteroid Belt Assault.

Finally, we have the `AddLargeExplosion()` method, which just varies the parameters passed to `AddExplosion()` to create an explosion with faster moving pieces that will cover more area before they fade. We will use this explosion when we create a rocket launcher weapon by stacking a few of these larger explosions slightly offset from each other when the rocket explodes.

Time for action – spark effects

1. Add the `AddSparkEffect()` method to the **Public Methods** region of the `EffectsManager` module:

```
Public Sub AddSparksEffect(
    location As Vector2,
    impactVelocity As Vector2)

    Dim particleCount As Integer = _rand.Next(10, 20)
    For x As Integer = 1 To particleCount
        Dim spark As Particle = New Particle(
            location - (impactVelocity / 60),
            _texture,
            _ParticleFrame,
            randomDirection(CSng(_rand.Next(10, 20))),
            Vector2.Zero,
            60,
            20,
            Color.Yellow,
            Color.Orange)
        _effects.Add(spark)
    Next
End Sub
```

2. In the `LoadContent()` method of the `Game1` class, initialize `EffectsManager` after the `Player` has been initialized:

```
EffectsManager.Initialize(
    spriteSheet,
    New Rectangle(0, 288, 2, 2),
    New Rectangle(0, 256, 32, 32),
    3)
```

3. In the `Update()` method of the `Game1` class, update `EffectsManager` after the `Player` has been updated:

```
EffectsManager.Update(gameTime)
```

4. In the `Draw()` method of the `Game1` class, draw `EffectsManager` after the
`Player` has been drawn:

```
EffectsManager.Draw(spriteBatch)
```

What just happened?

When a spark effect is added, a random number of particles are created. In order to place
the explosion right before the wall instead of embedding into it, the velocity passed to the
method is divided by 60 and subtracted from the location. Since the velocities are stored
on the sprites in pixels per second, dividing by 60 represents the approximate distance the
sprite would travel in one frame (at 60 frames per second). Effectively, the spark effect will
be generated at the position of the shot on the previous frame:

The effect itself is just a random number (ten to nineteen) of point-sprite particles that start
off yellow and progress to orange over the course of 20 frames. This will result in a small,
generally circular burst of sparks around the impact point.

Adding weaponry

Now that we can create special effects for our weaponry, we need to actually add the
weapons to the game! We will begin with a basic cannon, and then modify the `Player`
module to support the upgraded weaponry.

The WeaponManager

Once again, we will use a manager module to handle the shots fired in the game. This time
though, we will only be dealing with player fired because the enemy tanks must actually
collide with the player to inflict damage.

Time for action – beginning the WeaponManager module

1. Add a new module called WeaponManager to the Robot Rampage project.

2. Add declarations to the WeaponManager module:

```
#Region "Declarations"
Public WeaponSpeed As Single = 600

Private _shots As List(Of Particle) = new List(Of Particle)
Private _shotRectangle As Rectangle = New Rectangle(0, 128, 32,
32)
Private _shotTimer As Single = 0
Private _shotMinTimer As Single = 0.15
#End Region
```

3. Add properties to the WeaponManager module:

```
#Region "Properties"
Public Property Texture As Texture2D

Public ReadOnly Property WeaponFireDelay As Single
    Get
        Return _shotMinTimer
    End Get
End Property

Public ReadOnly Property CanFireWeapon As Boolean
    Get
        Return (_shotTimer >= WeaponFireDelay)
    End Get
End Property
#End Region
```

4. Add the AddShot() method to the WeaponManager module:

```
#Region "Shot Management Methods"

Private Sub AddShot(
    Location As Vector2,
    Velocity As Vector2,
    Frame As Integer)

    Dim shot As Particle = New Particle(
        location,
        Texture,
```

```
        _shotRectangle,
        velocity,
        Vector2.Zero,
        400F,
        120,
        Color.White,
        Color.White)

    shot.AddFrame(New Rectangle(
        _shotRectangle.X + _shotRectangle.Width,
        _shotRectangle.Y,
        _shotRectangle.Width,
        _shotRectangle.Height))

    shot.Animate = false
    shot.Frame = frame
    shot.RotateTo(velocity)
    _shots.Add(shot)
End Sub
#End Region
```

5. Add the `FireWeapon()` method to the `WeaponManager` module:

```
#Region "Weapons Management Methods"
Public Sub FireWeapon(location As Vector2, velocity As Vector2)
    AddShot(location, velocity, 0)
    _shotTimer = 0
End Sub
#End Region
```

6. Add the `Update()` and `Draw()` methods to the `WeaponManager` module:

```
#Region "Update and Draw"
Public Sub Update(gameTime As GameTime)
    Dim elapsed As Single
    elapsed = CSng(gameTime.ElapsedGameTime.TotalSeconds)
    _shotTimer += elapsed

    For x As Integer = _shots.Count - 1 To 0 Step - 1
        _shots(x).Update(gameTime)

        If _shots(x).Expired Then
            _shots.RemoveAt(x)
        End If
    Next
End Sub
```

```
Public Sub Draw(spriteBatch As SpriteBatch)
    For Each shot As Particle in _shots
        shot.Draw(spriteBatch)
    Next
End Sub
#End Region
```

7. In the `Player` module, in the `HandleInput()` method, update the `if` statement block that reads `If fireAngle <> Vector2.Zero Then` and replace it with:

```
If fireAngle <> Vector2.Zero Then
    fireAngle.Normalize()
    turretAngle = fireAngle

    If WeaponManager.CanFireWeapon Then
        WeaponManager.FireWeapon(
            TurretSprite.WorldLocation,
            fireAngle * WeaponManager.WeaponSpeed)
    End If
End If
```

8. In the `LoadContent()` method of the `Game1` class, add the following line to initialize the `Texture` property of the `WeaponManager` after the `spriteSheet` has been loaded:

```
WeaponManager.Texture = spriteSheet
```

9. In the `Game1` class, add a line to the `Update()` method to update the `WeaponManager` module right after the `Player` module is updated:

```
WeaponManager.Update(gameTime)
```

10. Still in the `Game1` class, add a line to the `Draw()` method to render the `WeaponManager` module. This time, place the call right before the `Player` is drawn:

```
WeaponManager.Draw(spriteBatch)
```

11. Launch Robot Rampage and drive your tank around. When using the right thumb stick or the numeric keypad, you can now launch volleys of projectiles:

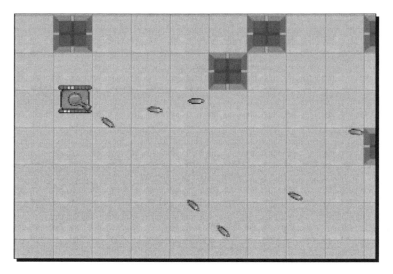

What just happened?

Each player shot is stored as a Particle in the `_shots` list. We are using Particles instead of Sprites so that we can take advantage of the automatic expiration of a Particle after a given time frame. That way, if a shot is fired into a wide open area and travels off the screen, it will simply clean itself up.

The `WeaponSpeed` value will be used to scale the velocity of the shots the player fires, and defaults to 600 pixels per second. The shots on the screen will be moving fairly quickly!

The `_shotTimer` and `_shotMinTimer` member variables, along with the `WeaponFireDelay` and `CanFireWeapon` properties work in conjunction to implement the timing mechanism we have used previously to control the rate at which new shots are added to the game.

When the time comes to actually add the shot, the `AddShot()` method creates the new `Particle` object. The sprite sheet we are using for the game has two different weapon graphics: one for a normal shot, and one for a missile. These two frames are added to the particle, and it is set not to animate between them. When `AddShot()` is passed a zero for the frame parameter, a normal shot will be fired. When it is passed a one, the second frame will be used, resulting in a missile being fired. We will implement weapon upgrades shortly—right now, the player can only fire normal shots.

Currently, the `FireWeapon()` method simply calls `AddShot()` and resets the `_shotTimer` variable. We will be expanding upon this method when we add multiple weapon types.

Finally, the `Update()` and `Draw()` methods contain our standard code to loop through the objects in the `_shots` list and handle them.

The only updates we need to make to the `Player` module to allow the player to fire weapons are to actually call the `FireWeapon()` method, assuming that `CanFireWeapon` is true. `FireWeapon()` is passed the current position of the player's turret, and the angle that the turret is pointing at multiplied by the weapon speed.

Weapon upgrades

In addition to the normal fire mode of the player's cannon, we are going to add two more weapon types: a triple cannon, which fires three shots at a spread angle and a rocket launcher, which destroys all the enemies in a small area surrounding its point of impact.

Time for action – new weapons

1. Add the following declarations to the `WeaponManager` module:

```
Public Enum WeaponType
    Normal
    Triple
    Rocket
End Enum

Public CurrentWeaponType As WeaponType = WeaponType.Triple
Public WeaponTimeRemaining As Single = 30
private _weaponTimeDefault As Single = 30
Private _rocketMinTimer As Single = 0.5
Private _tripleWeaponSplitAngle As Single = 15
```

2. Replace the current `WeaponFireDelay` property with the following:

```
Public ReadOnly Property WeaponFireDelay  As Single
    Get
        If CurrentWeaponType = WeaponType.Rocket Then
            Return _rocketMinTimer
        Else
            Return _shotMinTimer
        End If
    End Get
End Property
```

3. Replace the current `FireWeapon()` method with the following:

```
Public Sub FireWeapon(location As Vector2, velocity As Vector2)
    Select Case CurrentWeaponType

        Case WeaponType.Normal
            AddShot(location, velocity, 0)

        Case WeaponType.Triple
            AddShot(location, velocity, 0)

            Dim baseAngle As Single = CSng(Math.Atan2(
                velocity.Y,
                velocity.X))

            Dim offset As Single = MathHelper.ToRadians(
                _tripleWeaponSplitAngle)

            AddShot(
                location,
                New Vector2(
                    CSng(Math.Cos(baseAngle - offset)),
                    CSng(Math.Sin(baseAngle - offset))
                ) * velocity.Length(),
                0)

            AddShot(
                location,
                new Vector2(
                    CSng(Math.Cos(baseAngle + offset)),
                    CSng(Math.Sin(baseAngle + offset))
                ) * velocity.Length(),
                0)

        Case WeaponType.Rocket:
            AddShot(location, velocity, 1)
    End Select

    _shotTimer = 0.0
End Sub
```

4. Add the `checkWeaponUpgradExpire()` method to the **Weapon Management Methods** region of the `WeaponManager` module:

```
Private Sub checkWeaponUpgradeExpire(elapsed As Single)
    If CurrentWeaponType <> WeaponType.Normal Then
        WeaponTimeRemaining -= elapsed
        If WeaponTimeRemaining <= 0 Then
```

```
            CurrentWeaponType = WeaponType.Normal
        End If
    End If
End Sub
```

5. Modify the `Update()` method of the `WeaponManager` module to call `checkWeaponUpgradeExpire()` right after the `_shotTimer` variable is updated:

`checkWeaponUpgradeExpire(elapsed)`

6. Launch your game and fire your weapons. For thirty seconds after starting the game, you will have the triple cannon weapon, firing three shots at a time:

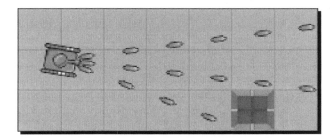

7. Stop the game and modify the `CurrentWeaponType` variable in the `WeaponManager` module to change its default value to `WeaponType.Rocket`.

8. Launch the game again, and shoot rockets from your cannon:

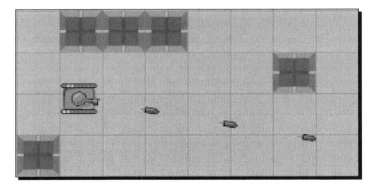

9. Stop the game and modify the `CurrentWeaponType` variable to change its default value to `WeaponType.Normal` and set the `WeaponTimeRemaining` value to `0`.

What just happened?

Rockets fire a bit slower than normal shots do, so the `WeaponFireDelay` property returns the delay value appropriate to the currently active weapon.

The `FireShot()` method treats normal shots and rockets almost identically, the only difference being that the normal shots are fired with a frame number of zero, while the rockets receive a frame number of one.

For the triple cannon, we calculate an offset from the current firing angle equal to the value of `_tripleWeaponSplitAngle` (which we default to 15 degrees), and after firing the base shot, simply fire two more shots, one adding the offset angle and one subtracting it from the base angle value.

Whenever the player picks up a new weapon, it will last for `_weaponTimeDefault` seconds, before their weapon reverts back to `WeaponType.Normal`. The `checkWeaponUpgradeExpire()` method enforces this rule.

Shot to map collisions

While we can let loose a barrage of weapons fire, so far our shots just pass right through the walls of the game world, flying off until the `Particle` class makes them expire. We need to implement collision detection with the tiles on the game map, thus allowing our shots to collide with walls and be destroyed.

Time for action – shots colliding with tiles

1. Add the `checkShotWallImpacts()` method to the `WeaponManager` module:

```
#Region "Collision Detection"
Private Sub checkShotWallImpacts(shot As Sprite)
    If shot.Expired Then
        Return
    End If

    If TileMap.IsWallTile(
        TileMap.GetSquareAtPixel(shot.WorldCenter)) Then

        shot.Expired = True

        If shot.Frame = 0 Then
            EffectsManager.AddSparksEffect(
                shot.WorldCenter,
                shot.Velocity)
        Else
            createLargeExplosion(shot.WorldCenter)
```

```
            End If
        End If
    End Sub
    #End Region
```

2. Add the `createLargeExplosion()` method to the **Shot Management Methods** region of the `WeaponManager` module:

```
Private Sub createLargeExplosion(location As Vector2)
    EffectsManager.AddLargeExplosion(
        location + New Vector2(-10, -10))
    EffectsManager.AddLargeExplosion(
        location + New Vector2(-10, 10))
    EffectsManager.AddLargeExplosion(
        location + New Vector2(10, 10))
    EffectsManager.AddLargeExplosion(
        location + New Vector2(10, -10))
    EffectsManager.AddLargeExplosion(location)
End Sub
```

3. Modify the `Update()` method of the `WeaponManager` class and replace the `for` loop that updates the `_shots` list with the following code:

```
For x As Integer = _shots.Count - 1 To 0 Step - 1
    _shots(x).Update(gameTime)

    checkShotWallImpacts(_shots(x))

    If _shots(x).Expired Then
        _shots.RemoveAt(x)
    End If
Next
```

4. Launch Robot Rampage and fire shots into the walls. They now erupt into a shower of sparks when they impact a wall tile:

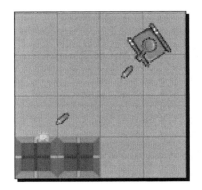

What just happened?

A shot that has already impacted something cannot impact a wall, so we check the `Expired` property of the sprite that is passed to the `checkShotWallImpact()` method and exit, if it has already been consumed.

If the shot is still active, the only thing we need to do to check for wall impacts is test the center pixel of the shot sprite to see if the map square it is on contains a wall tile. If it does, the shot has just entered a wall tile and we can mark it `Expired` and generate a graphical effect. If the shot's `Frame` property is zero, we know the shot is a `WeaponType.Normal` bullet, so we call `AddSparksEffect()` at the shot's location.

If the shot is a rocket (in other words, its `Frame` is one), we call `createLargeExplosion()`, which calls `AddLargeExplosion()` five times, once for the center of the explosion and four times spread out around the center. The center explosion is generated last so that its graphics will be on top of the other four, providing a visual focal point for the explosion.

Power-ups

We can fire upgraded weapons, but currently there is no way for the player to actually get the upgraded weaponry. We will spawn power-ups at random locations around the game world that the player can drive over to activate their upgraded weaponry:

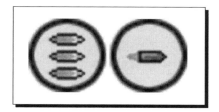

The power-ups we will spawn will be represented by yellow circles with the weapon type icon inside them. Up to five power-ups will be available at any given time.

Time for action – power-ups

1. Add the following declarations to the `WeaponManager` module:

```
Private _powerUps As List(Of Sprite) = New List(Of Sprite)
Private _maxActivePowerups As Integer = 5
Private _timeSinceLastPowerup As Single = 0.0
Private _timeBetweenPowerups As Single = 2.0
Private _rand As Random = new Random()
```

2. Add the `tryToSpawnPowerup()` method to the **Weapons Management Methods** region of the `WeaponManager` module:

```
Private Sub tryToSpawnPowerup(
    x As Integer,
    y As Integer,
    type As WeaponType)

    If _powerUps.Count >= _maxActivePowerups Then
        Return
    End If

    Dim thisDestination As Rectangle =
        TileMap.SquareWorldRectangle(New Vector2(x,y))

    For Each powerUp as Sprite in _powerUps
        If powerup.WorldRectangle = thisDestination Then
            Return
        End If
    Next

    If Not TileMap.IsWallTile(x,y) Then
        Dim newPowerup As Sprite = New Sprite(
            New Vector2(thisDestination.X, thisDestination.Y),
            Texture,
            New Rectangle(64, 128, 32, 32),
            Vector2.Zero)
        newPowerup.Animate = False
        newPowerup.CollisionRadius = 14
        newPowerup.AddFrame(new Rectangle(96, 128, 32, 32))
        If type = WeaponType.Rocket Then
            newPowerup.Frame = 1
        End If
        _powerUps.Add(newPowerup)
        _timeSinceLastPowerup = 0
    End If
End Sub
```

3. Add the `checkPowerupSpawns()` method to the **Weapons Management Methods** region of the `WeaponManager` module:

```
Private Sub checkPowerupSpawns(elapsed As Single)
    _timeSinceLastPowerup += elapsed
    If _timeSinceLastPowerup >= _timeBetweenPowerups Then
        Dim type As WeaponType = WeaponType.Triple
        If _rand.Next(0, 2) = 1 Then
```

```
                    type = WeaponType.Rocket
            End If
            tryToSpawnPowerup(
                _rand.Next(0, TileMap.MapWidth),
                _rand.Next(0, TileMap.MapHeight),
                type)
        End If
    End Sub
```

4. Add the `checkPowerupPickups()` method to the **Collision Detection** region of the `WeaponManager` module:

```
Private Sub checkPowerupPickups()
    For x As Integer = _powerUps.Count - 1 To 0 Step - 1
        If Player.BaseSprite.IsCircleColliding(
            _powerUps(x).WorldCenter,
            _powerUps(x).CollisionRadius) Then

            Select Case _powerUps(x).Frame
                case 0
                    CurrentWeaponType = WeaponType.Triple

                case 1
                    CurrentWeaponType = WeaponType.Rocket
            End Select
            WeaponTimeRemaining = _weaponTimeDefault
            _powerUps.RemoveAt(x)
        End If
    Next
End Sub
```

5. Modify the `Update()` method of the `WeaponManager` module, adding the following lines as the last two lines of the method:

```
checkPowerupSpawns(elapsed)
checkPowerupPickups()
```

6. Modify the `Draw()` method of the `WeaponManager` module, adding the following loop below the existing loop that draws the shots:

```
For Each powerUp as Sprite in _powerUps
    powerUp.Draw(spriteBatch)
Next
```

7. Launch Robot Rampage and drive around on the game map. Up to five power-ups will spawn on the map. Driving over one will activate the upgraded weapon and remove the power-up from the map:

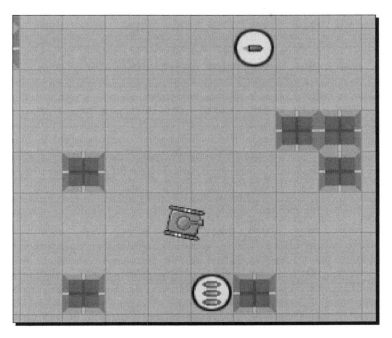

What just happened?

As with most of our game objects, we will use a List to store the power-ups that are currently active in the game world. By setting _maxActivePowerups, we can control the number that can be in the game world at any one time. New power-ups will spawn every two seconds (according to the _timeBetweenPowerups member variable) whenever there are less than five active in the world.

During the Update() method, the checkPowerupSpawns() method is called, which checks to see if the timer indicates that a new power-up should be spawned. If enough time has elapsed, a weapon type (triple or rocket) is randomly determined, and tryToSpawnPowerup() is called, passing the weapon type and a random map location.

The tryToSpawnPowerup() method checks to make sure that we do not already have the maximum number of power-ups in the world. If we do, it simply returns without doing anything. The same is true, if the method checks the existing power-ups and finds one already at the location passed to it. There is no benefit to stacking power-ups on top of each other, after all.

Finally, `tryToSpawnPowerup()` verifies that the tile we are going to place the power-up on is not a wall. The new power-up is generated as a Sprite object, and just like we did with the player's weapon fire, we use the frame number to determine if the power-up contains the triple cannon image or the rocket image. The power-up is added to the `_powerUps` list, and the spawn timer is reset to zero.

The `checkPowerupPickups()` method checks for a circle-based collision between the player and each of the active power-ups. If a collision is detected, the `CurrentWeaponType` member is set to the appropriate value based on the `Frame` property of the power-up (zero for triple cannons, one for rockets), `WeaponTimeRemaining` is set to the value of `_weaponTimeDefault`, and the power-up is removed from the `_powerUps` list.

It should be noted that `tryToSpawnPowerup()` does just that—attempt to spawn a power-up, if it does not detect any problems with its placement. If it runs into a problem, it returns without doing anything. Since the `checkPowerupSpawns()` method will be run again during the next frame, this does not pose a problem. If we are not able to create a power-up in a given frame, we will catch up over the next couple of frames. Why not just keep generating values until we find one that works? Hold that thought because...

We still have a problem...

We now have advanced weaponry and a way to get that weaponry into the player's hands. We even check to make sure the power-ups do not spawn inside walls, so what could possibly go wrong? The answer lies in the following picture:

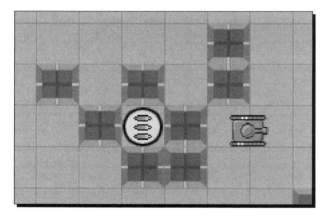

Since our map is randomly generated, it is quite possible that power-ups (and later on, enemy robots and computer terminals) will be spawned inside areas that the player cannot reach. In order to prevent that, we need to come up with a way to make sure that the square we decide to generate a game object in is actually reachable from the player's position.

Pathfinding

To resolve this problem, we need to implement a path-finding system that will allow us to easily determine the shortest route between any two squares on the tile map. The path needs to take walls into account, and needs to be fast enough that several enemy tanks can run the check without bogging down the game because in addition to verifying the placement of game objects, the same code will be used to allow the enemy robots to move towards the player and attempt to destroy him.

The A* Pathfinding algorithm

The A* path-finding method we will implement for Robot Rampage is called A* (pronounced "A Star"). This path-finding system is fairly straightforward and relatively fast, as it uses an educated guess system to try out potential paths between two points.

In order to implement A*, we need a few pieces of information:

◆ A way to identify nodes that objects can move between

◆ A starting node

◆ An ending node

◆ A method of determining the direct cost of moving between nodes

◆ A method of determining the indirect cost of moving between nodes

We can easily satisfy the first condition: each node in our path-finding system is represented by a square on the tile map grid. Similarly, defining a starting and ending point is straightforward as well. In the following example diagram, object A (located at (2, 4) on the grid) wishes to move to the position of object Z (3, 2):

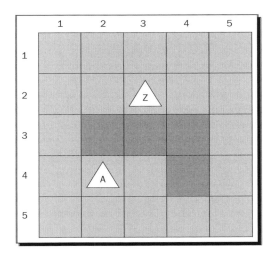

That just leaves determining the cost of moving between squares. A* uses two different costs that, together, allow it to determine the shortest path between two points. The first type of cost is a direct movement cost. This cost will always be the same for any two squares with the same relationship to each other.

If your pathing algorithm only allowed horizontal and vertical movement (no diagonals), then the direct cost could always be assumed to be the same. The direct cost is used to represent the advantage of diagonal movement over a two-step movement.

For example, if object A wants to move one square down and to the right to location (3, 5) it could do so in one of the following three ways. It could move right, and then down. It could move down, and then right or it could move diagonally right and down.

If we assign horizontal and vertical movement an arbitrary cost of 10 units (units of what is not really important), we can assign moving diagonally a cost that is between the cost to move one square (10 units) and the cost of moving two squares (20 units). We will split the difference and call the cost of moving diagonally 15 units. All things being equal, we can now define that moving diagonally is five units cheaper than moving straight twice to arrive at the same location.

This leaves the indirect cost of movement. This can be thought of as, "How much closer does this movement get me to where I want to be?" In our case, this is a very simple question to answer—all we need is to measure the distance between the square we are considering moving to and the destination square.

To keep the discussion simple, we will consider the Manhattan distance between our squares, or the distance if you could only move in straight lines. This can be calculated simply by adding the difference between the X positions and the difference between the Y positions together.

Manhattan versus linear distance

We are using Manhattan distance (the term comes from the distance you would need to walk in a city arranged in blocks, where you would walk so-many-blocks east and then so-many-blocks north to reach a destination, since you cannot walk through buildings) because it keeps the distances we are discussing in whole numbers.

When diagonal movement is allowed, linear distance becomes a little more accurate than Manhattan distance and we will use that in our path-finding code. This is simply the direct distance between the two points. In the case of A and Z in our diagram, the direct distance is approximately 2.24, calculated by using the Pythagorean theorem.

In our example image, the Manhattan distance between A and Z is 3 squares. They are one square apart horizontally and two squares apart vertically. If we consider the square directly to the right of object A, the distance to object Z is only 2 squares. From the square to the left of object A, the distance to the destination has increased to 4 squares (two up and two across).

In order to actually find a path with A*, we keep two lists of nodes. On the open list, we store all of the nodes that we have identified as possible moves but that we have not evaluated yet.

The second list, called the closed list, stores all of the nodes we have already checked. When we evaluate a node, we will move it from the open list to the closed list.

When we initiate the path-finding check, we begin by adding the starting node to the open list, and then check all of the adjacent nodes to see if we can move into them. In the case of our diagram, the node directly above the starting point, along with the node diagonally above and to the right, are walls, so they are not possible movement nodes. The other six nodes are not walls, but because we would need to partially move through the wall above the starting point to reach the node diagonally above and to the left of A, we will not consider moving there diagonally as a valid move.

That leaves five nodes, marked in the following diagram, that are valid movement locations from the starting node. The direct cost of moving to nodes B, C, and E is 10, and the direct cost of moving to nodes D and F is 15 based on our assignments for straight and diagonal moves:

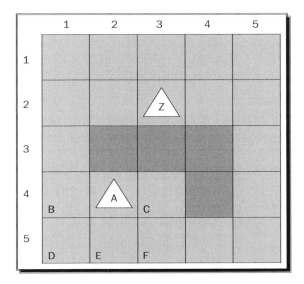

Next we must determine the indirect costs (again we will use Manhattan costs). We simply count the squares up and across from each node to reach node Z. Once we have these costs, we can add the direct and indirect costs to get the total cost for moving to the node:

Node	Direct Cost	Indirect Cost	Total Cost
B	10	4	14
C	10	2	12
D	15	5	20
E	10	4	14
F	15	3	18

All of the nodes are then added to the open list, which we will process in the lowest-cost-first order. In this case, square C has the lowest total cost, so it would be the next square to be evaluated. Square A is added to the closed list, since we have already evaluated everywhere we can go from there.

Whenever a square is evaluated, the cost of getting to that square is considered in the costs of moving to any of the other squares it is adjacent to. So from node C we could move to squares E or F. In fact, because we are blocked to the right and eliminate the diagonal movement right and downward due to that block, these are the only moves that we can make from square C. However, the costs to move from C to either E or F would be:

Node	Previous Cost	Direct Cost	Indirect Cost	Total Cost
E	12	15	4	31
F	12	10	3	25

Since we can reach both E and F for much lower costs directly from A (they are already on the open list at a lower cost), we discard these possibilities and move on, checking the next lowest cost node on the open list, which is a tie between B and E. Node B ends up adding the square above it to the open list at a total cost of 27 (built-in cost of 14, direct cost of 10, and indirect cost of 3) and no other nodes:

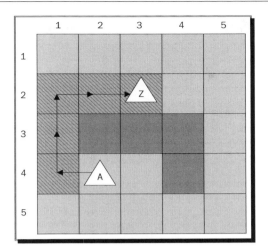

This process of evaluating nodes continues until the target square has been reached. Since we have taken the lowest cost available move at every opportunity, the path taken to reach the destination square will be the shortest available on the grid. The resulting path, shown in the previous diagram, moves around the obstacle to reach the destination in as few moves as possible.

Implementing A*

Now that we have the theoretical background on A* in place, let's implement it in Visual Basic for use in our game. Our first task is defining a node within our pathing structure.

Time for action – the PathNode class

1. Add a new class called PathNode to the Robot Rampage project.

   ```
   #Region "Declarations"
   Public ParentNode As PathNode
   Public EndNode As PathNode
   Public TotalCost As Single
   Public DirectCost As Single

   Private _gridLocation As Vector2
   #End Region
   ```

2. Add properties to the PathNode class:

   ```
   #Region "Properties"
   Public Property GridLocation As Vector2
       Get
           Return _gridLocation
   ```

```
        End Get
        Set(ByVal Value as Vector2)
            _gridLocation = new Vector2(
                CSng(MathHelper.Clamp(value.X,0F,CSng(TileMap.
                    MapWidth))),
                CSng(MathHelper.Clamp(value.Y,0F,CSng(TileMap.
                    MapHeight)))))
        End Set
    End Property

    Public ReadOnly Property GridX As Integer
        Get
            Return CInt(Int(GridLocation.X))
        End Get
    End Property

    Public ReadOnly Property GridY As Integer
        Get
            Return CInt(Int(GridLocation.Y))
        End Get
    End Property
    #End Region
```

3. Add a constructor to the `PathNode` class:

```
#Region "Constructor"
Public Sub New (
    parentNode As PathNode,
    endNode As PathNode,
    gridLocation As Vector2,
    cost As Single)

    Me.ParentNode = parentNode
    Me.GridLocation = gridLocation
    Me.EndNode = endNode
    DirectCost = cost
    If Not IsNothing(endNode) Then
        TotalCost = DirectCost + LinearCost()
    End If
End Sub
#End Region
```

4. Add a helper method to determine the indirect cost for a node:

```
#Region "Helper Methods"
Public Function LinearCost() As Single
    Return Vector2.Distance(EndNode.GridLocation, Me.GridLocation)
End Function
#End Region
```

5. Add public methods to allow the node to be compared with other nodes:

```
#Region "Public Methods"
Public Function IsEqualToNode(node As PathNode) As Boolean
    Return Me.GridLocation = node.GridLocation
End FUnction
#End Region
```

What just happened?

When building a chain of nodes that represent a path, each node needs to know what node it was arrived at from. The `ParentNode` member variable stores the reference to that node, while the `EndNode` member stores the node that the search system is seeking as the destination. This information will be needed in calculating the indirect cost of the node.

The `_gridLocation` member and its associated `GridLocation` property represent the X and Y coordinates of the node on the tile map, identifying the node's position in the game world. The `GridX` and `GridY` properties provide a shortcut for accessing the individual components of the `GridLocation` vector.

When a new `PathNode` is created, its direct cost (the cost associated with either a horizontal or vertical move) is stored in the `DirectCost` variable. If the `endNode` passed to the constructor is not equal to `Nothing` (which will be the case when the end node itself is created), the `TotalCost` member is calculated by adding the `DirectCost` and the result of the `LinearCost()` function, which measures the distance between the node and the end node. We could make the `TotalCost` a property that adds the two values and returns the result, but the `Vector2.Distance()` method is relatively intensive when it is run hundreds of times comparing costs, so caching the value will give us a slight edge in performance.

The `IsEqualToNode()` method is needed because our classes are reference types, meaning that the variables in our program are really pointers to objects in memory. Assigning a reference type to a new variable does not make a copy of the whole object, but rather it simply copies the pointer and creates a new reference to the same object.

In order to determine if two different instances of the PathNode class represent the same square on the map, `IsEqualToNode()` checks to see if the `GridLocation` properties of the two nodes match. Since a Vector2 is a value type, the comparison happens between the actual data values in the Vector2 instead of reference pointers.

Now it is time to build the actual path-finding code, which we are going to do in a few stages for clarity. To begin, let's create a new module which will handle pathing for our game.

Time for action – beginning the implementation of A*

1. Add a new module called `PathFinder` to the Robot Rampage project.

2. Add declarations to the `PathFinder` module:

```
#Region "Declarations"
Private Enum NodeStatus
  Open
  Closed
End Enum

Private statusTracker As Dictionary(Of Vector2, NodeStatus) =
    New Dictionary(Of Vector2, NodeStatus)()

Private Const CostStraight As Integer = 10
Private Const CostDiagonal As Integer = 15

Private openList As List(Of PathNode) = New List(Of PathNode)()

Private costTracker As Dictionary(Of Vector2, Single) =
    New Dictionary(Of Vector2, Single)()
#End Region
```

3. Add the `addNodeToOpenList()` method to the `PathFinder` module:

```
#Region "Helper Methods"
Private Sub addNodeToOpenList(node As PathNode)
    Dim index As Integer = 0
    Dim cost As Single = node.TotalCost

    Do While (openList.Count() > index) AndAlso
        (cost < openList(index).TotalCost)
        index += 1
    Loop

    openList.Insert(index, node)
    costTracker(node.GridLocation) = node.TotalCost
    statusTracker(node.GridLocation) = NodeStatus.Open
End Sub
#End Region
```

What just happened?

For readability purposes, we have defined an enum for tracking the status of each node, along with a Dictionary object called `statusTracker` that will hold the current status of any nodes we have either checked already (closed nodes) or that we are interested in checking (open nodes).

The CostStraight and CostDiagonal constants will be used with our lists of nodes. With these costs, we can see that a diagonal move is 5 units cheaper than the same move made as two straight moves. This difference in cost will ensure that the path finder selects diagonal movement whenever possible.

In addition to the statusTracker dictionary, we also define openList, which will store all of the nodes that the algorithm has identified as possible movement locations. While it is true that open node information is available in the statusTracker dictionary, we give up a bit of memory for the speed increase of maintaining the openList as a separate, sorted list instead of searching the statusTracker dictionary. Recall that we always want to investigate the lowest cost node on the open list next, so keeping a sorted list will allow us to pick the lowest cost item immediately, instead of comparing the entire contents of the dictionary against one another.

The costTracker dictionary represents a similar trade-off of memory for performance. The openList allows us to quickly answer the question "What is the lowest cost option?", but when we want to know "What is the cost of the node at position X, Y?", we would have to search the whole openList for that particular node. We will store costs in their own dictionary indexed by the node position vector to provide fast access to the node costs.

In step 3, we move the index value up the list until we reach a cost that is lower than the one we are inserting, and then place the node at that location. In effect, this generates a list of nodes sorted by cost. At the same time, as the item is inserted into the openList, we set the costTracker and statusTracker dictionaries to their corresponding values.

And versus AndAlso

In the addNodeToOpenList() method, we use the operator AndAlso instead of a simple And when evaluating the location in the list in which we will place the node on the list. AndAlso performs a short-circuit evaluation of the condition, meaning that if the first part of the statement (openList.Count() > index) is false, the second part (cost < openList(index).TotalCost) will not be evaluated at all.

Without this short-circuit evaluation, we would encounter an error because Visual Basic would still try to evaluate the second part of the statement when the first node is added to the list and no values currently exist. The same type of short-circuit evaluation exists for Or statements as well, using the OrElse operator.

Time for action – finding the path

1. Add the `FindPath()` method to the `PathFinder` module:

```
#Region "Public Methods"
Public Function FindPath(
    startSquare As Vector2,
    endSquare As Vector2) As List(Of Vector2)

    If TileMap.IsWallTile(endSquare) Or
        TileMap.IsWallTile(startSquare) Then

        Return Nothing
    End If

    openList.Clear()
    costTracker.Clear()
    statusTracker.Clear()

    Dim startNode As PathNode
    Dim endNode As PathNode

    endNode = new PathNode(Nothing, Nothing, endSquare, 0)
    startNode = new PathNode(Nothing, endNode, startSquare, 0)

    addNodeToOpenList(startNode)

    Do While openList.Count > 0
        Dim currentNode As PathNode = openList(openList.Count - 1)

        If currentNode.IsEqualToNode(endNode) Then
            Dim bestPath As List(Of Vector2) = New List(Of
Vector2)()
            Do While Not IsNothing(currentNode)
                bestPath.Insert(0, currentNode.GridLocation)
                currentNode = currentNode.ParentNode
            Loop
            Return bestPath
        End If

        openList.Remove(currentNode)
        costTracker.Remove(currentNode.GridLocation)

        For Each pNode as PathNode in
          findAdjacentNodes(currentNode, endNode)
            If statusTracker.ContainsKey(pNode.GridLocation) Then
                If statusTracker(pNode.GridLocation) =
                    NodeStatus.Closed Then
```

```
                    Continue
                End If

            If statusTracker(pNode.GridLocation) =
                NodeStatus.Open Then
                If pNode.TotalCost >=
                    costTracker(pNode.GridLocation) Then

                    Continue
                End If
            End If
        End If

        addNodeToOpenList(pNode)
    Next

    statusTracker(currentNode.GridLocation)=NodeStatus.Closed
Loop

Return Nothing
End Function
#End Region
```

What just happened?

The `FindPath()` method is the heart of the `PathFinder` module, and begins by checking to determine if either the start or the end node contains a wall tile. If either of these squares is a wall, it is impossible to find a path between them, so the method immediately returns `Nothing` to the caller.

With that initial check out of the way, the `openList`, `costTracker`, and `statusTracker` collections are cleared in preparation for testing the path between the two points. The two passed vectors are then converted into `PathNode` objects called `startNode` and `endNode`. Recall that we will need to pass `endNode` to every `PathNode` object that we create so that the nodes can measure their indirect costs. Normal nodes contain a reference to their parent node, which is the node we moved to this node from. Neither the `startNode` nor the `endNode` requires a parent node, and the `endNode` does not require a reference to itself, so all of these parameters are passed as `Nothing`.

Next, we add the starting node to the `openList`, and begin a `Do While` loop, which will continue until we run out of nodes to check, or until we find the path that we are looking for. The loop begins by getting the lowest-cost node from the `openList` (recall that it is sorted in highest-to-lowest order, so that the last item on the list will be the lowest-cost node).

If the node we just pulled from the openList is the endNode, we have reached the destination and can return the path to the calling code. We do this by inserting the GridLocation of the current node at index location zero into the bestPath list and then moving to the ParentNode of the current node and repeating the process until we run out of parent nodes. The result is that we have a list of vectors sorted in order from the starting point to the ending square.

Assuming that the current node is not the node we are trying to reach, we remove the current node from the openList, and remove the associated item from the costTracker dictionary (because the dictionary is used to track the costs for items on the openList, and the current node was just removed from that list).

Now, we need to check all of the surrounding squares on the tile map and see if we are able to move into any of them. The findAdjacentNodes() method (which we will be adding in a moment) returns a list of all of the nodes that it is legal to move into from the current node.

Each of these possible nodes is then checked to see if it is already on the closed list. If it is, there is no need to examine this node further, so a Continue statement is executed to proceed to the next item in the loop. The same is true for a node that is already on the open list at a lower cost. It needs no further processing either and another Continue is executed.

If neither of the If statements above resulted in a Continue (which would skip the rest of that iteration of the loop), the node is added to the openList as somewhere we need to potentially investigate for movement. After we have finished processing all of the potential new nodes, the current node's status is marked as NodeStatus.Closed.

If we make it all the way to the end of the FindPath() method, it means we have run out of nodes on the open list without finding a path from the starting node to the ending node. In this case, we return Nothing, just like we did in the case of starting or ending on a wall.

Time for action – adjacent squares

1. Add the findAdjacentNodes() method to the **Helper Methods** region of the PathFinder module:

```
Private Function findAdjacentNodes(
    currentNode As PathNode,
    endNode As PathNode) As List(Of PathNode)

    Dim adjacentNodes As List(Of PathNode) = New List(Of PathNode)()

    Dim X As Integer = currentNode.GridX
    Dim Y As Integer = currentNode.GridY
```

```
Dim upLeft As Boolean = True
Dim upRight As Boolean = True
Dim downLeft As Boolean = True
Dim downRight As Boolean = True

If ((X > 0) And (Not TileMap.IsWallTile(X - 1, Y))) THen
    adjacentNodes.Add(new PathNode(
            currentNode,
            endNode,
            New Vector2(X - 1, Y),
            CostStraight + currentNode.DirectCost))
Else
    upLeft = False
    downLeft = False
End If

If ((X < TileMap.MapWidth) And
    (Not TileMap.IsWallTile(X + 1, Y))) Then

    adjacentNodes.Add(new PathNode(
            currentNode,
            endNode,
            New Vector2(X + 1, Y),
            CostStraight + currentNode.DirectCost))
Else
    upRight = False
    downRight = False
End If

If ((Y > 0) And (Not TileMap.IsWallTile(X, Y - 1))) Then
    adjacentNodes.Add(new PathNode(
        currentNode,
        endNode,
        New Vector2(X, Y - 1),
        CostStraight + currentNode.DirectCost))
Else
    upLeft = False
    upRight = False
End If

If ((Y < TileMap.MapHeight) And
    (Not TileMap.IsWallTile(X, Y + 1))) Then

    adjacentNodes.Add(new PathNode(
        currentNode,
        endNode,
        New Vector2(X, Y + 1),
        CostStraight + currentNode.DirectCost))
Else
```

```
            downLeft = False
            downRight = False
        End If

    If ((upLeft) And (Not TileMap.IsWallTile(X-1,Y-1))) Then
        adjacentNodes.Add(new PathNode(
            currentNode,
            endNode,
            New Vector2(X - 1, Y - 1),
            CostDiagonal + currentNode.DirectCost))
    End If

    If ((upRight) And (Not TileMap.IsWallTile(X + 1, Y - 1))) Then
        adjacentNodes.Add(new PathNode(
            currentNode,
            endNode,
            New Vector2(X + 1, Y - 1),
            CostDiagonal + currentNode.DirectCost))
    End If

    If ((downLeft) And (Not TileMap.IsWallTile(X - 1, Y + 1)))
Then
        adjacentNodes.Add(new PathNode(
            currentNode,
            endNode,
            New Vector2(X - 1, Y + 1),
            CostDiagonal + currentNode.DirectCost))
    End If

    If ((downRight) And (Not TileMap.IsWallTile(X + 1, Y + 1)))
Then
        adjacentNodes.Add(new PathNode(
            currentNode,
            endNode,
            new Vector2(X + 1, Y + 1),
            CostDiagonal + currentNode.DirectCost))
    End If

    Return adjacentNodes
End Function
```

2. In the `Game1` class file, add the following line to the `Initialize()` method:

```
Me.IsMouseVisible = True
```

3. In the `Draw()` method of the `Game1` class, add the following code snippet right before the `spriteBatch.End()` call:

```
' Temporary Code Begin
Dim mouseLocation As Vector2 = New Vector2(
    Mouse.GetState().X, Mouse.GetState().Y)
```

```
mouseLocation += Camera.Position

Dim path As List(Of Vector2) = PathFinder.FindPath(
    TileMap.GetSquareAtPixel(mouseLocation),
    TileMap.GetSquareAtPixel(Player.BaseSprite.WorldCenter))

If Not IsNothing(path) Then
    For Each node As Vector2 In path
        spriteBatch.Draw(
            spriteSheet,
            TileMap.SquareScreenRectangle(
                CInt(Int(node.X)),
                CInt(Int(node.Y))),
            new Rectangle(0, 288, 32, 32),
            new Color(128, 0, 0, 80))
    Next
End If
' Temporary Code End
```

4. Execute Robot Rampage. Move your mouse around on the screen to see the highlighted path generated by the `PathFinder` module. Note that if your player tank starts out on top of a wall square, you will need to move it off the wall using the W-A-S-D movement keys to see the path:

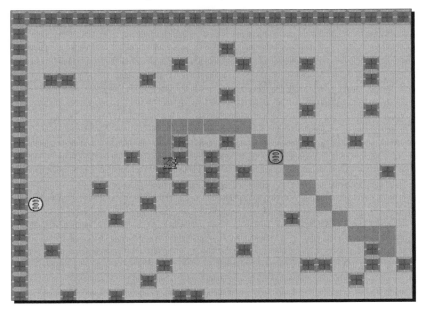

5. After you have finished viewing the path, remove the line you added to the `Initialize()` method and the temporary code from the `Draw()` method.

What just happened?

After caching the X and Y grid coordinates of the node, we want to check into local integer variables, the `findAdjacentNodes()` method creates four Boolean variables representing the four diagonal directions and defaults them to `True`. This starts off with the assumption that each of the diagonal moves is valid.

In order for a diagonal move to be allowed, both of the adjoining squares need to be floor tiles as well as the diagonal square, otherwise the object moving along the path would pass partially through a wall tile on its way diagonally to the destination square.

Next, a series of four `if` statements check each of the axis-aligned directions (right, left, up, and down) for wall tiles. If the square in question is not a wall tile, it is added to the `adjacentNodes` list, which will be returned from the function. Whenever a node is added, its cost is set to the direct cost of the movement (either `CostStraight` or `CostDiagonal`) plus the cost of reaching the current square.

If the square does contain a wall tile, it is not added to the `adjacentNodes` list and the two diagonals next to it are also set to `False`, meaning they will not be valid either. For example, if we are evaluating the square above the current square, and it contains a wall, the diagonal moves up/right and up/left will be invalidated.

After the four `if` statements for the straight-line moves have been evaluated, any of the diagonal direction Boolean values that remain `True` are checked in the same manner. If the square does not contain a wall tile, it is added to the `adjacentNodes` list.

Once all eight directions have been evaluated, the `adjacentNodes` list is returned from the function to be processed by the `FindPath()` method.

In steps 2 and 3, we added some demo code to activate the mouse cursor in the game, and executed the `FindPath()` method during each draw cycle, using the mouse cursor location as the starting point, and the current player position as the ending point of the path. Each square along the path is then drawn using the empty white square on the tile sheet to colorize the square on the screen with a half-transparent red color.

When the mouse position is retrieved, it is in screen coordinates, relative to the upper-left corner of the display window. Since we need to convert it to world coordinates, we have to add the current `Camera.Position` value to the mouse location. This is just the opposite of what the `Camera.Transform()` method does, which converts world coordinates to screen coordinates.

Safely placing power-ups

Now that we can find a path between two points, we can update our `WeaponManager` module to take pathing into account when generating power-ups.

Time for action – updating the WeaponManager class

1. Add a property to the `Player` module to create a shortcut to the square the player is currently located in:

```
#Region "Properties"
Public ReadOnly Property PathingNodePosition As Vector2
    Get
        Return TileMap.GetSquareAtPixel(BaseSprite.WorldCenter)
    End Get
End Property
#End Region
```

2. Modify the `tryToSpawnPowerup()` method of the `WeaponManager` module and replace the `If` statement that checks to see if the square the power-up is being placed on contains a wall tile (it currently reads "`If Not TileMap.IsWallTile(x,y) Then`") with the following code:

```
If Not IsNothing(PathFinder.FindPath(
    New Vector2(x,y),
    Player.PathingNodePosition)) Then
```

3. Execute Robot Rampage and explore the map, looking for the power-ups.

What just happened?

Since the `FindPath()` method returns `Nothing` immediately if either the starting or ending square is a wall, this new condition will cover trying to place a power-up on a wall tile as well as accounting for unreachable tiles on the map.

We talked in the power-ups section about not repeatedly attempting to generate a power-up by coming up with new locations until we find one that works, and the potential speed impact of the `FindPath()` method is the reason we do not do this. If we got unlucky and ended up needing to run `FindPath()` a few times when attempting to generate a power-up, it might cause the game to stutter as the path-finding code can be processor-intensive over long distances.

Player goals

The player's purpose in the game world is two-fold. First, they need to destroy the enemy robots that are trying to destroy them. Second, they need to shut down the computer terminals that are building the enemy tanks. Since the computers spawn the tanks, we will implement the terminals first and then add our robotic enemies.

Computer terminals

Our path-finding code will be put to the same use in the generation of computer terminals that it was for power-ups. After all, the player cannot shut down a terminal that they are unable to reach:

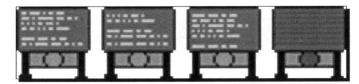

Each terminal will be represented by a Sprite that plays a multi-frame animation when active. When the player shuts down a terminal, the sprite will be replaced by an inactive terminal image.

Time for action – building a computer terminal

> **1.** Add a new class called `ComputerTerminal` to the Robot Rampage project.
>
> **2.** Add declarations to the `ComputerTerminal` class:
>
> ```
> #Region "Declarations"
> Private _activeSprite As Sprite
> Private _inactiveSprite As Sprite
> Public MapLocation As Vector2
> Public Active As Boolean = True
> Public LastSpawnCounter As Single = 0
> Public MinSpawnTime As Single = 6
> #End Region
> ```
>
> **3.** Add a constructor to the `ComputerTerminal` class:
>
> ```
> #Region "Constructor"
> Public Sub New(
>     activeSprite As Sprite,
>     inactiveSprite As Sprite,
>     mapLocation As Vector2)
>
>     _activeSprite = activeSprite
>     _inactiveSprite = inactiveSprite
>     Me.MapLocation = mapLocation
> End Sub
> #End Region
> ```

4. Add public methods to the `ComputerTerminal` class:

```vbnet
#region "Public Methods"
Public Function IsCircleColliding(
    otherCenter As Vector2,
    radius As Single) As Boolean

    If Not Active Then
        Return False
    End If

    Return _activeSprite.IsCircleColliding(otherCenter, radius)
End Function

Public Sub Deactivate()
    Active = False
End Sub

Public Sub Update(gameTime As GameTime)
    If Active Then
        Dim elapsed As Single
        elapsed = CSng(gameTime.ElapsedGameTime.TotalSeconds)

        LastSpawnCounter += elapsed
        If LastSpawnCounter > minSpawnTime Then
            LastSpawnCounter = 0
        End If

        _activeSprite.Update(gameTime)
    Else
        _inactiveSprite.Update(gameTime)
    End If
End Sub

Public Sub Draw(spriteBatch As SpriteBatch)
    If Active Then
        _activeSprite.Draw(spriteBatch)
    Else
        _inactiveSprite.Draw(spriteBatch)
    End If
End Sub
#End Region
```

What just happened?

The two possible states of each `ComputerTerminal` are represented by the two sprites `_activeSprite` and `_inactiveSprite`. We also cache the map-square-based location of the `ComputerTerminal` in the `MapLocation` vector. We will use this variable when we spawn enemy robots.

Other than `Update()` and `Draw()`, we have two public methods. The `IsCircleColliding()` method returns `False`, if the terminal is not active. Otherwise, it passes the call on to the `IsCircleColliding()` method of `_activeSprite`. The `Deactivate()` method simply sets `Active` to `False`.

During the `Update()` method, we check to see if the sprite is active. If it is, the spawn time mechanism is updated. Currently, when it is time to spawn a new robot our `Update()` code just resets the timer. We will be revisiting this method after we have constructed our enemy robots. Either `_activeSprite` or `_inactiveSprite` (depending on the state of the `Active` variable) is passed the `Update()` call before the method exits.

Similarly, the `Draw()` method uses the `Active` variable to determine which of the Sprite objects to pass the `Draw()` call to.

Spawning computer terminals

Now that we have defined the `ComputerTerminal` class, we need to create a way for them to appear on the game map. We will do this with a new module called `GoalManager`, which will be responsible for spawning computer terminals in accessible locations and monitoring to see when the player has shut down a computer terminal.

Time for action – the GoalManager module

1. Add a new module called `GoalManager` to the Robot Rampage project.

2. Add declarations to the `GoalManager` module:

```
#Region "Declarations"
Private _computerTerminals As List(Of ComputerTerminal) =
    New List(Of ComputerTerminal)()
Private _activeCount As Integer = 0

Private _minDistanceFromPlayer As Integer = 250

Private _rand As Random = new Random()

Private _texture As Texture2D
Private _initialActiveFrame As Rectangle
```

```
Private _initialDisabledFrame As Rectangle
Private _activeFrameCount As Integer
Private _disabledFrameCount As Integer
#End Region
```

3. Add a read-only property to the GoalManager module:

```
#Region "Properties"
Public ReadOnly Property ActiveTerminals As Integer
    Get
        Return _activeCount
    End Get
End Property
#End Region
```

4. Add the Initialize() method to the GoalManager module:

```
#Region "Initialization"
Public Sub Initialize(
    textureSheet As Texture2D,
    initialActiveRectangle As Rectangle,
    initialDisabledRectangle As Rectangle,
    activeFrames As Integer,
    disabledFrames As Integer)

    _texture = textureSheet
    _initialActiveFrame = initialActiveRectangle
    _initialDisabledFrame = initialDisabledRectangle
    _activeFrameCount = activeFrames
    _disabledFrameCount = disabledFrames
End Sub
#End Region
```

5. Add methods to manage ComputerTerminals to the GoalManager module:

```
#Region "Terminal Management"
Public Function TerminalInSquare(
    mapSquare As Vector2) As ComputerTerminal

    For Each terminal As ComputerTerminal In _computerTerminals
        If terminal.MapLocation = mapSquare Then
            Return terminal
        End If
    Next

    Return Nothing
End Function
```

```
Public Sub DetectShutdowns()
    For Each terminal As ComputerTerminal In _computerTerminals
        If terminal.Active Then
            If (terminal.IsCircleColliding(
                Player.BaseSprite.WorldCenter,
                Player.BaseSprite.CollisionRadius)) Then

                terminal.Deactivate()
                _activeCount -= 1
            End If
        End If
    Next
End Sub

Public Sub AddComputerTerminal()
    Dim startX As Integer = _rand.Next(2, TileMap.MapWidth - 2)
    Dim startY As Integer = _rand.Next(0, TileMap.MapHeight - 2)

    Dim tileLocation As Vector2 = New Vector2(startX, startY)

    If (Not IsNothing(TerminalInSquare(tileLocation))) OrElse
        (TileMap.IsWallTile(tileLocation)) Then

        Return
    End If

    If (Vector2.Distance(
        TileMap.GetSquareCenter(startX, startY),
        Player.BaseSprite.WorldCenter) < _minDistanceFromPlayer)
Then

        Return
    End If

    Dim path As List(Of Vector2) =
        PathFinder.FindPath(
            New Vector2(startX, startY),
            TileMap.GetSquareAtPixel(
                Player.BaseSprite.WorldCenter))

    If Not IsNothing(path) Then
        Dim squareRect As Rectangle =
            TileMap.SquareWorldRectangle(startX, startY)

        Dim activeSprite As Sprite = New Sprite(
            New Vector2(squareRect.X, squareRect.Y),
            _texture,
            _initialActiveFrame,
            Vector2.Zero)
```

```
            For x As Integer = 1 to 2
                activeSprite.AddFrame(
                    New Rectangle(
                    _initialActiveFrame.X + (x *
                        _initialActiveFrame.Width),
                    _initialActiveFrame.Y,
                    _initialActiveFrame.Width,
                    _initialActiveFrame.Height))
            Next

            activeSprite.CollisionRadius = 15

            Dim disabledSprite As Sprite = new Sprite(
                New Vector2(squareRect.X, squareRect.Y),
                    _texture,
                    _initialDisabledFrame,
                    Vector2.Zero)

            Dim terminal As ComputerTerminal = new ComputerTerminal(
                    activeSprite,
                    disabledSprite,
                    New Vector2(startX, startY))

            Dim timerOffset As Single = CSng(_rand.Next(1, 100))
            terminal.LastSpawnCounter = timerOffset / 100F

            _computerTerminals.Add(terminal)

            _activeCount += 1
        End If
    End Sub
#End Region
```

6. Add public methods to the `GoalManager` module:

```
#Region "Public Methods"
Public Sub GenerateComputers(computerCount As Integer)
    _computerTerminals.Clear()
    _activeCount = 0

    Do While _activeCount < computerCount
        AddComputerTerminal()
    Loop
End Sub

Public Sub Update(gameTime As GameTime)
    DetectShutdowns()
```

```
        For Each terminal As ComputerTerminal in _computerTerminals
            terminal.Update(gameTime)
        Next
    End Sub


    Public Sub Draw(spriteBatch As SpriteBatch)
        For Each terminal As ComputerTerminal in _computerTerminals
            terminal.Draw(spriteBatch)
        Next
    End Sub
    #End Region
```

7. In the `LoadContent()` method of the `Game1` class, initialize the `GoalManager` module and generate 10 computer terminals:

```
GoalManager.Initialize(
    spriteSheet,
    new Rectangle(0, 7 * 32, 32, 32),
    new Rectangle(3 * 32, 7 * 32, 32, 32),
    3,
    1)


GoalManager.GenerateComputers(10)
```

8. Still in the `LoadContent()` method of `Game1`, modify the call to `Player.Initialize()` and change the player's initial position to ensure that they will never end up on a block that contains a wall:

```
Player.Initialize(
    spriteSheet,
    new Rectangle(0, 64, 32, 32),
    6,
    new Rectangle(0, 96, 32, 32),
    1,
    new Vector2(32, 32))
```

9. In the `Update()` method of the `Game1` class, call the `Update()` method of `GoalManager` right after `EffectsManager` has been updated:

```
GoalManager.Update(gameTime)
```

10. In the `Draw()` method of the `Game1` class, call the `Draw()` method of `GoalManager` right after `EffectsManager` has been drawn:

```
GoalManager.Draw(spriteBatch)
```

11. Execute Robot Rampage and verify that the computer terminals have been spawned in appropriate locations. Moving over an active terminal switches it off.

What just happened?

The basics of our `GoalManager` should be very familiar by now. The individual terminals are stored in a list that is updated and drawn via loops in the `Update()` and `Draw()` methods.

During the `Initialize()` method, we establish all of the values that will let us create the sprites needed to represent the `ComputerTerminals` that will be created by the `AddComputerTerminal()` method.

When generating terminals, we will want to make sure that we do not place two terminals at the same map location, so the `TerminalInSquare()` method returns `ComputerTerminal` that occupies a given map square, if one exists. By checking this method when we generate a new computer, we can verify that all of the terminals end up in different locations.

The `DetectShutdowns()` method iterates through each of the terminals in the `_computerTerminals` list, checking to see if the player has collided with them. Remember that inactive terminals will always return a `False` for `IsCircleColliding()`. If the player has collided with a terminal, that terminal's `Deactivate()` method is called to shut it down.

The heart of the `GoalManager` class is the `AddComputerTerminal()` method, which begins by generating a random location on the map to place the terminal. If the randomly determined map square already contains a terminal, or if it is a wall square, the `AddComputerTerminal()` method returns without generating a computer.

We also check to make sure we are not generating the computer within 250 pixels of the player's current location. Given that the computers will be generated at the beginning of a game level, this will result in computers not being placed within 250 pixels of the player's starting location, which is the upper-left corner of the map.

Assuming the square passes all of these checks, a path-finding call is made to make sure that the space being considered can be reached from the player's current location. Once again, if it cannot, the method exits without generating the computer.

If everything checks out OK, the two Sprite objects are created and then the terminal object is built using the two new Sprites. The `LastSpawnCounter` for the terminal is adjusted by the randomly generated `timerOffset` value. By introducing a small random variation to the time at which terminals will spawn enemies, we can spread out the path-finding checks that will be required during the spawns to minimize the processing hit that would take place, if all of the terminals spawned enemies during the same frame.

Finally, the terminal is added to the `_computerTerminals` list and the `_activeCount` variable is incremented.

The GenerateComputers() method, which will be called when a level is generated, clears the _computerTerminals list and adds terminals until _activeCount reaches the number of computers passed to the GenerateComputers() method.

In addition to its normal responsibility to update all of the items in the _computerTerminals list, the Update() method also calls the DetectShutdowns() method, allowing the player to turn the computer terminals off.

Enemy robots

The last component we need to make our game playable is the actual enemy robots generated at the computer terminals. Visually, these robots are distinct from the player's tank not only by color, but also by wheel and turret design. The enemy robots are four-wheeled vehicles with rotatable claw-like arms. They will pursue the player through the game map, attempting to physically contact the player and destroy their tank:

Enemy basics

As with most of our game objects, we will build both the Enemy class, and a manager for the class that will handle updating and drawing the enemy robots as well as coordinating them with the rest of the game.

Time for action – building the Enemy class

1. Add a new class called Enemy to the Robot Rampage project.

2. Add declarations to the Enemy class:

```
#Region "Declarations"
Public EnemyBase As Sprite
Public EnemyClaws As Sprite
Public EnemySpeed As Single = 60
Public CurrentTargetSquare As Vector2
Public Destroyed As Boolean = False
Private _collisionRadius As Integer = 14
#End Region
```

3. Add a constructor to the `Enemy` class:

```
#Region "Constructor"
Public Sub New(
    worldLocation As Vector2,
    texture As Texture2D,
    initialFrame As Rectangle)

    EnemyBase = new Sprite(
        worldLocation,
        texture,
        initialFrame,
        Vector2.Zero)

    EnemyBase.CollisionRadius = _collisionRadius

    Dim turretFrame As Rectangle = initialFrame

    turretFrame.Offset(0, initialFrame.Height)
    EnemyClaws = new Sprite(
        worldLocation,
        texture,
        turretFrame,
        Vector2.Zero)
End Sub
#End Region
```

4. Add the `Update()` and `Draw()` methods to the `Enemy` class:

```
#region "Public Methods"
Public Sub Update(gameTime As GameTime)
    If Not Destroyed Then
        Dim direction As Vector2 = determineMoveDirection()
        direction.Normalize()

        EnemyBase.Velocity = direction * EnemySpeed
        EnemyBase.RotateTo(direction)
        EnemyBase.Update(gameTime)

        Dim directionToPlayer As Vector2 =
            Player.BaseSprite.WorldCenter - EnemyBase.WorldCenter
        directionToPlayer.Normalize()

        EnemyClaws.WorldLocation = EnemyBase.WorldLocation
        EnemyClaws.RotateTo(directionToPlayer)
    End If
End Sub
```

```
Public Sub Draw(spriteBatch As SpriteBatch)
    If Not Destroyed Then
        EnemyBase.Draw(spriteBatch)
        EnemyClaws.Draw(spriteBatch)
    End If
End Sub
#End Region
```

What just happened?

The `Enemy` class is similar in structure to the `Player` module. An enemy is composed of two different Sprites that will be overlaid to create the final enemy image. The enemies move at a slightly slower speed than the player.

Between frames, each enemy will keep track of the square it is currently trying to reach in the `CurrentTargetSquare` vector.

When the `Enemy` constructor runs, the base Sprite is created using the parameters passed to the constructor, while the Sprite representing the enemy robot's claws is created by offsetting the initial frame down one row of images on the sprite sheet.

Both the `Update()` and the `Draw()` methods only take action, if the enemy has not been destroyed. During `Update()`, the `determineMoveDirection()` method (which we have not yet written) is called. The job of this method will be to return a vector representing the direction that the enemy should be moving in during this frame.

Given that information, the enemy is moved in the same way that the player is moved. The `EnemyBase` Sprite is rotated to the direction of movement, and its velocity is set taking the `EnemySpeed` variable into account.

When the `EnemyClaws` Sprite is updated, it is rotated to face the player's current position, resulting in the enemy always reaching for the player.

Moving enemies

Before we can successfully compile the `Enemy` class, we need to fill in the missing `determineMoveDirection()` method. This method, along with its two helper methods, will utilize the `PathFinder` module to determine what direction the enemy tank should move in order to chase down the player.

Time for action – enemy AI methods

1. Add movement-related methods to the Enemy class:

```
#Region "AI Methods"
Private Function determineMoveDirection() As Vector2
    If reachedTargetSquare() Then
        CurrentTargetSquare = getNewTargetSquare()
    End If

    Dim squareCenter As Vector2 = TileMap.GetSquareCenter(
        currentTargetSquare)

    Return squareCenter - EnemyBase.WorldCenter
End Function

Private Function reachedTargetSquare() As Boolean
    Return Vector2.Distance(EnemyBase.WorldCenter,
            TileMap.GetSquareCenter(currentTargetSquare)) <= 2
End Function

Private Function getNewTargetSquare() As Vector2
    Dim path As List(Of Vector2) = PathFinder.FindPath(
        TileMap.GetSquareAtPixel(EnemyBase.WorldCenter),
        TileMap.GetSquareAtPixel(Player.BaseSprite.WorldCenter))

    If path.Count > 1 Then
        Return New Vector2(path(1).X, path(1).Y)
    Else
        Return TileMap.GetSquareAtPixel(
            Player.BaseSprite.WorldCenter)
    End If
End Function
#End Region
```

What just happened?

The first thing determineMoveDirection() does is call reachedTargetSquare() to decide whether the enemy tank has reached the square represented by CurrentTargetSquare or not. This determination is made by taking the distance between the center of the target square and the center of the enemy sprite. If the distance is within two pixels, we assume that we have reached the target square.

If the target square has been reached, we need to decide what the new target square should be, based on the latest positions of both the enemy and the player.

The `getNewTargetSquare()` method uses the `PathFinder.FindPath()` method, passing it the current location of the enemy and the location of the player. The list that is returned represents the shortest path between the two.

If there is more than one entry in the path list, we know we have not reached the player, so we return the second element in the path list (the first element, element number zero will be the location the enemy tank currently resides in).

If only one entry exists in the path list, then the starting and ending squares are the same square, meaning that we have reached the player. We can simply return the player's current square as the destination square.

As implemented, our enemy AI will always move in complete squares, from the center of one square towards the center of the next square along its path. Every time a new square center has been reached, the whole path is re-evaluated since the player may have moved while the enemy was making its way to the current square.

Since our enemies move based on the results of the `PathFinder` module, we do not even need to check for enemy-to-wall collisions, because the path-finding code will not return squares that contain wall tiles as potential destinations for our enemy tanks.

The enemy manager

Our `EnemyManager` module will be very straightforward. Its only responsibilities are to track the active `Enemy` objects in the game and add them when requested. We will also need to update the `ComputerTerminals` class to actually trigger enemy spawns.

Time for action – the enemy manager

1. Add a new module called `EnemyManager` to the Robot Rampage project.

2. Add declarations to the `EnemyManager` module:

```
#Region "Declarations"
Public Enemies As List(Of Enemy) = new List(Of Enemy)()
Private _texture As Texture2D
Private _initialFrame As Rectangle
Public MaxActiveEnemies As Integer = 30
#End Region
```

3. Add the `Initialize()` method to the `EnemyManager` module:

```
#Region "Initialization"
Public Sub Initialize(
    texture As Texture2D,
    initialFrame As Rectangle)
```

```
    _texture = texture
    _initialFrame = initialFrame
End Sub
#End Region
```

4. Add the `AddEnemy()` method to the `EnemyManager` module:

```
#region "Enemy Management"
Public Sub AddEnemy(squareLocation As Vector2)
    Dim startX As Integer = CInt(Int(squareLocation.X))
    Dim startY As Integer = CInt(Int(squareLocation.Y))

    Dim squareRect As Rectangle =
        TileMap.SquareWorldRectangle(startX, startY)

    Dim newEnemy As Enemy = New Enemy(
        New Vector2(squareRect.X, squareRect.Y),
        _texture,
        _initialFrame)

    newEnemy.CurrentTargetSquare = squareLocation
    Enemies.Add(newEnemy)
End Sub
#End Region
```

5. Add the `Update()` and `Draw()` methods to the `EnemyManager` module:

```
#Region "Update and Draw"
Public Sub Update(gameTime As GameTime)
    For x As Integer = Enemies.Count - 1 To 0 Step - 1
        Enemies(x).Update(gameTime)
        If Enemies(x).Destroyed Then
            Enemies.RemoveAt(x)
        End IF
    Next
End Sub

Public Sub Draw(spriteBatch As SpriteBatch)
    For Each enemyTank as Enemy in Enemies
        enemyTank.Draw(spriteBatch)
    Next
End Sub
#End Region
```

6. In the `ComputerTerminal` class, replace the `Update()` method with the following:

```
Public Sub Update(gameTime As GameTime)
    If Active Then
        Dim elapsed As Single
        Elapsed = CSng(gameTime.ElapsedGameTime.TotalSeconds)

        LastSpawnCounter += elapsed
        If LastSpawnCounter > minSpawnTime Then
            If Vector2.Distance(_activeSprite.WorldCenter,
                Player.BaseSprite.WorldCenter) > 128 Then
                If EnemyManager.Enemies.Count <
                    EnemyManager.MaxActiveEnemies Then

                    EnemyManager.AddEnemy(MapLocation)
                    LastSpawnCounter = 0
                End If
            End If
        End IF

        _activeSprite.Update(gameTime)
    Else
        _inactiveSprite.Update(gameTime)
    End If
End Sub
```

7. In the `LoadContent()` method of the `Game1` class, initialize the `EnemyManager`:

```
EnemyManager.Initialize(
    spriteSheet,
    New Rectangle(0, 160, 32, 32))
```

8. In the `Update()` method of the `Game1` class, update the `EnemyManager` right after the `GoalManager` had been updated:

```
EnemyManager.Update(gameTime)
```

9. In the `Draw()` method of the `Game1` class, draw the `EnemyManager` right after the `GoalManager` has been drawn:

```
EnemyManager.Draw(spriteBatch)
```

10. Execute Robot Rampage. The computer terminals now spawn robots, which pursue your player tank:

What just happened?

Most of the `EnemyManager` module is standard for our managers. When an enemy is added via the `AddEnemy()` method, the enemy's `CurrentTargetSquare` member is set to the square that the enemy has been spawned in, meaning that on its first `Update()` cycle, it will execute `PathFinder.FindPath()` to determine a path towards the player.

Updating the WeaponManager

It sure would be nice to be able to use our fancy weaponry to destroy those enemy tanks! We have all of the pieces in place to implement this capability, so let's tie them together and allow enemies to be blown to bits.

Time for action – destroying enemies

1. Add `checkShotEnemyImpacts()` and `checkRocketSplashDamage()` to the **Collision Detection** region of the `WeaponManager` module:

```
Private Sub checkShotEnemyImpacts(shot As Sprite)
    If shot.Expired Then
        Return
    End If

    For Each enemyTank As Enemy in EnemyManager.Enemies
        If Not enemyTank.Destroyed Then
            If (shot.IsCircleColliding(
                enemyTank.EnemyBase.WorldCenter,
                enemyTank.EnemyBase.CollisionRadius)) Then

                shot.Expired = True
                enemyTank.Destroyed = True
                If shot.Frame = 0 Then
                    EffectsManager.AddExplosion(
                        enemyTank.EnemyBase.WorldCenter,
                        enemyTank.EnemyBase.Velocity / 30)
                Else
                    If shot.Frame = 1
                        createLargeExplosion(shot.WorldCenter)
                        checkRocketSplashDamage(shot.WorldCenter)
                    End If
                End If
            End IF
        End If
    Next
End Sub

Private Sub checkRocketSplashDamage(location As Vector2)
    Dim rocketSplashRadius As Integer = 40

    For Each enemyTank As Enemy In EnemyManager.Enemies
        If Not enemyTank.Destroyed Then
            If (enemyTank.EnemyBase.IsCircleColliding(
                location, rocketSplashRadius)) Then

                enemyTank.Destroyed = true
                EffectsManager.AddExplosion(
```

```
                    enemyTank.EnemyBase.WorldCenter,
                    Vector2.Zero)
            End IF
        End If
    Next
End Sub
```

2. In the `checkShotWallImpacts()` method of the `WeaponManager` module, add a call to `checkRocketSplashDamage()` to allow rockets impacting walls to destroy nearby enemy tanks. Place this line after the call to `createLargeExplosion()`.

```
checkRocketSplashDamage(shot.WorldCenter)
```

3. In the `Update()` method of the `WeaponManager` class, add a call to check for collisions between shots and enemy tanks right after the existing call to `checkShotWallImpacts(_shots(X))`:

```
checkShotEnemyImpacts(_shots(x))
```

4. Execute the Robot Rampage game and blow away the bad guys.

What just happened?

When a shot collides with an enemy, the shot's `Frame` property is checked. Recall that we use a zero `Frame` value for regular shots, and one value for rockets. If the value indicates that the shot is a normal shot, the `AddExplosion()` method is called and given the location of the enemy tank.

If the shot is a rocket, the `createLargeExplosion()` method is executed, and followed up with a call to `checkRocketSplashDamage()`. Any enemies within 40 pixels of the detonation point of the rocket are destroyed, and their own small explosion effects triggered.

In either case (rocket or normal shot), the shot is marked as `Expired`, and any enemies destroyed by the shot are marked as `Destroyed`.

Game structure

The pieces of our game are all in place, so our final task is to wrap them in a game playing structure. The structure here will be deliberately simple, and you can expand upon it as you desire.

Time for action – the GameManager module

1. In the `EffectsManager` module, add the `ResetEffects()` method to the **Public Methods** region:

```
Public Sub ResetEffects()
    _effects.Clear()
End Sub
```

2. In the `WeaponsManager` module, add the `ResetWeaponSystems()` method:

```
#Region "Public Methods"
Public Sub ResetWeaponSystems
    CurrentWeaponType = WeaponType.Normal
    _shots.Clear()
    _powerUps.Clear()
End Sub
#End Region
```

3. Add a new module called `GameManager` to the Robot Rampage project.

4. Add declarations to the `GameManager` module:

```
#Region "Declarations"
Public Score As Integer = 0
Public CurrentWave As Integer = 0
Public BaseTerminalCount As Integer = 8
Public MaxTerminalCount As Integer = 15
Public CurrentTerminalCount As Integer = 8
Public PlayerStartLoc As Vector2 = New Vector2(32, 32)
#End Region
```

5. Add public methods to the `GameManager` module:

```
#Region "Public Methods"
Public Sub StartNewWave()
    CurrentWave += 1
    If CurrentTerminalCount < MaxTerminalCount Then
        CurrentTerminalCount += 1
    End If

    Player.BaseSprite.WorldLocation = PlayerStartLoc
    Camera.Position = Vector2.Zero
    WeaponManager.ResetWeaponSystems()
    EffectsManager.ResetEffects()
    EnemyManager.Enemies.Clear()
```

```
      TileMap.GenerateRandomMap()
      GoalManager.GenerateComputers(CurrentTerminalCount)
  End Sub

  Public Sub StartNewGame()
      CurrentWave = 0
      Score = 0
      StartNewWave()
  End Sub
  #End Region
```

What just happened?

We begin by adding a pair of public functions to the `WeaponsManager` and `EffectsManager` modules to allow our new `GameManager` module to clear out the various lists of items these manager modules contain when a new level is starting.

The `GameManager` module itself handles tracking the player's score and the wave (or level) the player is currently on. The `StartNewWave()` method resets all of the lists and control values to their defaults for a new level, generates a random map, and then generates computer terminals on the map.

The `StartNewGame()` method simply resets the `CurrentWave` and `Score` values, and then calls `StartNewWave()` to begin the first wave.

Keeping score

As our game stands, we do not award points to the player for their actions. We will change this by adding the necessary code to the `WeaponManager` and `GoalManager` classes.

Time for action – awarding points

1. In the `checkShotEnemyImpacts()` method of the `WeaponManager` module, add the following line after the line that reads `enemyTank.Destroyed = True`:

```
GameManager.Score += 10
```

2. In the `checkRocketSplashDamage()` method of the `WeaponManager` module, add the following line after the line that reads `enemyTank.Destroyed = True`:

```
GameManager.Score += 10
```

3. In the `DetectShutdowns()` method of the `GoalManager` module, add the following line right after the line that reads `_activeCount -= 1`:

```
GameManager.Score += 100
```

What just happened?

Since we can destroy enemies with either normal shots or rocket splash damage, we need to award points in either case. Shutting down a computer is worth ten times as many points as destroying a single enemy.

Updating Game1

Finally, to wrap our game in a game structure, we need to build it into the Game1 class.

We will include a game state tracker much like we used in Asteroid Belt Assault, with a similar division of code in the Update() and Draw() methods depending on the current game state.

Time for action – updating the Game1 class

1. Add the following declarations to the Game1 class:

```
Public Enum GameStates
    TitleScreen
    Playing
    WaveComplete
    GameOver
End Enum

Private gameState As GameStates = GameStates.TitleScreen

Private gameOverTimer As Single = 0
Private gameOverDelay As Single = 6

Private waveCompleteTimer As Single = 0
Private waveCompleteDelay As Single = 6
```

2. Remove the call to GoalManager.GenerateComputers() from the LoadContent() method of the Game1 class.

3. Add the checkPlayerDeath() method to the Game1 class:

```
Private Sub checkPlayerDeath()
    For Each enemyTank As Enemy In EnemyManager.Enemies
        If (enemyTank.EnemyBase.IsCircleColliding(
            Player.BaseSprite.WorldCenter,
            Player.BaseSprite.CollisionRadius)) Then

            gameState = GameStates.GameOver
        End If
    Next
End Sub
```

4. Replace the existing `Update()` method of the `Game1` class with the following code:

```
Protected Overrides Sub Update(gameTime As GameTime)
    ' Allows the game to exit
    If (GamePad.GetState(PlayerIndex.One).Buttons.Back =
        ButtonState.Pressed) Then
        Me.Exit()
    End If

    Select Case gameState
        Case GameStates.TitleScreen
            If ((GamePad.GetState(PlayerIndex.One).Buttons.A =
                ButtonState.Pressed) Or
                (Keyboard.GetState().IsKeyDown(Keys.Space))) Then

                GameManager.StartNewGame()
                gameState = GameStates.Playing
            End If


        Case GameStates.Playing
            Player.Update(gameTime)
            WeaponManager.Update(gameTime)
            EnemyManager.Update(gameTime)
            EffectsManager.Update(gameTime)
            GoalManager.Update(gameTime)
            If GoalManager.ActiveTerminals = 0 Then
                gameState = GameStates.WaveComplete
            End If

        Case GameStates.WaveComplete
            waveCompleteTimer +=
                CSng(gameTime.ElapsedGameTime.TotalSeconds)
            If waveCompleteTimer > waveCompleteDelay Then
                GameManager.StartNewWave()
                gameState = GameStates.Playing
                waveCompleteTimer = 0
            End If

        Case GameStates.GameOver
            gameOverTimer +=
                CSng(gameTime.ElapsedGameTime.TotalSeconds)
            If gameOverTimer > gameOverDelay Then
                gameState = GameStates.TitleScreen
```

```
                    gameOverTimer = 0
                End IF
        End Select

        MyBase.Update(gameTime)
    End Sub
```

5. Replace the current `Draw()` method of the `Game1` class with the following code:

```
Protected Overrides Sub Draw(gameTime As GameTime)
    GraphicsDevice.Clear(Color.CornflowerBlue)

    spriteBatch.Begin()

    If gameState = GameStates.TitleScreen Then
        spriteBatch.Draw(
            titleScreen,
            new Rectangle(0,0,800,600),
            Color.White)
    End If

    If ((gameState = GameStates.Playing) Or
        (gameState = GameStates.WaveComplete) Or
        (gameState = GameStates.GameOver))

        TileMap.Draw(spriteBatch)
        WeaponManager.Draw(spriteBatch)
        Player.Draw(spriteBatch)
        EnemyManager.Draw(spriteBatch)
        EffectsManager.Draw(spriteBatch)
        GoalManager.Draw(spriteBatch)

        checkPlayerDeath()

        spriteBatch.DrawString(
            pericles14,
            "Score: " + GameManager.Score.ToString(),
            new Vector2(30, 5),
            Color.White)

        spriteBatch.DrawString(
            pericles14,
            "Terminals Remaining: " +
                GoalManager.ActiveTerminals.ToString(),
            new Vector2(520, 5),
```

```
                    Color.White)
            End If

            If gameState = GameStates.WaveComplete Then
                spriteBatch.DrawString(
                    pericles14,
                    "Beginning Wave " +
                        (GameManager.CurrentWave+1).ToString(),
                    new Vector2(300, 300),
                    Color.White)
            End If

            If gameState = GameStates.GameOver Then
                spriteBatch.DrawString(
                    pericles14,
                    "G A M E O V E R!",
                    new Vector2(300,300),
                    Color.White)
            End If

            spriteBatch.End()

            MyBase.Draw(gameTime)
        End Sub
```

5. Execute your game!

What just happened?

Just as in Asteroid Belt Assault, we track a `gameState` variable that determines what happens during each `Update()` and `Draw()` cycle. The value of `GoalManager.ActiveComputers` is checked during each update cycle, and when the player completes a wave, there is a delay while **Beginning Wave...** is displayed, followed by a switch back to `GameStates.Playing`.

While playing, the `checkPlayerDeath()` method is executed during each cycle, checking to see if the player has collided with any enemy tanks. If so, the game state switches to `GameStates.GameOver`, which has its own delay before switching back to the `TitleScreen` state.

Have a go hero

There are a number of options for expanding on Robot Rampage. Here are a few suggestions:

◆ Robot Rampage is decidedly silent! Import the sound system from Asteroid Belt Assault and add new sound effects for Robot Rampage. Update the code to play sound effects when appropriate.

◆ As stated in the preceding text, the game state management system is fairly basic. Implement multiple player lives, allowing them to regenerate after they have been destroyed.

◆ Add a new weapon to the player's arsenal! Create a weapon that fires a large burst of 12 projectiles in an arc in front of the player tank, but give their particles a very short duration, so the shots will destroy a host of enemy tanks close up, but will not reach more than a few map squares away from the player.

Summary

Robot Rampage covers some important ground in the form of path finding and providing a basis for a very simple form of artificial intelligence for the enemy tanks. In addition, we looked at topics such as:

◆ Expanding the visual effects system we introduced in Asteroid Belt Assault

◆ Allowing the player to use different types of weaponry

◆ Adding enemy robots with the ability to chase the player through the tile-based game map

◆ Implementing goals for the player to accomplish to complete a game level

8

Gemstone Hunter - Put on your Platform Shoes

*In the Gemstone Hunter game, the player is a treasure-hunting archaeologist roaming the zombie-infested wilderness. Unlike the other games presented in this book, Gemstone Hunter will not automatically generate levels. For this reason, the game can be viewed more along the lines of a project starter to explore topics, such as **combining** Windows Forms and XNA, to produce a level editor, and an introduction to the basics of building a platform-style game.*

*The XNA Creator's Club website provides a number of **Starter Kits** that contain sample code and images to get you started on developing specific types of games. The Platform Starter Kit was introduced with XNA 3.1 and included the XNA Game Studio distribution. We are going to make use of some of the graphics from this Starter Kit in Gemstone Hunter. We will not use the actual starter kit itself, however, for a couple of reasons. First, all of the code in the Starter Kit is in C#, and second, we want to build on some of the code that we have established in our prior games and focus on key aspects of the platform genre.*

In this chapter, we will begin the development of Gemstone Hunter, by building a map editor for the game. In order to do so, we will cover:

- Expanding our existing tile map engine
- Adding multiple projects to a Visual Studio solution
- Adding a Windows Form to an XNA game project
- Communicating between Windows Forms and our game code
- Loading and saving map files through serialization

Borrowing graphics

While we may not be directly using XNA's Platform Starter Kit, we will be borrowing the graphical resources for the player's character and enemy monsters from the project. We will begin by creating the project that will eventually house our completed game:

Time for action – creating projects

1. Download `2403_08_GRAPHICPACK.zip` from the book's website, and extract the contents to a temporary folder. Leave this folder open in Windows Explorer.

2. Inside Visual Studio, select **New Project...** from the **File** menu.

3. Create a new **Windows Game (4.0)** project called `Gemstone Hunter`.

4. Right-click on the **Gemstone Hunter Content** project, and add a new folder called `Textures`.

5. Switch back to the **Windows Explorer** window, and highlight the `Sprites` folder, as well as the three .PNG files (`Gem.png`, `PlatformTiles.png`, and `TitleScreen.png`). Right-click on one of the highlighted files and select **Copy**.

6. Switch back to the **Visual Studio** window, right-click on the **Textures** folder in the content project, and select **Paste**. This should result in a **Sprites** folder under **Textures** folder and all three images being added to your project.

7. Right-click on the **Gemstone HunterContent** project, and add a new folder called `Fonts`.

8. Create a new `SpriteFont` object called `Pericles8` in the `Fonts` folder. Set the font name to `Pericles` and the size to `8`.

9. At the top of the **Solution Explorer** window, right-click on the solution (**Solution 'Gemstone Hunter'**) and select **Add | New Project...**.

10. From the new project window, select the **Windows Game Library (4.0)** template. Name the project `Tile Engine`, and add it to the solution:

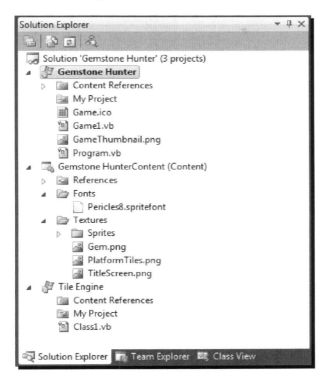

What just happened?

We now have three projects in our solution—The **Gemstone Hunter** game project, the associated content project, and the **Tile Engine** game library project. The game project itself will be detailed in the next chapter. The **Tile Engine** project will contain the code for, not surprisingly, the game's tile engine, which will be shared with yet another project, the **Level Editor**, which we will create shortly.

A more advanced tile engine

In Robot Rampage, we built a simple tile engine that displayed a single layer of tiles from a two-dimensional array of integers, which represented the tiles associated with each map square. For Gemstone Hunter, we will construct a new tile engine that handles multiple tile layers, including a layer of tiles that are drawn in the foreground, appearing in front of the player:

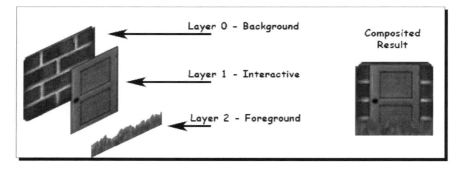

Since we need to store more information about an individual map square, we will begin by defining a class that will contain all of the information we need about a particular square.

Time for action – the MapSquare class

1. Add a new class called `MapSquare` to the **Tile Engine** project.

2. Modify the declaration of the `MapSquare` class by adding the `<Serializable()>` attribute before the class declaration. The class declaration should read:

   ```
   <Serializable()> Public Class MapSquare
   ```

3. Add the declarations region to the MapSquare class:

   ```
   #Region "Declarations"
      Public LayerTiles(3) As Integer
      Public CodeValue As String = "
      Public Passable As Boolean = True
   #End Region
   ```

4. Add a constructor to the MapSquare class:

   ```
   #Region "Constructor"
      Public Sub New(
         background As Integer,
         interactive As Integer,
         foreground As Integer,
   ```

```
        code As String,
        passable As Boolean)

      LayerTiles(0) = background
      LayerTiles(1) = interactive
      LayerTiles(2) = foreground
      CodeValue = code
      Me.Passable = passable
   End Sub
#End Region
```

4. Add the `TogglePassable()` method to the `MapSquare` class:

```
#Region "Public Methods"
   Public Sub TogglePassable()
      Passable = Not Passable
   End Sub
#End Region
```

What just happened?

In *step 2*, we added a new type of information to our code file called an **attribute**. Attributes indicate to the Visual Basic compiler that the item following it should be treated differently in some way compared to the norm for that item type.

In our case, we want to be able to save the tile map that we will be creating to a file and then load that file in both the editor and the game projects. To do this, we need to indicate to Visual Basic that the object is serializable—that is, the object can be converted into a byte-stream, which can be stored and reloaded at a later point.

Modifying serializable classes

We need to be fairly sure we have covered all of the bases with our `MapSquare` class, because once we have used the class to save map files, any changes made (even renaming variables) will cause reloading the saved data to either fail completely, or return corrupted results. This is because the binary serialization method that we will be using essentially grabs the in-memory representation of the data and saves it to disk, reloading it in the same manner. If the definition of the structure changes in any way, the binary format that was output will not match the new in-memory format, resulting in unpredictable problems with our loaded maps.

The `LayerTiles` array stores three integer values representing the tile images on the background, interactive, and foreground layers. Depending on the needs of your game, you could create any number of layers. When we draw them, we will use the index of the layer to determine the depth at which the sprite is drawn, ensuring that they appear in the correct order on the screen.

While building our map, we can associate a string value with each individual map square by setting the `CodeValue` variable. This variable will allow us to create special features, such as map transitions, traps, and invisible barriers to enemy movement.

Finally, to determine if the map square blocks player movement, we can check the `Passable` member variable. If it is `false`, the player cannot move into this square. The default for all `MapSquares` is to be open to movement (`Passable` set to `true`).

Rebuilding the camera

Just as we did in Robot Rampage, we will use a `Camera` module to represent the player's view of our game world and track all object positions in world-based coordinates.

Our `Camera` module is very similar to the module from Robot Rampage, with only minor changes which are detailed next.

Time for action – the Camera module

1. Create a new module `Camera` in the **Tile Engine** project.

2. Modify the declaration of the `Camera` module to make it public:

```
Public Module Camera
```

3. Add declarations to the `Camera` module:

```
#Region "Declarations"
  Private _position As Vector2 = Vector2.Zero
  Private _viewPortSize As Vector2 = Vector2.Zero
#End Region
```

4. Add properties to the `Camera` module:

```
#Region "Properties"
  Public Property WorldRectangle As Rectangle =
    New Rectangle(0, 0, 0, 0)

  Public Property ViewPortWidth As Integer
    Get
      Return CInt(Int(_viewPortSize.X))
```

```
      End Get
      Set(ByVal value As Integer)
        _viewPortSize.X = value
      End Set
    End Property

    Public Property ViewPortHeight As Integer
      Get
        Return CInt(Int(_viewPortSize.Y))
      End Get
      Set(ByVal value As Integer)
        _viewPortSize.Y = value
      End Set
    End Property

    Public Property Position As Vector2
      Get
        Return _position
      End Get
      Set(ByVal value As Vector2)
        _position = New Vector2(
          MathHelper.Clamp(value.X,
            WorldRectangle.X,
          WorldRectangle.Width - ViewPortWidth),
          MathHelper.Clamp(value.Y,
            WorldRectangle.Y,
          WorldRectangle.Height - ViewPortHeight))
      End Set
    End Property

    Public ReadOnly Property ViewPort As Rectangle
      Get
        Return New Rectangle(
          CInt(Int(Position.X)), CInt(Int(Position.Y)),
        ViewPortWidth, ViewPortHeight)
      End Get
    End Property
  #End Region
```

5. Add methods to the `Camera` module:

```
#Region "Public Methods"
  Public Sub Move(offset As Vector2)
    Position += offset
  End Sub
```

```
Public Function ObjectIsVisible(bounds As Rectangle) As Boolean
  Return ViewPort.Intersects(bounds)
End Function

Public Function WorldToScreen(worldLocation As Vector2) As
  Vector2
  Return worldLocation - Position
End Function

Public Function WorldToScreen(worldRect As Rectangle) As
  Rectangle
  Return New Rectangle(
    worldRect.Left - CInt(Int(Position.X)),
    worldRect.Top - CInt(Int(position.Y)),
    worldRect.Width,
  worldRect.Height)
End Function

Public Function ScreenToWorld(screenLocation As Vector2) As
  Vector2
  Return screenLocation + Position
End Function

Public Function ScreenToWorld(screenRect As Rectangle) As
  Rectangle
  Return New Rectangle(
    screenRect.Left + CInt(Int(Position.X)),
    screenRect.Top + CInt(Int(Position.Y)),
    screenRect.Width,
  screenRect.Height)
End Function
#End Region
```

What just happened?

The `Transform()` methods from the Robot Rampage Camera have been renamed to `WorldToScreen()`, and a new pair of methods called `ScreenToWorld()` have been added. We will need to respond to mouse events in the map editor, and the mouse position is reported in screen coordinates. These new methods will assist in determining the map square underneath the mouse cursor.

We saw in Robot Rampage that converting world coordinates to screen coordinates was a simple matter of subtracting the position of the camera from the coordinate. The reverse is also true. To convert from a screen coordinate to a world map coordinate, we add the position of the camera.

Constructing the Tile Engine

The basic concepts behind our original tile-based map engine are unchanged, and indeed most of the code for our new tile engine can be brought over from Robot Rampage. We need to make modifications to the way the map itself is stored, and the way we access (for both reading and setting) map tiles to accommodate the `MapSquare` class, instead of a simple array of integers.

Time for action – the TileMap module – part 1

1. In the **Tile Engine** project, rename the `Class1.vb` file that was generated by the **Game Library** project template to `TileMap.vb` by right-clicking on `Class1.vb` and selecting **Rename**. Visual Studio will ask if you wish to rename all references to the class as well. Go ahead and click on **Yes**. We have not referenced our new class anywhere, so no other code is actually updated.

2. Double-click on the newly renamed `TileMap.vb` file to open it in the editor.

3. Modify the declaration of the `TileMap` class to add two `Imports` directives and to change the class into a `Public Module`. The entire text of the file should now be:

```
Imports System.Runtime.Serialization.Formatters.Binary
Imports System.IO

Public Module TileMap
End Module
```

4. Add declarations to the TileMap module:

```
#Region "Declarations"
  Public Const TileWidth As Integer = 48
  Public Const TileHeight As Integer = 48
  Public Const MapWidth As Integer = 160
  Public Const MapHeight As Integer = 12
  Public Const MapLayers As Integer = 3
  Private Const skyTile As Integer = 2

  Private mapCells(mapWidth,mapHeight) As MapSquare

  Public EditorMode As Boolean = False

  Public spriteFont As SpriteFont
  Private tileSheet As Texture2D
#End Region
```

5. Add the `TilesPerRow` property to the `TileMap` module:

```
#Region "Properties"
  Public ReadOnly Property TilesPerRow As Integer
    Get
      Return CInt(Int(tileSheet.Width / TileWidth))
    End Get
  End Property
#End Region
```

6. Add the `Initialize()` method to the `TileMap` module:

```
#Region "Initialization"
  Public Sub Initialize(tileTexture As Texture2D)
    tileSheet = tileTexture

    For x As Integer = 0 To MapWidth - 1
      For y As Integer = 0 To MapHeight - 1
        For z As Integer = 0 To MapLayers - 1
          mapCells(x,y) = New MapSquare(skyTile, 0, 0, "", True)
        Next
      Next
    Next
  End Sub
#End Region
```

7. Add the `TileSourceRectangle()` function to the `TileMap` module:

```
#Region "Tile Handling Methods"
  Public Function TileSourceRectangle(index As Integer) As
    Rectangle
    Return New Rectangle(
      (index Mod TilesPerRow) * TileWidth,
      CInt(Int(index / TilesPerRow)) * TileHeight,
      TileWidth,
      TileHeight)
  End Function
#End Region
```

What just happened?

Before we continue with the implementation of the `TileMap` class, let's look at the difference we can see so far from the same class in Robot Rampage.

Right from the start, we have a directive that we have not used before: `Imports`. There are many, many namespaces (pre-defined pieces of code) supplied with the .Net Framework, and everything we have used up until this point has been accessible without using the `Imports` directive. All `Imports` does is tell the Visual Basic compiler that we will be using objects from the specified namespace and lets us avoid typing the entire namespace name whenever we want to use one of its components. The `System.Runtime.Serialization.Formatters.Binary` assembly provides a simple way for us to write our level files out to the disk (and read them back in again), by converting the array of `MapSquare` objects in memory into a format that can be written to a file.

Importing namespaces

`Imports` directives provide us with a shorthand way of using classes in namespaces that we would not normally access. Without it, we must enter the full name (`System.Runtime.Serialization.Formatters.Binary.BinaryFormatter`) of the class we wish to use, instead of simply using the class name (`BinaryFormatter`). Both approaches will work, but if we are accessing objects from a long namespace more than a couple of times in a code file, the `Imports` directive saves quite a bit of typing.

If you examine C# XNA code, you will often see several `using` directives at the top of each code file, with namespaces, such as `Microsoft.XNA.Framework.Graphics`. We do not need to import these in Visual Basic, as the project templates take care of this for us.

You may notice that both the declaration and initialization regions are quite a bit shorter than they were in Robot Rampage. In Gemstone Hunter, we will define a tile sheet image that contains the tiles we will use in the game. Unlike our previous games, we will not simply store all of our game's graphics on the same sprite sheet, but break it up into multiple sheets. We have a texture dedicated to the tile images for our game, and each type of game object has a texture file of its own:

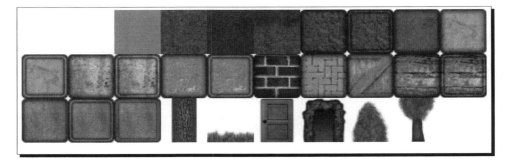

By defining a single sprite sheet to hold only tiles for the tile map, we can treat the sheet in a special manner and decide that the sheet will be evenly divided into as many tiles as will fit on the image. Our tile sheet image is `480x480` pixels, and with a `48x48` tile size, we have 10 rows of 10 tiles, for 100 total tiles available to our game. We could always increase the size of the image to add more tiles, though we would want to keep it to increments of 48 pixels in each direction, to make the math easier.

We will number the tiles starting with zero in the upper-left corner of the tile sheet and progressing across a row. When we reach the end of the row, we return to the left side of the image and start a new row. The `TilesPerRow` property and the `TileSourceRectangle` method replace the array of pre-defined tiles, by providing a way to locate the source rectangle for any tile we wish to draw on the tile sheet image.

Our map is still represented by an array, but around this time, it is a two-dimensional array of `MapSquare` objects, instead of simple integers. We have also rearranged our terminology to reflect the more complex nature of our tile map. What we referred to as squares in Robot Rampage, we now call cells. Any of our code that dealt with getting or setting information about map tiles in Robot Rampage will need to be updated to handle the entire `MapSquare` object in each cell, instead of a simple integer value.

The `TileMap` itself will include support for being used in editing mode, which can be toggled by setting the `EditorMode` member variable. While in editor mode, we will draw the contents of the `CodeValue` member of the `MapSquare` class on top of each square, so the `TileMap` class needs a `SpriteFont` for use with `SpriteBatch.DrawString()`.

Our `Initialize()` method is greatly simplified by the removal of the tiles array, allowing us to establish all of the `mapCells` as MapSquares, with empty tiles on each layer. Our tile sheet contains a fully transparent tile in the upper-left corner (tile zero) and a blue sky tile in the third position (tile two), so by filling the map with squares containing tile two on the background layer, and tile zero on the other two layers, we end up with an empty map with a blue sky background. This will simply save time when creating a new map with the map editor, by letting us skip drawing the sky on each map.

Time for action – the TileMap module – part 2

1. Add methods dealing with locating map cells to the `TileMap` module:

```
#Region "Information about Map Cells"
    Public Function GetCellByPixelX(pixelX As Integer) As Integer
        Return CInt(Int(pixelX / TileWidth))
    End Function

    Public Function GetCellByPixelY(pixelY As Integer) As Integer
        Return CInt(Int(pixelY / TileHeight))
    End Function
```

```vbnet
    Public Function GetCellByPixel(pixelLocation As Vector2) As
Vector2
      Return New Vector2(
        GetCellByPixelX(CInt(Int(pixelLocation.X))),
        GetCellByPixelY(CInt(Int(pixelLocation.Y))))
    End Function

    Public Function GetCellCenter(
      cellX As Integer,
      cellY As Integer) As Vector2

      Return New Vector2(
        CSng((cellX * TileWidth) + (TileWidth / 2)),
        CSng((cellY * TileHeight) + (TileHeight / 2)))
    End Function

    Public Function GetCellCenter(cell As Vector2) As Vector2
      Return GetCellCenter(
        CInt(Int(cell.X)),
        CInt(Int(cell.Y)))
    End Function

    Public Function CellWorldRectangle(
      cellX As Integer,
      cellY As Integer) As Rectangle

      Return New Rectangle(
        cellX * TileWidth,
        cellY * TileHeight,
        TileWidth,
      TileHeight)
    End Function

    Public Function CellWorldRectangle(cell As Vector2) As Rectangle

      Return CellWorldRectangle(
        CInt(Int(cell.X)),
      CInt(Int(cell.Y)))
    End Function

  Public Function CellScreenRectangle(
      cellX As Integer,
      cellY As Integer) As Rectangle

      Return Camera.WorldToScreen(CellWorldRectangle(cellX, cellY))
    End Function
```

```
Public Function CellSreenRectangle(cell As Vector2) As Rectangle
  Return CellScreenRectangle(CInt(Int(cell.X)),
    CInt(Int(cell.Y)))
End Function

Public Function CellIsPassable(
  cellX As Integer,
  cellY As Integer) As Boolean

  Dim square As MapSquare = GetMapSquareAtCell(cellX, cellY)

  If IsNothing(square) Then
    Return True
  Else
    Return square.Passable
  End If
End Function

Public Function CellIsPassable(cell As Vector2) As Boolean
  Return CellIsPassable(CInt(Int(cell.X)), CInt(Int(cell.Y)))
End Function

Public Function CellIsPassableByPixel(
  pixelLocation As Vector2) As Boolean

  Return CellIsPassable(
    GetCellByPixelX(CInt(Int(pixelLocation.X))),
  GetCellByPixelY(CInt(Int(pixelLocation.Y))))
End Function

Public Function CellCodeValue(
  cellX As Integer,
  cellY As Integer) As String

  Dim square As MapSquare = GetMapSquareAtCell(cellX, cellY)

  If IsNothing(square) Then
    Return ""
  Else
    Return square.CodeValue
  End If
End Function

Public Function CellCodeValue(cell As Vector2) As String
  Return CellCodeValue(CInt(Int(cell.X)), CInt(Int(cell.Y)))
End Function
#End Region
```

2. Add methods for manipulating `MapSquares` to the `TileMap` module:

```
#Region "Information about MapSquare objects"
  Public Function GetMapSquareAtCell(
    tileX As Integer,
    tileY As Integer) As MapSquare

    If ((tileX >= 0) And (tileX < MapWidth) And
      (tileY >= 0) And (tileY < MapHeight)) Then
      Return mapCells(tileX, tileY)
    Else
      Return Nothing
    End If
  End Function

  Public Sub SetMapSquareAtCell(
    tileX As Integer,
    tileY As Integer,
    square As MapSquare)

    If ((tileX >= 0) And (tileX < MapWidth) And
      (tileY >= 0) And (tileY < MapHeight)) Then
      mapCells(tileX, tileY) = square
    End If
  End Sub

  Public Sub SetTileAtCell(
    tileX As Integer,
    tileY As Integer,
    layer As Integer,
  tileIndex As Integer)

    If ((tileX >= 0) And (tileX < MapWidth) And
      (tileY >= 0) And (tileY < MapHeight)) Then
      mapCells(tileX, tileY).LayerTiles(layer) = tileIndex
    End If
  End Sub

  Public Function GetMapSquareAtPixel(
    pixelX As Integer,
    pixelY As Integer) As MapSquare

    Return GetMapSquareAtCell(
      GetCellByPixelX(pixelX),
    GetCellByPixelY(pixelY))
  End Function
```

```
Public Function GetMapSquareAtPixel(
  pixelLocation As Vector2) As MapSquare

  Return GetMapSquareAtPixel(
    CInt(Int(pixelLocation.X)),
  CInt(Int(pixelLocation.Y)))
End Function

#End Region
```

What just happened?

Much of the code we need for dealing with the tile map is unchanged from our simpler tile engine, aside from the changes to accommodate our new cell and `MapSquare` terminology. We also use the `MapSquare` type when getting and setting the contents of map cells instead of integers.

The `SetTileAtCell()` method may seem out of place among the methods dealing with `MapSquare` objects. Its purpose is to provide a way to change the tile index of a single layer in a cell, without repackaging the cell's entire `MapSquare` object. By passing `SetTileAtCell()` a cell location, layer number, and tile index, we can change the content of a single layer—exactly what we will need to do when building the map editor.

Because the game engine will need easy access to the `Passable` and `CodeValue` members of a cell (without the need to deal with the tile layer values), we have created the shortcut methods `CellIsPassable()` and `CellCodeValue()`. When the time comes to move the player and enemy objects during game play, we will make extensive use of these methods to determine what map squares are accessible to game entities.

Drawing the Tile Map

We are now ready to assemble the code necessary to draw the enhanced tile map to the screen. We need to account for all three layers of the map, ensuring that each will be drawn in the proper relationship to the others—the background layer appearing furthest away, the interactive layer drawn above it, and finally the foreground layer drawn nearest to the screen.

Time for action – the TileMap module – part 3

1. Add the `Draw()` method to the `TileMap` module:

```
#Region "Drawing"
  Public Sub Draw(spriteBatch As SpriteBatch)
    Dim startX As Integer
    startX = GetCellByPixelX(CInt(Int(Camera.Position.X)))
```

```vb
    Dim endX As Integer
    endX = GetCellByPixelX(CInt(Int(Camera.Position.X)) +
      Camera.ViewPortWidth)

    Dim startY As Integer
    startY = GetCellByPixelY(CInt(Int(Camera.Position.Y)))

    Dim endY As Integer
    endY = GetCellByPixelY(CInt(Int(Camera.Position.Y)) +
      Camera.ViewPortHeight)

    For x As Integer = startX To endX
      For y As Integer = startY To endY
        For z As Integer = 0 To MapLayers - 1
          If ((x >= 0) And (y >= 0) And
            (x < MapWidth) And (y < MapHeight)) Then
            spriteBatch.Draw(
              tileSheet,
              CellScreenRectangle(x,y),
              TileSourceRectangle(
                mapCells(x,y).LayerTiles(z)),
              Color.White,
              0.0,
              Vector2.Zero,
              SpriteEffects.None,
             1F - (CSng(z) * 0.1F))
          End If
        Next

        If EditorMode Then
          DrawEditModeItems(spriteBatch, x, y)
        End If
      Next
    Next
End Sub

Public Sub DrawEditModeItems(
  spriteBatch As SpriteBatch,
  x As Integer,
y As Integer)

  If ((x < 0) Or (x >= MapWidth) Or
    (y < 0) Or (y >= MapHeight)) Then
    Return
  End If
```

```
            If Not CellIsPassable(x,y) Then
              spriteBatch.Draw(
                tileSheet,
                CellScreenRectangle(x, y),
                TileSourceRectangle(1),
                New Color(255, 0, 0) * 0.4F,
                0.0,
                Vector2.Zero,
                SpriteEffects.None,
                0.0)
            End If

            If mapCells(x, y).CodeValue <> "" Then
              Dim screenRect As Rectangle = CellScreenRectangle(x, y)

              spriteBatch.DrawString(
                spriteFont,
                mapCells(x, y).CodeValue,
                New Vector2(screenRect.X, screenRect.Y),
                Color.White,
                0.0,
                Vector2.Zero,
                1.0,
                SpriteEffects.None,
                0.0)
            End If
        End Sub
    #End Region
```

What just happened?

Once again, the `Draw()` method is very familiar. We still use the position of the camera to determine the range of cells that need to be drawn to the screen, but this time we nest a third loop inside the horizontal and vertical loops, which draws the tiles from each of the three layers.

This `SpriteBatch.Draw()` call is unlike any of the others we have made, because this time we are specifying a layer depth as the last parameter of the call. In the past, when we have used the advanced form of the `Draw()` method, we have always left this parameter at a value of `0`.

Layer depths

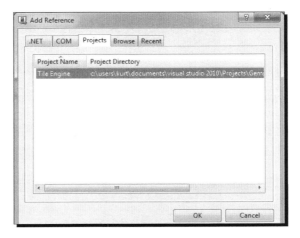

By specifying the layer depth at which to draw the sprite, we can execute the draw calls in any order and allow the graphics card to place them properly according to their sorted depth. In order for this to work, we need to specify some additional parameters to the `SpriteBatch.Begin()` method call we will use in the `Game1` class' `Draw()` method. We need to specify `SpriteSortMode.BackToFront` as the first parameter of the call. This tells the `SpriteBatch` object to pay attention to the layer depth information, otherwise the order in which the sprites are drawn will still be used for sorting, and the layer depths will be ignored. The `FrontToBack` reverses the meaning of the layer depth parameter, making items at `1.0` closer to the camera than items at `0.0`. None of the other modes (`Immediate`, `Deferred`, and `Texture`) will allow us to properly sort sprites, because they either rely on the drawing order (`Immediate` and `Deferred`) or group the drawn sprites in order by the source texture they come from (`Texture`).

If our tile engine is currently in editor mode, the `DrawEditModeItems()` method is called after each tile is drawn. This uses the white tile at tile index one to draw a semi-transparent red block over any square that is not passable by the player. Additionally, the method uses `SpriteBatch.DrawString()` to display the content of the `CodeValue` variable associated with each map cell, if it is not empty.

Time for action – adding the tile map to the game project

1. Right-click on the **Gemstone Hunter** project in **Solution Explorer**, and click on **Add Reference...**.

2. Click on the **Projects** tab in the **Add Reference** window, and ensure that the **Tile Engine** project is selected. Click on **OK**:

3. Open the Game1.vb file in the **Gemstone Hunter** project, and add the following Imports directive to the top of the file:

```
Imports Tile_Engine
```

4. Add the following to the LoadContent() method of the Game1 class:

```
TileMap.Initialize(
   Content.Load(Of Texture2D)("Textures\PlatformTiles"))
TileMap.SetTileAtCell(3, 3, 1, 10)

Camera.WorldRectangle = new Rectangle(0, 0, 160 * 48, 12 * 48)
Camera.Position = Vector2.Zero
Camera.ViewPortWidth = 800
Camera.ViewPortHeight = 600
```

5. Replace the current Draw() method of the Game1 class with the following:

```
Protected Overrides Sub Draw(gameTime As GameTime)
   GraphicsDevice.Clear(Color.Black)
   spriteBatch.Begin(
     SpriteSortMode.BackToFront,
   BlendState.AlphaBlend)
   TileMap.Draw(spriteBatch)
   spriteBatch.End()

   MyBase.Draw(gameTime)
End Sub
```

6. Execute the project.

What just happened?

By referencing the **Tile Engine** project from the **Gemstone Hunter** project, we can utilize the code from the **Tile Engine** project, by including an Imports directive referencing the Tile_Engine namespace.

During the LoadContent() method, we initialize the TileMap and Camera classes, and add a single tile to the map, so that we will see it when we run the application.

Finally, we see the special form of the SpriteBatch.Begin() call that we need to make, to display the different tile layers sorted in the proper order. In addition to specifying the sort mode, we also need to specify the way transparent sprites are blended together. The default is BlendState.AlphaBlend, which is what we want to keep. Since there is no SpriteBatch.Begin() call that allows us to specify only the sort mode, we must supply the blend mode, even though it is normally the default.

Why go to all of this trouble creating multiple projects and referencing them instead of including the `MapSquare`, `Camera`, and `TileMap` code directly into the Gemstone Hunter project? Since we are going to need to display the tile engine in both the game and the level editor, splitting it out into its own project and referencing it allows us to create only one set of source files for the map components. If we were to include the code directly in the game, we would need to make another copy of those three items for our map editor project. Any time we need to update the entities, we would need to remember to update them in both places, increasing the chance of introducing errors and inconsistencies into our project.

The map editor project

With the tile engine in place, we are now ready to begin building the map editor that we will use to create levels for the Gemstone Hunter game. The map editor will combine both an XNA Game and a Windows Forms form to take advantage of the Windows Forms controls (menus, buttons, checkboxes, and so on) to save us the time of recreating all of these controls within XNA.

Creating the map editor project

Since we know that we want to create a Windows Forms application for our level editor, it is tempting to use the Windows Forms application template that is included with Visual Studio. However, it is much easier to add a Windows Forms object to an XNA game project than to work the other way around, and try to incorporate all of the components of an XNA project into the Windows Forms template.

Time for action – creating the Level Editor project

1. In the **Solution Explorer** window, right-click on the top-most item that reads **Solution 'Gemstone Hunter' (3 Projects)**, and select **Add | New Project...**.

2. Select the **Windows Game (4.0)** project template.

3. Name the project `Level Editor`, and click on OK.

4. Right-click on the **Level Editor** project, and select **Add Reference...**.

5. On the **Projects** tab of the **Add** Reference window, select **Tile Engine**, and click on **OK**:

6. Right-click on the **Level Editor** project again, and select **Add Content Reference....**

7. Select the **Gemstone HunterContent (Content)** project, and click **OK**.

8. Right-click on the **Level Editor** project in the **Solution Explorer** window, and click on **Set as StartUp Project**.

What just happened?

Your solution now has five separate projects: the game project (simply called Gemstone Hunter), the game's **Content** project, the **Tile Engine** game library, the **Level Editor**, and the **Level EditorContent** project. Because we have created a content reference in the **Level Editor** project to the game's content project, all of the game's content will be available in the level editor as well. We will leave the **Level Editor Content** project empty, but if we needed content items available in the **Level Editor** that were not needed by the game, we could place them here.

By setting the **Level Editor** as the startup project, whenever we execute our code from the development environment, the **Level Editor** will be the application that starts (as opposed to starting the actual game). This setting is just a convenience for us while we work on the editor:

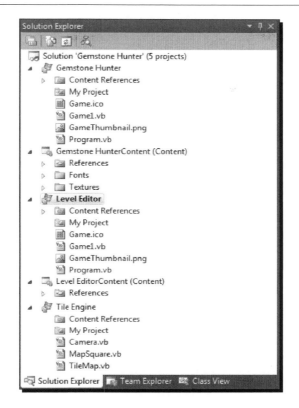

Just like our **Gemstone Hunter** project, the **Level Editor** project contains a reference to the **Tile Engine** project, allowing it to make use of the tile engine code without duplicating it.

Adding a form

We will begin the construction of the **Level Editor** by adding a Windows Form to our project and linking it to the XNA Game, to allow the output of the game to be displayed on a `PictureBox` control on the form.

Time for action – adding a form

1. Right-click on the **Level Editor** project in **Solution Explorer**, and select **Add | Windows Form**.

2. Name the form `MapEditor.vb`, and click on the **Add** button.

3. The **MapEditor** form will automatically open in **Design** mode as a blank window:

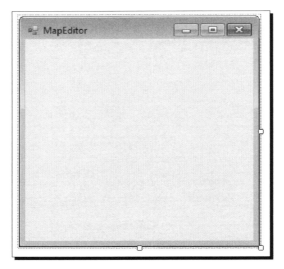

4. In the properties window (right-click on the form and select **Properties** if you have hidden the properties window), set the **Size** property to 700, 670 pixels.

5. On the left edge of the screen, open the **Toolbox** panel (**View | Other Windows | Toolbox** if it is hidden) and expand the **All Windows Forms** section. Locate the MenuStrip control and drag an instance of it onto the MapEditor form. Leave the menu items empty for now.

6. Drag a new PictureBox control from the **Toolbox** panel onto the form.

7. Click on the newly created PictureBox, and set the following properties in the **Properties** window:

- **Name**: pctSurface
- **Anchor**: Top, Bottom, Left, Right
- **Location**: 184, 27
- **Modifiers** : Public
- **Size**: 471, 576

8. Right-click on the MapEditor.vb file in **Solution Explorer**, and select **View Code** to open the source code for the MapEditor form.

9. Add the following `Imports` directives to the `MapEditor` class file:

```
Imports System.IO
Imports System.Drawing
Imports System.Drawing.Imaging
Imports System.Windows.Forms
Imports Tile_Engine
```

10. Add the following declaration to the `MapEditor` class:

```
Public game As Game1
```

11. In the **Level Editor** project, double-click on the `Program.vb` file, and replace the `Main()` method with the following:

```
Sub Main(ByVal args As String())
  Dim form As MapEditor = New MapEditor()
  form.Show()
  form.game = New Game1(
    form.pctSurface.Handle,
    form,
    form.pctSurface)
  form.game.Run()
End Sub
```

12. Still in the **Level Editor** project, open the `Game1.vb` class file, and add the following declarations to the declarations area:

```
Private drawSurface As IntPtr
Private parentForm As System.Windows.Forms.Form
Private pictureBox As System.Windows.Forms.PictureBox
```

13. Replace the `Game1` constructor with the following:

```
Public Sub New(drawSurface As IntPtr,
  parentForm As System.Windows.Forms.Form,
  surfacePictureBox As System.Windows.Forms.PictureBox)

  graphics = New GraphicsDeviceManager(Me)
  Content.RootDirectory = "Content"

  Me.drawSurface = drawSurface
  Me.parentForm = parentForm
  Me.pictureBox = surfacePictureBox

  AddHandler graphics.PreparingDeviceSettings,
  AddressOf graphics_PreparingDeviceSettings

  Mouse.WindowHandle = drawSurface
End Sub
```

14. Add the `graphics_PreparingDeviceSettings()` event handler to the `Game1` class:

```
Private Sub graphics_PreparingDeviceSettings(
  sender As object,
  e As PreparingDeviceSettingsEventArgs)

  With e.GraphicsDeviceInformation.PresentationParameters
    .DeviceWindowHandle = drawSurface
  End With
End Sub
```

15. Execute the project:

What just happened?

As it turns out, we can add a form to an XNA Game project in the same way we would add a form to a standard Windows application. The form will not show up by default, however. The `Program.vb` file is the driver behind the XNA `project`, and the `Main()` method gets executed when the application starts.

Other methods

This is not the only way to integrate Windows Forms and XNA. Check out the Winforms samples at the XNA Creators Club website (http://creators.xna.com/en-US/sample/winforms_series1) for additional information. The Creators Club website has many samples on other topics as well.

For a normal XNA Game, the Main() method creates an instance of the Game1 class and calls its Run() method. In order to combine our game with a Windows Form, we have altered this startup process.

Instead of creating an instance of the Game1 class in the Program module (where Main() lives), we create an instance of our MapEditor form class, and then create an instance of Game1 inside the form.

This will simplify addressing components of the Game1 class from the MapEditor form, allowing us to change properties in the game object in response to user interaction with form controls.

We pass the window handle of the PictureBox to the Game1 constructor. The window handle uniquely identifies the display area of PictureBox, allowing our code to redirect XNA's drawing commands from the original game window to the area defined by the PictureBox.

In order to tell XNA that the graphics we draw should be displayed on the PictureBox, we add an event handler to the PreparingDeviceSettings event of the GraphicsDeviceManager class. In this event handler, we simply set the DeviceWindowHandle associated with the graphics device to drawSurface, the value that we passed in when the instance of the Game1 class was created inside Program.vb.

The last thing the constructor does is tell XNA's Mouse class that it should report coordinates relative to the PictureBox that the game will be drawn onto. If we do not make this setting, we will not be able to determine where on our game display the mouse cursor is located.

Alas! We still have a few problems. The most obvious is that there is a big, empty window that shows up on top of our level editor window. This is the window that would normally contain the XNA game. We have moved the output of the XNA drawing commands to a new drawing surface, but the old window still gets created.

The second problem will not be apparent right away, but will cause us trouble when we resize the map editor form while it is running. When the size of the PictureBox changes, we need to let XNA know that the back-buffer size has changed and let our Camera module know that the view port on the display has changed as well.

To address both of these problems, we will add additional event handlers to the system events that occur when the visibility of the game's empty window changes and when the picture box is resized.

Event handlers

Just about everything that happens in Windows happens in response to events. When the user clicks on a button, resizes a window, selects an item from a menu, or any number of other actions, Windows notifies everything that might be impacted by that action that the event has taken place. All Windows Forms controls have event handlers that determine how they respond to those events. In Visual Basic, we can easily add an event handler to an object, even if it already has event handlers, using the AddHandler statement.

Time for action – adding event handlers

1. Add the following directive to the top of the **Level Editor** project's Game1 class:

```
Imports Tile_Engine
```

2. Add the following declaration to the declarations area of the Game1 class of the **Level Editor** project:

```
Private gameForm As System.Windows.Forms.Control
```

3. Add the following code to the constructor of the Game1 class:

```
gameForm = System.Windows.Forms.Control.
  FromHandle(Me.Window.Handle)
AddHandler gameForm.VisibleChanged, AddressOf
  gameForm_VisibleChanged
AddHandler pictureBox.SizeChanged, AddressOf
  pictureBox_SizeChanged
```

4. Add the two event handlers to the Game1 class:

```
Private Sub gameForm_VisibleChanged(sender As object, e as
  EventArgs)
  If gameForm.Visible Then
    gameForm.Visible = False
  End If
End Sub

Private Sub pictureBox_SizeChanged(sender As object, e As
  EventArgs)
  If (parentForm.WindowState <>
```

```
        System.Windows.Forms.FormWindowState.Minimized) Then
          graphics.PreferredBackBufferWidth = pictureBox.Width
          graphics.PreferredBackBufferHeight = pictureBox.Height
          Camera.ViewPortWidth = pictureBox.Width
          Camera.ViewPortHeight = pictureBox.Height
          graphics.ApplyChanges()
        End If
      End Sub
```

5. Execute the application.

6. To end the application, you will need to return to the Visual Studio interface and select **Stop Debugging** from the **Debug** menu.

What just happened?

At first, the `gameForm_VisibleChanged()` method may look odd. It may seem that it would prevent the game from ever being displayed, as it sets the `gameForm.Visible` property to `false`, if it ever ends up as `true`.

Remember, though, that the form (or window), which is automatically generated by XNA, will always be empty. Our game's display is now being redirected to the `PictureBox` on our `MapEditor` form. This means that we really do want to make sure that the game's form is never visible. Whenever its visibility changes, we ensure that `Visible` is set to `false`, to keep it from appearing.

When the size of the `PictureBox` changes—since it is anchored to the sides of the `MapEditor` form, resizing the form will resize the `PictureBox`—we want to update the game's `GraphicsDeviceManager` with the new size of our display area, and pass those updates along to the `Camera` module. We need to be careful to check the `WindowState` of the parent form when processing the resize event. Because the back-buffer width and height must be greater than zero, if we attempt to set them when the form has been minimized, the application will crash.

Clicking on the window close button or pressing *Alt + F4* to end the application will no longer work, because the hidden window that `Game1` would normally run in will not close automatically.

Filling out our form

Right now, we just have the familiar blue XNA window being displayed on our form. We need to add a number of other controls to the form to build a functional level editor.

Time for action – creating the menu bar

1. Double-click on the `MapEditor.vb` file in **Solution Explorer** to open the `MapEditor` form in the design window.

2. Click on the empty `MenuStrip` that you previously added to the form, and add menu entries for the following items (including the `&` symbols, which will create keyboard shortcuts for the menu entries):

    `&File`

    - ❏ `&Load Map`
    - ❏ `&Save Map`
    - ❏ `-`: A single dash, creating a separator line
    - ❏ `E&xit`

    &Tools

    - ❏ `&Clear Map`

    &Layer

    - ❏ `&Background`
    - ❏ `&Interactive`
    - ❏ `&Foreground`

3. Double-click on the **Exit** item under the **File** menu to have Visual Studio automatically generate an event handler for the **Exit** menu item.

4. Enter the following code into the `ExitToolStripMenuItem_Click()` event handler:

    ```
    game.Exit()
    Application.Exit()
    ```

What just happened?

We now have a standard Windows menu attached to our form with a few entries for our level editor. In order to add code to menu items other than the **Exit** command, we need to make modifications to our `Game1` class, so we will come back to them after we have laid out all of the items on our display.

What are all those ampersands?

In *step two*, each of the menu item entries contains an ampersand (`&`) character, usually as the first character in the entry. When the `MenuStrip` control sees these characters, instead of displaying them in the menu, it causes the next character in the name to be underlined and treated as a shortcut key. By labeling the **File** menu as &File, the item will be displayed as **File**, and pressing *Alt + F* will open the **File** menu. Items within the **File** menu can then be accessed by pressing their own shortcut keys (*L* for **Load**, *S* for **Save**, and so on).

Time for action – tile selection controls

1. Expand the `Textures` folder in the **Gemstone Hunter Content** project.

2. Click on the `PlatformTiles.png` file. The **Properties** window below **Solution Explorer** will update to display the properties of the image file.

3. Change the **Copy to Output Directory** property to **Copy if newer**.

4. Switch back to the **Design** mode view of the `MapEditor` form.

5. Add an `ImageList` control to the `MapEditor` form by double-clicking on the control in the **Toolbox** window. It will show up in the gray area below the form, as it is a non-visible control. Set the following properties on the `ImageList`:

   □ **Name**: `imgListTiles`
   □ **ColorDepth**: `Depth32Bit`
   □ **ImageSize**: 48, 48

6. Add a `ListView` control to the `MapEditor` form, and give it the following properties:

- **Name**: `listTiles`
- **HideSelection**: `False`
- **LargeImageList**: `imgListTiles`
- **Location**: `10, 27`
- **MultiSelect**: `False`
- **Size**: `173, 315`
- **TileSize**: `48, 48`
- **View**: `Tile`

7. Right-click on `MapEditor.vb` in **Solution Explorer**, and select **View Code**.

8. Add the following helper method to the `MapEditor` class:

```
Private Sub LoadImageList()
  Dim filepath As String
  Filepath = Application.StartupPath +
    "\Content\Textures\PlatformTiles.png"

  Dim tileSheet As Bitmap = New Bitmap(filepath)
  Dim tilecount As Integer = 0
  Dim y As Integer
  Dim x As Integer
  Dim tilesAcross As Integer
  Dim tilesDown As Integer

  tilesAcross = CInt(Int(tileSheet.Width / TileMap.TileWidth))
  tilesDown = CInt(Int(tileSheet.Height / TileMap.TileHeight))

  For y = 0 To tilesDown - 1
    For x = 0 To tilesAcross - 1
      Dim newBitmap As Bitmap
      Dim rect As Rectangle
      Rect = New Rectangle(
        x * TileMap.TileWidth,
        y * TileMap.TileHeight,
        TileMap.TileWidth,
      TileMap.TileHeight)

      newBitmap = tileSheet.Clone(
        rect,
      System.Drawing.Imaging.PixelFormat.DontCare)

      imgListTiles.Images.Add(newBitmap)
      Dim itemName As String = ""
      If tilecount = 0 Then
        itemName = "Empty"
      End If
      If tilecount = 1 Then
        itemName = "White"
      End If
      listTiles.Items.Add(new ListViewItem(itemName, tilecount))
      tileCount += 1
    Next
  Next
End Sub
```

9. Double-click on the `MapEditor.vb` file to reopen the **Design** mode view of the form.

10. Double-click on the title bar for the `MapEditor` window, causing Visual Studio to automatically generate an event handler for the `MapEditor_Load` event.

11. Add the following line to the `MapEditor_Load()` event handler:

```
LoadImageList()
```

12. Execute the application:

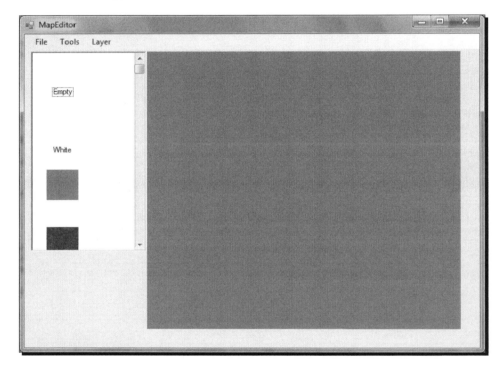

13. End the application by selecting **Exit** from the **File** menu.

What just happened?

After executing the project, you should have a scrollable view of the tiles in the tile set in the `ListView` control in the upper-left corner of the editor window. The `LoadImageList()` helper method reads the `PlatformTiles.png` file, and splits it up into tile-sized chunks, which it stores inside the `imgListTiles ImageList` control.

Notice that we needed to modify the properties of the `PlatformTiles.png` file so that it gets copied to the output directory, because normally the content pipeline would convert the PNG file into an XNB file, which is unreadable by the standard Windows Bitmap class. The XNB file will still be created and copied, but the PNG file will also be placed in the output folder where our `MapEditor` code can find it.

As each image is added to the `imgListTiles` control, entries are also added to the `listTiles ListView` control. The first and second tiles are given special labels in the `ListView` (`Empty` and `White`), as they will both appear to be empty white squares since the background of the `ListView` itself is white.

The `MapEditor_Load()` event handler runs when the form is loaded, as its name implies. We will be expanding on this event handler as we add more controls to the form, since it gives us a convenient place to perform initialization.

Time for action – scroll bars

1. Double click on the `MapEditor.vb` file in **Solution Explorer** to reopen the map editor in the design view if it is not already open.

2. In the **Toolbox** window, double-click on the `VScrollBar` control, to add it to the form. Give it the following properties:
    - ❑ **Name:** `VScrollBar1`
    - ❑ **Anchor:** `Top, Bottom, Right`
    - ❑ **LargeChange:** `48`
    - ❑ **Location:** `658, 27`
    - ❑ **Size:** `17, 576`

3. In the Toolbox window, double-click on the `HScrollBar` control to add it to the form. Give it the following properties:
    - ❑ **Name:** `HScrollBar1`
    - ❑ **Anchor:** `Bottom, Left, Right`
    - ❑ **LargeChange:** `48`
    - ❑ **Location:** `184, 606`
    - ❑ **Size:** `474, 17`

4. Switch back to the code view for the `MapEditor.vb` file, and add the `FixScrollBarScales()` helper method to the `MapEditor` class:

```
Private Sub FixScrollBarScales()
    Camera.ViewPortWidth = pctSurface.Width
    Camera.ViewPortHeight = pctSurface.Height
```

```
Camera.Move(Vector2.Zero)

VScrollBar1.Minimum = 0
VScrollBar1.Maximum =
  Camera.WorldRectangle.Height -
  Camera.ViewPortHeight

HScrollBar1.Minimum = 0
HScrollBar1.Maximum =
  Camera.WorldRectangle.Width -
  Camera.ViewPortWidth
End Sub
```

5. Edit the `MapEditor_Load()` method to include a call to `FixScrollBarScales()`:

```
FixScrollBarScales()
```

6. Double-click on `MapEditor.vb` in **Solution Explorer** to reopen the **Design** mode view of the `MapEditor` form.

7. Click on the title bar of the `MapEditor` window to select the form as the active control.

8. In the **Properties** window, ensure that the drop-down box at the top of the window reads **MapEditor System.Windows.Forms.Form**.

9. Still in the **Properties** widow, click on the yellow lightning bolt button in the toolbar to switch the view from properties to event handlers:

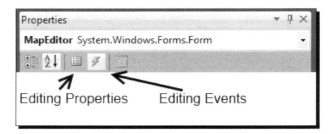

10. Scroll down to locate the **Resize** event, and double-click on the empty box to the right of the event name, causing Visual Studio to automatically generate an event handler for the `MapEditor_Resize` event.

11. Add the following to the `MapEditor_Resize()` method:

```
FixScrollBarScales()
```

12. Switch back to properties view in the **Properties** window by going back to the **Design** mode view of the form and clicking on the small page icon to the left of the lightning bolt icon in the **Properties** window toolbar.

What just happened?

We now have scroll bars attached to the sides of the game's display area. When the form is initially displayed, and then again whenever it is resized, the scroll bars will be rescaled so that they cover the entire area of the game's tile map.

We will use these scroll bars to move around on the map while editing, though their actual implementation will again be tied to changes to the Game1 class.

Time for action – final controls

1. Add a GroupBox to the MapEditor form, and give it the following properties:

- ❑ **Name**: groupBoxRightClick
- ❑ **Location**: 10, 346
- ❑ **Size**: 173, 103
- ❑ **Text**: Right Click Mode

2. Add a RadioButton control inside the groupBoxRightClick GroupBox by dragging it from the **Toolbox** window and dropping it inside the Groupbox. Give it the following properties:

- ❑ **Name**: radioPassable
- ❑ **Checked**: True
- ❑ **Location**: 6, 17
- ❑ **Text**: Toggle Passable

3. Add another RadioButton control inside the groupBoxRightClick control with the following properties:

- ❑ **Name**: radioCode
- ❑ **Location**: 6, 35
- ❑ **Text**: Code

4. Add a `TextBox` control inside the `groupBoxRightClick` control, with the following properties:

- ❑ **Name**: `txtNewCode`
- ❑ **Location**: `62, 36`
- ❑ **Size**: `103, 20`

5. Add a `Label` control inside the `groupBoxRightClick`, with the following properties:

- ❑ **Name**: `lblCurrentCode`
- ❑ **Location**: `60, 59`
- ❑ **Text**: `---`

6. Add a `ComboBox` control inside the `groupBoxRightClick`, with the following properties:

- ❑ **Name**: `cboCodeValues`
- ❑ **DropDownStyle**: `DropDownList`
- ❑ **Location**: `5, 75`
- ❑ **Size**: `160, 21`

7. Add a `Label` control below the group box, with the following properties:

- ❑ **Name**: `lblMapNumber`
- ❑ **Location**: `12, 452`
- ❑ **Text**: `Map Number`

8. Add a `ComboBox` control below the group box, with the following properties:

- ❑ **Name**: `cboMapNumber`
- ❑ **DropDownStyle**: `DropDownList`
- ❑ **Location**: `81, 452`
- ❑ **Size**: `94, 21`

9. Modify the `MapEditor_Load()` method of the `MapEditor` class, by adding the following to the existing code:

```
cboCodeValues.Items.Clear()
cboCodeValues.Items.Add("Gemstone")
cboCodeValues.Items.Add("Enemy")
cboCodeValues.Items.Add("Lethal")
```

```
cboCodeValues.Items.Add("EnemyBlocking")
cboCodeValues.Items.Add("Start")
cboCodeValues.Items.Add("Clear")
cboCodeValues.Items.Add("Custom")

For x As Integer = 0 To 99
  cboMapNumber.Items.Add(x.ToString().PadLeft(3, CChar("0")))
Next

cboMapNumber.SelectedIndex = 0

TileMap.EditorMode = True
```

10. Return to the **Design** view of the `MapEditor` form, and double-click on the `cboCodeValues` combo box (the combo box inside the group box). Update the automatically generated event handler to read:

```
Private Sub cboCodeValues_SelectedIndexChanged(
  sender As System.Object, e As System.EventArgs
  ) Handles cboCodeValues.SelectedIndexChanged

  txtNewCode.Enabled = False
  Select Case (
    cboCodeValues.Items(cboCodeValues.SelectedIndex).ToString())

    Case "Gemstone"
      txtNewCode.Text = "GEM"

    Case "Enemy"
      txtNewCode.Text = "ENEMY"

    Case "Lethal"
      txtNewCode.Text = "DEAD"

    Case "EnemyBlocking"
      txtNewCode.Text = "BLOCK"

    Case "Start"
      txtNewCode.Text = "START"

    Case "Clear"
      txtNewCode.Text = ""

    Case "Custom"
      txtNewCode.Text = ""
      txtNewCode.Enabled = True
  End Select
End Sub
```

11. Execute the application:

What just happened?

We now have all of the interactive controls that we need for our level editor. The codes drop-down box provides a number of standard code values that we will use during level creation, with the ability to add custom codes, which are entered in the textbox above it.

Updating the Game1 class

We currently have a Windows form that contains our XNA Game display, but the two pieces of the level editor application do not yet share any information, or allow the user to actually edit maps. It is time to begin updating our game to support level editing.

Time for action – updating Game1

1. Double-click on the Game1.vb file in the **Level Editor** project to open it in the editor.

2. Add the following declarations to the Game1 declarations area:

```
Public DrawLayer As Integer = 0
Public DrawTile As Integer = 0
Public EditingCode As Boolean = False
```

```
Public CurrentCodeValue As String = ""
Public HoverCodeValue As String = ""

Public lastMouseState As MouseState
Private vscroll As System.Windows.Forms.VScrollBar
Private hscroll As System.Windows.Forms.HScrollBar
```

3. Add the following lines to the Game1 constructor:

```
vscroll = CType(parentForm.Controls("VScrollBar1"),
  System.Windows.Forms.VScrollBar)

hscroll =CType(parentForm.Controls("HScrollBar1"),
  System.Windows.Forms.HScrollBar)
```

4. Modify the LoadContent() method of the Game1 class to read:

```
Protected Overrides Sub LoadContent()
  spriteBatch = new SpriteBatch(GraphicsDevice)

  Camera.ViewPortWidth = pictureBox.Width
  Camera.ViewPortHeight = pictureBox.Height
  Camera.WorldRectangle =
    New Rectangle(
      0,
      0,
      TileMap.TileWidth * TileMap.MapWidth,
      TileMap.TileHeight * TileMap.MapHeight
    )

  TileMap.Initialize(
    Content.Load(Of Texture2D)("Textures\PlatformTiles"))

  TileMap.spriteFont =
    Content.Load(Of SpriteFont)("Fonts\Pericles8")

  lastMouseState = Mouse.GetState()

  pictureBox_SizeChanged(Nothing, Nothing)
End Sub
```

5. Modify the Draw() method of the Game1 class to read:

```
Protected Overrides Sub Draw(gameTime As GameTime)
  GraphicsDevice.Clear(Color.Black)
```

```
    spriteBatch.Begin(
      SpriteSortMode.BackToFront,
    BlendState.AlphaBlend)
    TileMap.Draw(spriteBatch)
    spriteBatch.End()

    MyBase.Draw(gameTime)
  End Sub
```

What just happened?

To simplify communications between the Windows Form and the XNA Game, we have declared a number of public member variables that our Windows Form code will be able to update in response to user-generated events. We have also loaded a SpriteFont to draw code values with, and a MouseState variable to hold the state of the mouse between frames.

Finally, we declare two objects that reference the scroll bars on the level editor form. We will use these to sync-up the display of the tile map to the location of the scroll bars.

The LoadContent() method is fairly standard, setting the size of the tile map, and loading the tile images and sprite font. The TileMap class spriteFont member is set to the font we loaded, and the lastMouseState member is initialized. Right before exiting, the LoadContent() method calls the pictureBox_SizeChanged() method, to make sure that the graphics device has the proper dimensions for the display window.

In our Draw() method, we have again used the expanded form of the SpriteBatch. Begin() call in order to specify the SpriteSortMode.BackToFront parameter.

Time for action – the Game1 Update method

1. Replace the current Update() method in the Game1 class with the following:

```
Protected Overrides Sub Update(gameTime As GameTime)
  Camera.Position = new Vector2(hscroll.Value, vscroll.Value)

  Dim ms As MouseState  = Mouse.GetState()

  if ((ms.X > 0) And (ms.Y > 0) And
    (ms.X < Camera.ViewPortWidth) And
    (ms.Y < Camera.ViewPortHeight)) Then
    Dim mouseLoc As Vector2 = Camera.ScreenToWorld(
      new Vector2(ms.X, ms.Y))
```

```
    If Camera.WorldRectangle.Contains(
      CInt(mouseLoc.X), CInt(mouseLoc.Y)) Then
      If ms.LeftButton = ButtonState.Pressed Then
        TileMap.SetTileAtCell(
          TileMap.GetCellByPixelX(CInt(mouseLoc.X)),
          TileMap.GetCellByPixelY(CInt(mouseLoc.Y)),
          DrawLayer,
        DrawTile)
      End If

      If (ms.RightButton = ButtonState.Pressed) And
        (lastMouseState.RightButton = ButtonState.Released) Then

        If EditingCode Then
          TileMap.GetMapSquareAtCell(
          TileMap.GetCellByPixelX(CInt(mouseLoc.X)),
          TileMap.GetCellByPixelY(CInt(mouseLoc.Y))
          ).CodeValue = CurrentCodeValue
        Else
          TileMap.GetMapSquareAtCell(
            TileMap.GetCellByPixelX(CInt(mouseLoc.X)),
            TileMap.GetCellByPixelY(CInt(mouseLoc.Y))
          ).TogglePassable()
        End If
      End If

      HoverCodeValue =
        TileMap.GetMapSquareAtCell(
          TileMap.GetCellByPixelX(
            CInt(mouseLoc.X)),
          TileMap.GetCellByPixelY(
            CInt(mouseLoc.Y))).CodeValue
    End If
  End If

  lastMouseState = ms

  MyBase.Update(gameTime)
End Sub
```

2. Execute the application. Attempting to draw tiles at this point results in black holes being punched in the all-blue map:

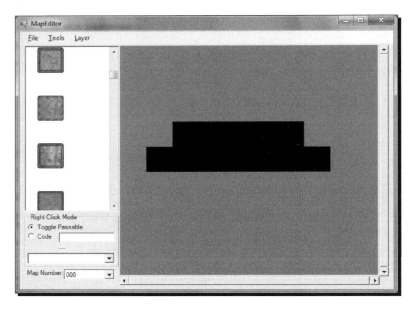

What just happened?

The first thing our Update() method does is to set the game's camera position, based on the current values of the horizontal and vertical scroll bars on the level editor form. When we scroll the scroll bars, the game map will scroll as well.

Next, we verify that the mouse coordinates are within the view port of the camera and thus within the PictureBox control on the editor form. If they are, we determine the world-based coordinates of the mouse cursor.

If the left mouse button has been pressed, we update the tile under the cursor on the current DrawLayer with the current DrawTile. The right mouse button is a bit more complicated.

We will use the right mouse button to set two different types of information—either toggling on and off the Passable property of the MapSquare, or setting its CodeValue property, depending on the mode selected on the MapEditor form.

In either case, we will only make a change to the underlying tile if the right mouse button is pressed during this frame and was not pressed during the previous frame. This eliminates updating the same square multiple times on a single button press (which would make toggling passability on and off difficult!) During the first frame after the button is pressed, the MapSquare will be updated. Until the button is released, no other updates will occur.

The `HoverCodeValue` member is set to the `CodeValue` of the `MapSquare` under the mouse cursor. This value will be used by the `MapEditor` form and displayed on a label on the screen to provide an alternative method of viewing the code for an individual square.

Finally, `lastMouseState` is updated to the current mouse state, and the `Update()` method is completed.

Connecting the form to the game

As we saw at the end of the last section, attempting to draw tiles to the map at this point only leaves empty spaces. This is because the `DrawLayer` and `DrawTile` integers both default to zero, so we are drawing a fully-transparent tile onto the background layer.

Now that we have made the necessary updates to the XNA side of the level editor, we need to flesh out the event handlers for the controls we placed on the `MapEditor` form to update the control variables inside the `Game1` class.

Time for action – completing the editor – part 1

1. Open the `MapEditor` form in **Design** mode.

2. Double-click on the `listTiles` ListView control to automatically generate an event handler for the `SelectedIndexChanged` event. Update the event code to read:

```
Private Sub listTiles_SelectedIndexChanged(
    sender As System.Object,
    e As System.EventArgs) Handles listTiles.SelectedIndexChanged

    If listTiles.SelectedIndices.Count > 0 Then
        game.DrawTile = listTiles.SelectedIndices(0)
    End If
End Sub
```

3. Return to the **Design** view of the `MapEditor` form, and double-click on the radio button labeled **Toggle Passable** to generate a handler for the `CheckChanged` event. Update the event handler to read:

```
Private Sub radioPassable_CheckedChanged(
    sender As System.Object,
    e As System.EventArgs) Handles radioPassable.CheckedChanged

    If Not IsNothing(game) Then
        If radioPassable.Checked Then
            game.EditingCode = False
        Else
```

```
      game.EditingCode = True
    End If
  End If
End Sub
```

4. Return to the **Design** view, and double-click on the **Code** radio button. Update the `CheckChanged` event handler to read:

```
Private Sub radioCode_CheckedChanged(
  sender As System.Object,
  e As System.EventArgs) Handles radioCode.CheckedChanged

  If Not IsNothing(game) Then
    If radioPassable.Checked Then
      game.EditingCode = False
    Else
      game.EditingCode = True
    End If
  End If
End Sub
```

5. Return to the **Design** view, and double-click on the `txtNewCode` textbox. Update the `TextChanged` event handler to read:

```
Private Sub txtNewCode_TextChanged(
  sender As System.Object,
  e As System.EventArgs) Handles txtNewCode.TextChanged

  game.CurrentCodeValue = txtNewCode.Text
End Sub
```

6. Return to the **Design** view, and double-click on the **Background** menu item under the **Layer** menu. Update the `Click` event handler to read:

```
Private Sub BackgroundToolStripMenuItem_Click(
  sender As System.Object,
  e As System.EventArgs) Handles BackgroundToolStripMenuItem.Click

  game.DrawLayer = 0
  backgroundToolStripMenuItem.Checked = True
  interactiveToolStripMenuItem.Checked = False
  foregroundToolStripMenuItem.Checked = False
End Sub
```

7. Generate a `Click` event handler for the **Interactive** layer menu item, and update it to read:

```
Private Sub InteractiveToolStripMenuItem_Click(
  sender As System.Object,
  e As System.EventArgs) Handles
  InteractiveToolStripMenuItem.Click

  game.DrawLayer = 1
  backgroundToolStripMenuItem.Checked = False
  interactiveToolStripMenuItem.Checked = True
  foregroundToolStripMenuItem.Checked = False
End Sub
```

8. Generate a `Click` event handler for the **Foreground** layer menu item, and update it to read:

```
Private Sub ForegroundToolStripMenuItem_Click(
  sender As System.Object,
  e As System.EventArgs) Handles ForegroundToolStripMenuItem.Click

  game.DrawLayer = 2
  backgroundToolStripMenuItem.Checked = False
  interactiveToolStripMenuItem.Checked = False
  foregroundToolStripMenuItem.Checked = True
End Sub
```

9. In the `MapEditor_Load()` method, add the following to the end of the method to indicate the starting layer for the editor:

```
backgroundToolStripMenuItem.Checked = True
```

10. Execute the application, and use the editor to draw tiles to the map:

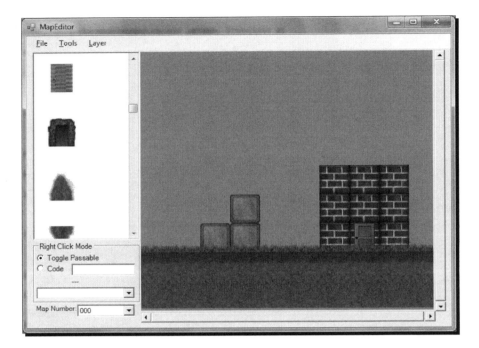

11. Maximize the display window, and attempt to use the scroll bars to scroll around the map display.

What just happened?

All of our event handlers for the form controls simply pass information along to the appropriate variables in the Game1 class. Selecting a layer from the menu bar updates the DrawLayer value, while the radio buttons toggle the EditingCode variable between true and false. We need to wrap these statements in "If Not IsNothing(game) Then" statements, because the first time these events will be executed is before the game object has been created.

Any time the txtNewCode control's Text property is changed, the current contents of the TextBox are copied to the CurrentCodeValue member of the Game1 class.

In *step 11*, you probably noticed that the game window does not update the current position when you are scrolling through the scroll bars until you release the mouse button, even though the scroll bar's marker moves the whole time. This happens because the movement of the scroll bar is preventing the game loop from executing while the user is in the process of manipulating the scroll bars.

In addition, the scroll bars do not match up to the map window until we resize the display at least once. This is because the form's Load event happens prior to the initialization of the Game1 instance (if you go back and look at Program.vb, the form is created and shown first, and then the game is initialized), so the WorldRectangle property of the Camera module is {0, 0, 0, 0}. This results in FixScrollBarScales() setting negative numbers for the maximum values of the scroll bars.

We can fix both of these problems by adding a **timer** to the form that initially calls FixScrollBarScales() and repeatedly calls the game's Tick() method.

Time for action – fixing the scrolling delay

1. Reopen the **Design** mode view of the MapEditor window.

2. Double-click on the timer control in the **Toolbox** window to add a new instance to the MapEditor form. As with the ImageList control, the timer is not visible and will appear in the editor as an icon and label below the design window. Give the timer control the following properties:

- ❏ **Name**: timerGameUpdate
- ❏ **Enabled**: True
- ❏ **Interval**: 20

3. Double-click on the timerGameUpdate control to generate a Tick event handler, and add the following code to it:

```
Private Sub timerGameUpdate_Tick(
  sender As System.Object,
  e As System.EventArgs) Handles timerGameUpdate.Tick

  If hScrollBar1.Maximum < 0 Then
    FixScrollBarScales()
  End If

  game.Tick()

  If game.HoverCodeValue <> lblCurrentCode.Text Then
    lblCurrentCode.Text = game.HoverCodeValue
  End If
End Sub
```

4. Execute the application. Draw a few tiles on the map, and use the scroll bars to verify that they function as expected.

What just happened?

Using the scroll bars does not prevent the timer control from firing its `Tick` event, so by executing the game's `Tick()` method from within the `timerGameUpdate_Tick()` event handler, we can force the game's `Update()` and `Draw()` methods to run even when they normally would not.

The last item in the `timerGameUpdate_Tick()` handler checks to see if the `HoverCodeValue` inside the `Game1` class has been updated, since it was last copied to the label displaying it on the Windows Form. If it has, the form label is updated as well.

Loading and saving maps

The last thing we need to address to complete the Gemstone Hunter Level Editor is how we will load and save our map files. There are a number of ways we could store our level maps, but we will implement a very simple method that does not require parsing XML or creating a textfile with a special format to store the map.

Time for action – implementing loading and saving

1. In the **Tile Engine** project, open the `TileMap.vb` module file.

2. Add the **Loading and Saving Maps** region to the `TileMap` module:

```
#Region "Loading and Saving Maps"
  Public Sub SaveMap(fileToSave As FileStream)
    Dim formatter As BinaryFormatter = new BinaryFormatter()
    formatter.Serialize(fileToSave, mapCells)
    fileToSave.Close()
  End Sub

  Public Sub LoadMap(fileToLoad As FileStream)
    Try
      Dim formatter As BinaryFormatter = new BinaryFormatter()
      mapCells = CType(formatter.Deserialize(fileToLoad),
        MapSquare(,))
      fileToLoad.Close()
    Catch
      ClearMap()
    End Try
  End Sub

  Public Sub ClearMap()
    For x As Integer = 0 To MapWidth - 1
      For y As Integer = 0 To MapHeight - 1
```

```
            For z As Integer = 0 To MapLayers - 1
               mapCells(x, y) = New MapSquare(2, 0, 0, "", True)
            Next
         Next
      Next
   End Sub
#End Region
```

3. Back in the **Level Editor** project, open the `MapEditor` form in **Design** mode.

4. Double-click on the **Load Map** item in the **File** menu to create the `Click` event handler, and update its code to read:

```
Private Sub LoadMapToolStripMenuItem_Click(
   sender As System.Object,
   e As System.EventArgs) Handles LoadMapToolStripMenuItem.Click

   Try
      TileMap.LoadMap(New FileStream(
         Application.StartupPath + "\MAP" +
         cboMapNumber.Items(cboMapNumber.SelectedIndex).ToString() +
         ".MAP",
      FileMode.Open))
   Catch
      System.Diagnostics.Debug.Print("Unable to load map file")
   End Try
End Sub
```

5. Double-click on the **Save Map** item in the **File** menu, and update its `Click` handler to read:

```
Private Sub SaveMapToolStripMenuItem_Click(
   sender As System.Object,
   e As System.EventArgs) Handles SaveMapToolStripMenuItem.Click

   TileMap.SaveMap(New FileStream(
      Application.StartupPath + "\MAP" +
      cboMapNumber.Items(cboMapNumber.SelectedIndex).ToString() +
      ".MAP",
   FileMode.Create))
End Sub
```

6. Double-click on the **Clear** Map item in the **Tools** menu, and update its `Click` handler to read:

```
Private Sub ClearMapToolStripMenuItem_Click(
    sender As System.Object,
    e As System.EventArgs) Handles ClearMapToolStripMenuItem.Click

    TileMap.ClearMap()
End Sub
```

7. Execute the application and create a simple map. Save it to disk, update the map, and reload it.

What just happened?

When a map is saved, we create a `FileStream` object, which represents our file on disk. We then create an instance of the `BinaryFormatter` class and call its `Serialize()` method, passing in the stream to serialize the data from the object we wish to serialize. In our case, it is the array containing the `MapSquare` objects that represent our game map.

When loading the map, the process is exactly the same, except that we use the `Deserialize()` method of the `BinaryFormatter` class to reverse the process, converting the binary data on disk back into its in-memory representation. By surrounding the attempt to load the map with a `Try...End Try` block, we can take action (clearing the map to an empty blue sky) instead of simply crashing the level editor.

From the Windows Form side of the system, we call the new `LoadMap()` and `SaveMap()` methods, passing in the `FileStream` object that is created based on the `cboMapNumber` drop-down list. Our maps will be saved in files named `"MAP###.MAP"`, with the three-digit number taken from the `cboMapNumber` list. While using our maps in the **Level Editor**, they will be stored in the same directory our **Level Editor** executable is running from (normally, the `Visual Studio 2010\Projects\Gemstone Hunter\Level Editor\Level Editor\ bin\x86\debug` folder inside your `Documents` folder). In the following screenshot, we have created a sample map using the level editor. This map currently has no passability or code information on it, and it contains only tile information for now:

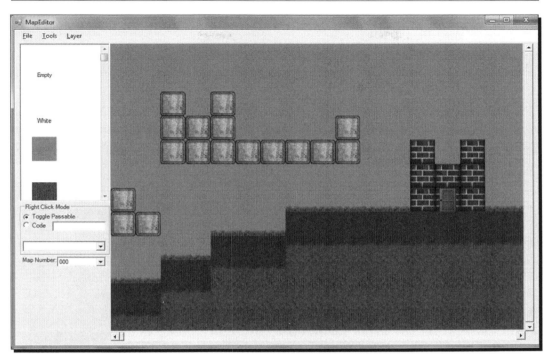

Passability

When building maps, we will use the right mouse button to toggle each individual map square as either passable or impassable. When a square is marked as impassable, it will be tinted red by the editor, indicating that both the monster and the player will treat the square as a solid wall, no matter what visual representation the square has.

Without this information, the player would fall straight through the level and off the map—something we will need to account for in the game engine when we build it in the next chapter.

Map codes

Each `MapSquare` can be assigned a code value that will allow the game to implement special behavior for that square. We have pre-defined a handful of code values including:

- **Gemstone** (GEM): A gem will be spawned at this location for the player to collect.
- **Enemy** (ENEMY): An enemy will be spawned at this location.
- **Lethal** (DEAD): Contacting this square will kill the player.

◆ **Enemy Blocking** (BLOCK): Players can move through these squares, but enemies will treat them as walls. This allows us to confine enemies to an elevated platform, for example.

◆ **Start** (START): If no position is set because of a map transition, the player will start the map in this square.

In addition, we will define a special code for map transitions. In the following image, we have a code value of T-001-03-10 on the MapSquare containing the door into the brick building. At runtime, we will interpret this code value to mean: *Transition (T) to map 001, at location 03, 10*. In this way, we can link maps together and allow the player to move between them:

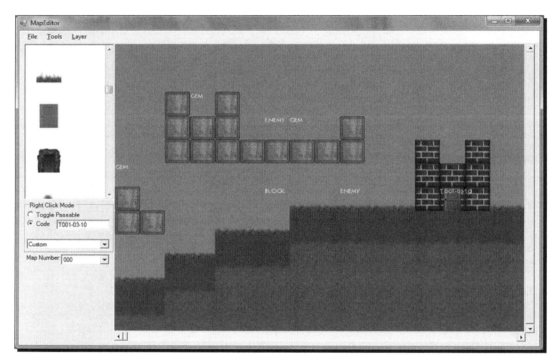

This image shows the map from the previous section with both passability and code information filled in. In Editor mode, the TileEngine class displays the code values as text blocks on each map square. These codes mean nothing to the editor, so just like passability information, we will need to account for it in the game engine.

One last issue

Remember way back when we hid the empty `Game1` form, the one where we added code to the **Exit** menu item to properly terminate the application? We can clear up what happens when the user clicks on the **X** button in the upper-right corner of the window to close the application.

Time for action – handling the FormClosed event

1. Open the `MapEditor` form in **Design** mode.

2. Select the form as the current object by clicking on the form's title bar in the **Design** window.

3. Switch to **Event editing** mode in the **Properties** window by clicking on the lightning bolt button.

4. Scroll down to the `FormClosed` event, and double-click in the empty box to the right of the event name to create the `MapEditor_FormClosed()` event handler.

5. Add the following code to the `MapEditor_FormClosed()` event handler:

```
game.Exit()
Application.Exit()
```

What just happened?

When the form closes, we need to shut down both the XNA game and the overall application, otherwise the system will not release the resources, and the program will still be running invisibly in the background.

Have a go hero

The **Gemstone Hunter Level Editor** project is fairly rough around the edges. It is not exactly a model example of Windows Forms development, but then few purpose-built internal game development tools are.

If you feel like diving further into Windows Forms development, here are a few suggestions for improving on the level editor:

◆ Currently, the level editor does not alert you if you try to load a map after you have made changes to the current map. By adding checks to the `Update()` method of the `Game1` class, you could flag the map as having changed and issue the appropriate warnings to the user when they try to load a new map.

◆ Marking squares as impassable requires an individual click on each square. You could expand the number of radio buttons to include marking squares as passable and impassable as separate tasks, thus allowing the user to hold down the mouse button and draw large blocks of impassable squares.

◆ On the more game-focused side of things, try creating a few levels! The level editor supports up to 100 levels (000 through 099), so there is plenty of room to experiment.

Summary

We now have a working—if not pretty—level editor. In this chapter, we:

◆ Added multiple layers and other types of data to the `TileMap` class that we built for ·Robot Rampage

◆ Created a multi-project Visual Studio solution that shares code between projects

◆ Added a Windows Forms form to our XNA Game Studio project and modified the program's startup process to render the form to a `PictureBox` control on the form

◆ Implemented methods to allow communication between the Windows Form and the XNA game, including synchronized scroll bars, and updating member variables in the `Game1` class in response to Windows Forms controls events

◆ Implemented methods to load and save map files through the `BinaryFormatter` class

In the next chapter, we will flesh out the Gemstone Hunter project and cover the basics of building a platform-style game using the maps that we created with the level editor from this chapter.

9
Gemstone Hunter—Standing on your Own Two Pixels

With our level editor completed, we can now move on to build the Gemstone Hunter game itself. As with the other games in this book, we will build on what we have learned in the previous projects and introduce some new concepts.

In this chapter, we will cover the following topics:

- ◆ A new approach to animating game objects using named animation strips
- ◆ A more object-oriented approach to game objects
- ◆ Platform game physics, allowing the player to run, jump, and squash enemies
- ◆ Processing map codes when a map is loaded to spawn objects in the game world
- ◆ Using map codes at runtime to generate in-game effects

Animation strips

In all of the other game projects in this book, our graphical resources have been confined to a single sprite sheet, onto which we have consolidated all of the images needed for our gameplay elements.

This works well for many small games, but it is certainly not the only way to organize your content. Since we are borrowing content from the XNA Platform Starter Kit, we will use it in the format it has been provided to us instead of creating new sprite sheets.

For each type of entity we will display in Gemstone Hunter, we have one or more PNG files containing multiple image frames for a single animation. For example, the `Run.png` file for the main character from the Platform Starter Kit looks as follows:

Each frame is of the same size (48 x 48 pixels in this case), and the size of the image file itself determines the number of frames contained in the animation. The run animation is 480 pixels wide, at 48 pixels per frame, so there are 10 frames in the animation.

Time for action – building the AnimationStrip class

1. In the Gemstone Hunter project, add a new class called `AnimationStrip`.

2. Add declarations to the `AnimationStrip` class:

```
#Region "Declarations"
Private _frameTimer As Single = 0
Private _currentFrame As Integer
Private _finishedPlaying As Boolean = False
#End Region
```

3. Add properties to the `AnimationStrip` class:

```
#Region "Properties"
Public Property FrameWidth As Integer
Public Property FrameHeight As Integer
Public Property Texture As Texture2D
Public Property Name As String
Public Property NextAnimation As String
Public Property LoopAnimation As Boolean = True
Public Property FrameLength as Single = 0.05

Public ReadOnly Property FinishedPlaying As Boolean
    Get
        Return _finishedPlaying
    End Get
End Property

Public ReadOnly Property FrameCount As Integer
    Get
        Return CInt(Int(texture.Width / frameWidth))
```

```
        End Get
    End Property

    Public ReadOnly Property FrameRectangle As Rectangle
        Get
            Return New Rectangle(
                _currentFrame * FrameWidth,
                0,
                FrameWidth,
                FrameHeight)
        End Get
    End Property
#End Region
```

4. Add a constructor to the `AnimationStrip` class:

```
#Region "Constructor"
Public Sub New(
    texture As Texture2D,
    frameWidth As Integer,
    name As String)

    Me.Texture = texture
    Me.FrameWidth = frameWidth
    Me.frameHeight = texture.Height
    Me.Name = name
End Sub
#End Region
```

5. Add public methods to the `AnimationStrip` class:

```
#Region "Public Methods"
Public Sub Play()
    _currentFrame = 0
    _finishedPlaying = False
End Sub

Public Sub Update(gameTime As GameTime)
    Dim elapsed As Single
    elapsed = CSng(gameTime.ElapsedGameTime.TotalSeconds)

    _frameTimer += elapsed

    If _frameTimer >= FrameLength Then
        _currentFrame += 1
```

```
            If _currentFrame >= FrameCount Then
                If LoopAnimation Then
                    _currentFrame = 0
                Else
                    _currentFrame = FrameCount - 1
                    _finishedPlaying = True
                End If
            End If

            _frameTimer = 0
        End If
    End Sub
#End Region
```

What just happened?

Each `AnimationStrip` is defined primarily by the `Texture2D` object that contains the images for the animation and the frame size information passed into the constructor. From these two pieces of information, we can play a basic animation by including the timing loop logic that we have used many times previously.

The `Play()` method sets the `_currentFrame` variable to zero and `_finishedPlaying` to false, resulting in future calls to the `Update()` method advancing the frame until the last frame in the image is reached.

What happens after the last frame is displayed is dependent on the value of `LoopAnimation`. If this `Boolean` property is `True`, the `_currentFrame` counter will be set back to zero, and the animation will continue to play in a continuous loop.

If `LoopAnimation` is false, the animation will continue to display the last frame of the animation, setting `_finishedPlaying` to `True`. We can check the associated `FinishedPlaying` property from our game code to determine what we should do after an animation has finished playing.

In order to help decide what to play next, each `AnimationStrip` has `Name` and `NextAnimation` string properties. For example, the graphics for the player's character in the Platform Starter Kit contains an animation for jumping. When we load this animation, we can specify that the jump animation's `NextAnimation` property is `idle`.

When we build our game objects, we can watch for an animation to finish playing and then start playing the animation specified by `NextAnimation` to present a smooth transition between animated states.

It is important to note that the `AnimationStrip` class does not do any drawing. It simply provides a texture source and frame rectangle to another object that will perform the actual drawing to the display. The game objects themselves will keep track of their positions and current animation states, requesting the appropriate information from their `AnimationStrip` when they need to be drawn.

Animated game objects

The basis for all of our game objects apart from the tile-based map (the player, enemies, and gemstones) will be a class called `GameObject`. This class will provide support for playing animations and collision detection with the tile map.

In many ways, the `GameObject` class is similar to the `Sprite` class we built for our other games. Since the `GameObject` class does not hold texture information like the `Sprite` class did, we have given it a new name to better describe its functionality.

Just as we did in Robot Rampage, we will track the position of all of our game objects in world coordinates, translating those to screen coordinates as necessary with the `Camera` module.

Time for action – building the GameObject class – part 1

1. Add a new class called `GameObject` to the Gemstone Hunter project.

2. Add the following `Imports` directive to the top of the `GameObject` class file:

    ```
    Imports Tile_Engine
    ```

3. Add declarations to the `GameObject` class:

    ```
    #Region "Declarations"
    Protected _frameWidth As Integer
    Protected _frameHeight As Integer

    Protected _collisionRectangle As Rectangle
    Protected _collideWidth As Integer
    Protected _collideHeight As Integer

    Protected _animations As Dictionary(Of String, AnimationStrip) =
        New Dictionary(Of String, AnimationStrip)()
    Protected _currentAnimation As String
    #End Region
    ```

4. Add properties to the `GameObject` class:

```
#Region "Properties"
Public Property Enabled As Boolean
Public Property Flipped As Boolean = False
Public Property OnGround As Boolean = False
Public Property CodeBasedBlocks As Boolean = True
Public Property WorldLocation As Vector2
Public Property Velocity As Vector2
Public Property DrawDepth As Single = 0.85

Public ReadOnly Property CurrentAnimation As String
    Get
        Return _currentAnimation
    End Get
End Property

Public ReadOnly Property WorldCenter As Vector2
    Get
        Return New Vector2(
           CInt(WorldLocation.X) + CInt(_frameWidth/2),
           CInt(WorldLocation.Y) + CInt(_frameHeight/2))
    End Get
End Property

Public ReadOnly Property WorldRectangle As Rectangle
    Get
        Return New Rectangle(
            CInt(WorldLocation.X),
            CInt(WorldLocation.Y),
            _frameWidth,
            _frameHeight)
    End Get
End Property

Public Property CollisionRectangle As Rectangle
    Get
        Return New Rectangle(
            CInt(WorldLocation.X) + _collisionRectangle.X,
            CInt(WorldRectangle.Y) + _collisionRectangle.Y,
            _collisionRectangle.Width,
            _collisionRectangle.Height)
    End Get
    Set(ByVal value As Rectangle)
```

```
        _collisionRectangle = value
    End Set
  End Property
  #End Region
```

What just happened?

As we can see, most of the properties of the GameObject class are carried over from the Sprite class from our previous games. The properties ,such as WorldLocation, WorldCenter, and CollisionRectangle all have the same meaning for GameObject as they did for Sprite.

However, we do have some new additions. All of the animation strips for our characters represent the character facing to the left. When the character should be facing right, we will use a parameter of the SpriteBatch.Draw() method to flip the image horizontally. The Flipped property will keep track of the character's current facing.

Our player will have the ability to jump, but logically should only be able to jump when standing on the ground. Jumping while already in the air would certainly produce strange results. The OnGround property will be set to True whenever the player has come to rest on a solid floor block, indicating to the jump code that a jump is allowed.

Recall that in our level editor we created a CodeValue entry called **Enemy Blocking**, which indicates that a particular square is impassable to enemies, while not restricting player movement the way the Passable flag does. If the CodeBasedBlocks variable is set to True, our collision detection code will take these blocks into account when detecting impassable walls and floors. For all game objects except the player, this value will be True, so that is the default set in the declaration.

In order to draw the GameObject to the screen and have it displayed at the appropriate depth compared to the tile map layers, we need to specify Single that will be passed as the layerDepth parameter to the SpriteBatch.Draw() method. In this case, the DrawDepth property is set to 0.85. When our tile layers are drawn, they are drawn at depths of 1.0 and 0.9 for the background and interactive layers, and 0.7 for the foreground layer.

This means that game objects will be drawn behind the foreground layer but above the background and interactive layers, allowing for objects such as doors to be placed on the interactive layer over a background and still have the player walk in front of them.

Unlike a Sprite, the GameObject does not contain any texture data of its own, so the last piece of information we need to track is the list of available animations for the object. These are stored in the _animations Dictionary object, indexed by the name we will assign to the animation when it is loaded—names such as idle, run, and jump. The _currentAnimation string variable holds the name of the currently playing animation.

Drawing, animation, and movement

Now that we have the basics of the GameObject class, we need to be able to draw the appropriate AnimationStrip to the display and allow the object to move.

Time for action – building the GameObject class – part 2

1. Add the updateAnimation() helper method to the GameObject class:

```
#Region "Helper Methods"
Private Sub updateAnimation(gameTime As GameTime)
    If _animations.ContainsKey(CurrentAnimation) Then
        If _animations(CurrentAnimation).FinishedPlaying Then
            PlayAnimation(_animations(CurrentAnimation).
                NextAnimation)
        Else
            _animations(CurrentAnimation).Update(gameTime)
        End If
    End If
End Sub
#End Region
```

2. Add a new region called **Public Methods** to the GameObject class:

```
#Region "Public Methods"
#End Region
```

3. Inside the **Public Methods** region, add the PlayAnimation() method:

```
Public Sub PlayAnimation(name As String)
    If Not IsNothing(name) AndAlso _animations.ContainsKey(name)
Then
        _currentAnimation = name
        _animations(name).Play()
    End If
End Sub
```

4. Still in the **Public Methods** region, add the Update() method:

```
Public Overridable Sub Update(gameTime As GameTime)
    If Not Enabled Then
        Return
    End If

    Dim elapsed As Single
    Elapsed = CSng(gameTime.ElapsedGameTime.TotalSeconds)
```

```
    updateAnimation(gameTime)

    If Velocity.Y <> 0 Then
        OnGround = False
    End If

    Dim moveAmount As Vector2 = velocity * elapsed

    moveAmount = horizontalCollisionTest(moveAmount)
    moveAmount = verticalCollisionTest(moveAmount)

    Dim newPosition As Vector2 = worldLocation + moveAmount

    newPosition = new Vector2(
        MathHelper.Clamp(newPosition.X, 0,
          Camera.WorldRectangle.Width - _frameWidth),
        MathHelper.Clamp(newPosition.Y, 2*(-TileMap.TileHeight),
          Camera.WorldRectangle.Height - _frameHeight))

    worldLocation = newPosition
End Sub
```

5. Still in the **Public Methods** region, add the `Draw()` method:

```
Public Overridable Sub Draw(spriteBatch As SpriteBatch)
    If Not Enabled Then
        Return
    End If

    If _animations.ContainsKey(CurrentAnimation) Then
        Dim effect As SpriteEffects = SpriteEffects.None

        If Flipped Then
            effect = SpriteEffects.FlipHorizontally
        End If

        spriteBatch.Draw(
            _animations(currentAnimation).Texture,
            Camera.WorldToScreen(WorldRectangle),
            _animations(currentAnimation).FrameRectangle,
            Color.White, 0.0, Vector2.Zero, effect, DrawDepth)
    End If
End Sub
```

What just happened?

The `updateAnimation()` helper method is called from the `Update()` method itself and is broken up for the sake of readability. The method first checks to make sure that an animation with the name corresponding to the value of `CurrentAnimation` actually exists in the animations dictionary. If it does, and the current animation has finished playing, the `updateAnimation()` method will use the `PlayAnimation()` method to begin playing the animation indicated by the `NextAnimation` property of the currently playing `AnimationStrip`.

If the current animation has not completed, its own `Update()` method is called, allowing the `AnimationStrip` to advance to the current frame.

The `PlayAnimation()` method itself also checks to make sure if the value passed to it is a valid animation for this `GameObject`. If it is, the object's `_currentAnimation` is set, and the named animation's `Play()` method is executed.

When the `Update()` method of the `GameObject` is called, it verifies that the object is `Enabled` and calls the `updateAnimation()` helper method. Next, the `Update()` method checks to see if the object's current velocity has a Y component that is not zero. If it does, we know that we cannot be on the ground and set the `OnGround` variable to `False`.

In order to determine where our `GameObject` will move during this frame, we multiply the velocity (in our standard pixels per second scale) by the elapsed game time for this frame, resulting in the movement we wish the `GameObject` to have for the frame.

This movement, however, can be restricted by surrounding game tiles. In order to determine which portions of our movement are available to us, we will call the `horizontalCollisionTest()` and `verticalCollisionTest()` methods, which we will implement in just a moment. The result of these two methods is to modify the `moveAmount` variable to account for any potential collisions, so after they have been tested we can add the move amount to the current position of the `GameObject`.

However, we do not apply it directly. First, we create a `Vector2` variable called `newPosition` and then use `MathHelper.Clamp()` to limit the object's position to the area of the game board, with the exception of the top of the screen. By specifying `2*(-TileMap.TileHeight)` as the minimum value for the vertical component of the `newPosition` vector, we allow the `GameObject` to actually be positioned up to two tiles above the top of the game map. This will allow our player (in a manner very similar to a certain red-clad plumber who has been known to run about in a tile-based world from time to time) to jump slightly above the screen.

When the `GameObject` is drawn, we establish a value for the `SpriteEffects` parameter of the `SpriteBatch.Draw()` call by examining the `Flipped` property. The texture for the object is retrieved from the currently playing `AnimationStrip`, and the sprite is drawn at the predefined drawing depth.

Map-based collision detection

As we did with Robot Rampage, we split map-based collision detection into horizontal and vertical components. We process the horizontal component first, and then the vertical component based upon the results of the horizontal check.

Why perform these checks separately? Consider the following diagram showing the requested movement of the player's character:

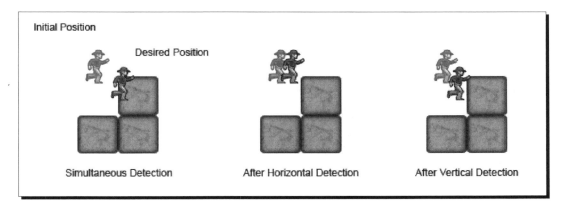

If we process both the horizontal and vertical collision checks at the same time, the GameObject will become suspended in mid-air, unable to fall downwards because the horizontal component of the object's movement would place the object inside a wall. Simply checking the new collision box will result in the entirety of the movement being negated.

By checking the horizontal movement first, the player can bump up against the wall block, stopping his horizontal movement. When the vertical component of the movement is then checked separately, the player can fall downwards toward the floor because the collision box has been adjusted for the new horizontal movement (or lack thereof) and will not result in a wall collision when testing for vertical movement.

Time for action – building the GameObject class – part 3

1. Add the map-based collision detection methods to the GameObject class:

```
#Region "Map-Based Collision Detection Methods"
Private Function horizontalCollisionTest(
    moveAmount As Vector2) As Vector2

    If moveAmount.X = 0 Then
        Return moveAmount
    End If
```

```
    Dim afterMoveRect As Rectangle = CollisionRectangle
    afterMoveRect.Offset(CInt(moveAmount.X),0)
    Dim corner1 As Vector2
    Dim corner2 As Vector2

    If moveAmount.X < 0 Then
        corner1 = New Vector2(afterMoveRect.Left,
                              afterMoveRect.Top + 1)
        corner2 = New Vector2(afterMoveRect.Left,
                              afterMoveRect.Bottom - 1)
    Else
        corner1 = New Vector2(afterMoveRect.Right,
                              afterMoveRect.Top + 1)
        corner2 = New Vector2(afterMoveRect.Right,
                              afterMoveRect.Bottom - 1)
    End If

    Dim mapCell1 As Vector2 = TileMap.GetCellByPixel(corner1)
    Dim mapCell2 As Vector2 = TileMap.GetCellByPixel(corner2)

    If (Not TileMap.CellIsPassable(mapCell1)) Or
        (Not TileMap.CellIsPassable(mapCell2)) Then
        moveAmount.X = 0
        _Velocity.X = 0
    End If

    If CodeBasedBlocks Then
        If (TileMap.CellCodeValue(mapCell1) = "BLOCK") Or
            (TileMap.CellCodeValue(mapCell2) = "BLOCK") Then

            moveAmount.X = 0
            _Velocity.X = 0
        End If
    End If

    Return moveAmount
End Function

Private Function verticalCollisionTest(
    moveAmount As Vector2) As Vector2

    If moveAmount.Y = 0 Then
        Return moveAmount
    End If
```

```
        Dim afterMoveRect As Rectangle = CollisionRectangle
        afterMoveRect.Offset(CInt(moveAmount.X), CInt(moveAmount.Y))
        Dim corner1 As Vector2
        Dim corner2 As Vector2

        If moveAmount.Y < 0 Then
            corner1 = new Vector2(afterMoveRect.Left + 1,
                                afterMoveRect.Top)
            corner2 = new Vector2(afterMoveRect.Right - 1 ,
                                afterMoveRect.Top)
        Else
            corner1 = new Vector2(afterMoveRect.Left + 1,
                                afterMoveRect.Bottom)
            corner2 = new Vector2(afterMoveRect.Right - 1 ,
                                afterMoveRect.Bottom)
        End If

        Dim mapCell1 As Vector2 = TileMap.GetCellByPixel(corner1)
        Dim mapCell2 As Vector2 = TileMap.GetCellByPixel(corner2)

        If (Not TileMap.CellIsPassable(mapCell1)) Or
           (Not TileMap.CellIsPassable(mapCell2)) Then

            If moveAmount.Y > 0 Then
                OnGround = True
            End If

            moveAmount.Y = 0
            _Velocity.Y = 0
        End If

        If CodeBasedBlocks Then
            If (TileMap.CellCodeValue(mapCell1) = "BLOCK") Or
               (TileMap.CellCodeValue(mapCell2) = "BLOCK") Then

                If moveAmount.Y > 0 Then
                    OnGround = true
                End If

                moveAmount.Y = 0
                _Velocity.Y = 0
            End If
        End IF

        Return moveAmount
    End Function

#End Region
```

What just happened?

Our collision detection methods begin by building a rectangle that represents the location that the GameObject will be in if the requested movement is completed. They do this by taking a copy of the current CollisionRectangle property for the object and offsetting it by the movement amount.

In the case of horizontal movement, which is checked first, only the X component of the movement is considered. When afterMoveRect is constructed for the vertical movement check, we also apply the horizontal movement, since it would have been corrected for horizontal collision detection already.

In order to actually test for collisions, we only need to check the two outermost pixels of the new movement area. For example, in the previous diagram, the player's character is moving to the right. By checking the upper-right and lower-right pixels during the horizontal collision detection method, we will cover moving right into any impassable map square, because our character is the same size as a map tile.

After determining the pixel locations of these two corners, we can retrieve their tile map values and check CellIsPassable() to determine if the square should block movement. If this game entity is also blocked by invisible CodeValue blocks (CodeBasedBlocks is true), we also check to see if the squares we are testing against contain the code **BLOCK** and disallow movement into them, if so.

We have one special case to handle for vertical movement—setting the value of OnGround when the player is standing on a surface. By setting this value to True whenever we detect an impassable block while travelling in a positive Y direction, we can indicate to the later code that the player can jump from their current position.

The player

Now that we have the GameObject class to base the components of our game world on, we can begin creating the entities that will populate the game. We will start with the player and put enough temporary code into place in the Game1 class to move and animate the brown-clad archaeologist adventurer.

Time for action – creating the Player class

1. In the Gemstone Hunter project, add a new class called Player.

2. Add the following Imports directive to the top of the Player class file:

```
Imports Tile_Engine
```

3. Modify the declaration of the Player class to inherit from the GameObject class:

```
Public Class Player
    Inherits GameObject
```

4. Add declarations to the Player class:

```
#Region "Declarations"
Private _fallSpeed As Vector2 = new Vector2(0, 20)
Private _moveScale As Single = 180
Private _dead As Boolean = false
#End Region
```

5. Add the Dead property to the Player class:

```
#Region "Properties"
Public ReadOnly Property Dead As Boolean
    Get
        Return _dead
    End Get
End Property
#End Region
```

6. Create a constructor for the Player class:

```
#Region "Constructor"
Public Sub New(content As ContentManager)
    _animations.Add("idle",
      new AnimationStrip(
        content.Load(Of Texture2D)("Textures\Sprites\Player\
Idle"),
        48,
        "idle"))
    _animations("idle").LoopAnimation = True

    _animations.Add("run",
      new AnimationStrip(
        content.Load(Of Texture2D)("Textures\Sprites\Player\Run"),
        48,
        "run"))
    _animations("run").LoopAnimation = True

    _animations.Add("jump",
      new AnimationStrip(
        content.Load(Of Texture2D)("Textures\Sprites\Player\
Jump"),
```

```
        48,
        "jump"))
    _animations("jump").LoopAnimation = False
    _animations("jump").FrameLength = 0.08
    _animations("jump").NextAnimation = "idle"

    _animations.Add("die",
      new AnimationStrip(
        content.Load(Of Texture2D)("Textures\Sprites\Player\Die"),
        48,
        "die"))
    _animations("die").LoopAnimation = False

    _frameWidth = 48
    _frameHeight = 48
    CollisionRectangle = New Rectangle(9, 1, 30, 46)

    DrawDepth = 0.825f

    Enabled = True
    codeBasedBlocks = False
    PlayAnimation("idle")
  End Sub
#End Region
```

7. In the `Game1` class for the Gemstone Hunter project, add a declaration for an instance of the `Player` class:

```
Private _player As Player
```

8. In the `Initialize()` method of the `Game1` class, set the window size for the game:

```
Me.graphics.PreferredBackBufferWidth = 800
Me.graphics.PreferredBackBufferHeight = 600
Me.graphics.ApplyChanges()
```

9. In the `LoadContent()` method of the `Game1` class that was carried over from Chapter 8, *Gemstone Hunter—Put on your Platform Shoes*, remove the line that reads `TileMap.SetTileAtCell(3,3,1,10)`.

10. Still in the `LoadContent()` method, add the following to initialize the player:

```
_player = New Player(Content)
_player.WorldLocation = New Vector2(350, 300)
```

11. Add the following to the `Update()` method of the `Game1` class:

```
_player.Update(gameTime)
```

12. Add the following code to the `Draw()` method of the `Game1` class inside the existing `spriteBatch.Begin()` and `spriteBatch.End()` block:

```
_player.Draw(spriteBatch)
```

13. Right-click on the Gemstone Hunter project in Solution Explorer and select **Set as StartUp Project**.

14. Execute the Gemstone Hunter project to view the player:

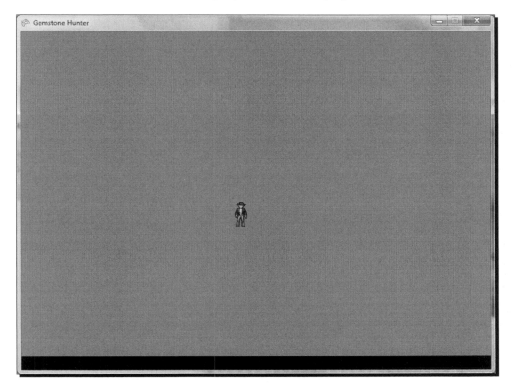

What just happened?

Our `Player` class currently needs only three member variables beyond those that already exist in the `GameObject` class— `_fallSpeed` to determine the rate of acceleration when the player is falling, `_moveScale` to determine how fast the player runs when moving along the X axis, and `_dead` to flag when the character has been killed. We will be adding a few more items to this list in later sections as we expand on the features of the game.

The constructor for the `Player` class does all of the work of initializing various `AnimationStrip` used by the class, including an animation for running, jumping, player death, and standing idle. Individual properties are set on these animations based on how we wish to play them.

For example, the idle and running animations have their `LoopAnimation` property set to true. While these animations are active, we want them to cycle in a continuous loop until we set the current animation to something else. Because these animations loop, there is no need to specify a `NextAnimation` value. It will never be activated.

The jumping animation, on the other hand, should only be played once when the player jumps. After completing, the animation will default back to idle, assuming the player is not pressing any movement keys at the time the animation ends.

Finally, the animation named `die` neither loops, nor has a `NextAnimation` setting. In this case, we want the animation to play once, and then continue to display the final frame of the player lying on the ground until we take an action to respawn the player, reload the level, or transition to a **Game Over** state.

In steps 7 through 12, we implement just enough code to allow us to display the player object to the screen, setting up the game world, and creating the player object inside it. Of course, at the moment the player cannot move, run, jump, or animate!

Running...

We will override the `Update()` method of the `GameObject` in the `Player` class to handle user input and handle switching between animations as appropriate. We will build the `Update()` method in several stages, adding functionality with each iteration.

Time for action – overriding the Update() method – part 1

1. Create a new region in the `Player` class for `Public Methods`:

```
#Region "Public Methods"
#End Region
```

2. Add the initial `Update()` override method to the `Public Methods` region of the `Player` class:

```
Public Overrides Sub Update(gameTime As GameTime)
   If Not Dead Then
      Dim newAnimation As String = "idle"

      Velocity = New Vector2(0, Velocity.Y)

      Dim padState As GamePadState = GamePad.GetState(PlayerIndex.
One)
```

```
      Dim keyState As KeyboardState = Keyboard.GetState()

      If (keyState.IsKeyDown(Keys.Left) Or
          (padState.ThumbSticks.Left.X < -0.3F)) Then
          Flipped = False
          newAnimation = "run"
          Velocity = New Vector2(-_moveScale, Velocity.Y)
      End If

      If (keyState.IsKeyDown(Keys.Right) Or
          (padState.ThumbSticks.Left.X > 0.3F)) Then
          Flipped = True
          newAnimation = "run"
          Velocity = New Vector2(_moveScale, Velocity.Y)
      End If

      If newAnimation <> CurrentAnimation Then
          PlayAnimation(newAnimation)
      End IF
    End If

  MyBase.Update(gameTime)
End Sub
```

3. Execute the Gemstone Hunter project and move the player left and right:

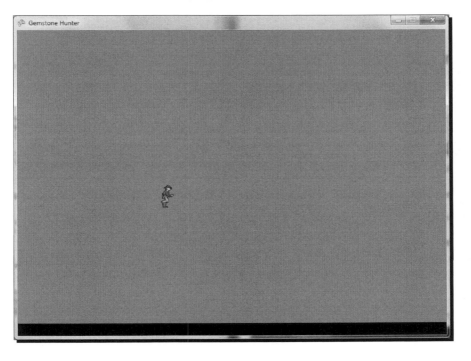

What just happened?

The animation that the player object will display will be determined by the current input state. By default, we will assume that there is no input and the animation should be changed to idle.

We then zero out the X component of the player's velocity, again assuming that there is no input and, therefore, no lateral movement. The state of the gamepad and the keyboard are captured and then the current input values are evaluated.

If the player indicates via the keyboard or the gamepad that they wish to move left or right, we set the `newAnimation` variable to run and set the X component of the velocity vector to the `_moveScale` value, negating it for left movement and leaving the value positive for right movement.

When moving left, the `Flipped` property is set to false. Moving right sets the property to true. If neither left nor right movement is made, the value of `Flipped` is left unchanged. Recall that when the `AnimationStrip` is drawn, `Flipped` will be used to produce both left and right images from the same bitmap.

Finally, right before calling `MyBase.Update()` to allow the normal `GameObject` update process to take place, the value that we wish to assign for animation is checked against the animation that is currently playing. If they are already the same, no change is made. If the `newAnimation` value is different from `CurrentAnimation`, the new animation is played. Without this check, a player running would always display the first frame of the running animation, appearing to glide without animating because the animation would be restarted (by the `Play()` method) in every frame.

...and jumping

Currently, our player begins near the center of an empty screen and can run left or right but has no vertical movement capability. In order to allow the player to jump, we will also need to allow the player to fall.

Time for action – overriding the Update() method – part 2

1. Inside the `Public Methods` region of the `Player` class, add the `Jump()` method:

```
Public Sub Jump()
    Velocity = New Vector2(Velocity.X, -500)
End Sub
```

2. Add the following code to the `Update()` method right after the `if` statement for detecting movement to the right, and before the check for which animation to play:

```
If (keyState.IsKeyDown(Keys.Space) Or
    (padState.Buttons.A = ButtonState.Pressed)) Then
```

```
        If OnGround Then
            Jump()
            newAnimation = "jump"
        End If
    End If

    If CurrentAnimation = "jump" Then
        newAnimation = "jump"
    End If
```

3. Still in the `Update()` method, add the following line right before the call to `MyBase.Update()` (outside of the conditional for the player being dead—being dead will not prevent the player's body from falling due to gravity):

```
    Velocity += _fallSpeed
```

4. Execute the Gemstone Hunter project. Use the *Space* bar or the A button on the gamepad to jump.

What just happened?

When you execute the game, the player will fall with increasing speed and land on the bottom of the window. Even though we are not currently displaying a map, the bounds of the map are considered impassable.

Our simple simulation of gravity (adding 20 downward pixels per second to the player's current velocity) means that all we need to do to initiate a jump is to set the Y component of the player's velocity to a larger negative number. As the player rises, our gravity will slow them down, eventually stopping and reversing the movement upward.

Finally, notice that no matter what we have indicated from other movement commands, the jump animation will override them. Additionally, if the jump animation is already playing (`CurrentAnimation = "jump"`), we also set `newAnimation` to jump, so as not to interrupt it.

The jump animation has a `NextAnimation` property, which will ensure that it runs once and then returns to idle. Just as before, this check is to make the animation appear smoothly. Without it, the first frame of the jump animation would play, and if the player were pressing the left or right arrow keys at that time, the run animation would take over, preventing the full jump animation from playing. The full jump animation looks like this:

Staying on the screen

One issue that is evident right away is that you can simply run straight off the right edge of the screen, and the game's camera does not follow your character. We can fix this by adding a helper method to the player class.

Time for action – repositioning the camera

1. Add the `Helper Methods` region and the `repositionCamera()` method to the `Player` class:

```
#Region "Helper Methods"
Private Sub repositionCamera()
    Dim screenLocX As Integer
    screenLocX = CInt(Int(Camera.WorldToScreen(worldLocation).X))

    If screenLocX > 500 Then
        Camera.Move(New Vector2(screenLocX - 500, 0))
    End If

    If screenLocX < 200 Then
        Camera.Move(New Vector2(screenLocX - 200, 0))
    End If
End Sub
#End Region
```

2. In the `Update()` method of the `Player` class, add a call to reposition the camera right before the call to `MyBase.Update()`:

```
repositionCamera()
```

3. Execute the Gemstone Hunter application and move towards the right side of the screen.

What just happened?

During each update frame, the current screen position of the character is checked. If the character has gotten too close to the edge of the screen (200 pixels from the left edge, or 300 pixels from the right edge), the camera's position is adjusted to keep the character within those bounds.

If the camera is already as far in either direction as it can go, nothing will happen—this behavior is built into the `Camera` class. This allows the character to move to the edge of the map instead of requiring us to impose some kind of artificial barrier in the game world.

At the moment, however, we are still running around on a huge empty expanse. It may be a bit difficult to recognize that the camera is in fact scrolling when you get near the edge of the screen. To resolve that problem, we need to begin displaying our level map.

Loading levels

Included in the content package for the Gemstone Hunter game are a few `.MAP` files in their own folder. These maps were created using the **Level Editor**, and we will use them to implement level loading. Feel free to replace these files with the levels of your own design!

The LevelManager module

Initially, our `LevelManager` module will only be responsible for loading MAP files into the `TileEngine`. As we add entities (enemies and gemstones) to the game, `LevelManager` will be expanded to track and control them as well.

Time for action – building the LevelManager module

1. Right-click on the **Gemstone Hunter Content** project and add a new folder called `Maps`.

2. Add the `MAP000.MAP` and `MAP001.MAP` sample maps from `0669_08_GRAPHICPACK` to the `Maps` folder.

3. Click on each .MAP file in the Solution Explorer and, in the Properties window, set the **Build Action** to **None** and the **Copy to Output Directory** property to **Copy if newer**.

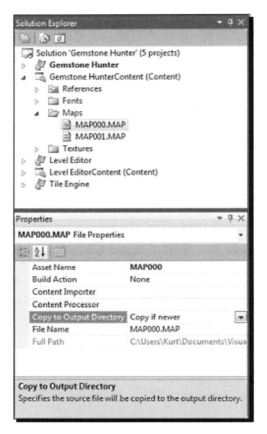

4. Add a new module called LevelManager to the **Gemstone Hunter** project.

5. Add the following Imports directive to the top of the LevelManager module file:

```
Imports Tile_Engine
```

6. Modify the declaration of the LevelManager module to make it Public:

```
Public Module LevelManager
```

7. Add declarations to the `LevelManager` module:

```
#Region "Declarations"
Private _content As ContentManager
Private _player As Player
Private _currentLevel As Integer
#End Region
```

8. Add the properties to the `LevelManager` module:

```
#Region "Properties"
Public ReadOnly Property CurrentLevel As Integer
    Get
        Return _currentLevel
    End Get
End Property

Public Property RespawnLocation As Vector2
#End Region
```

9. Add the `Initialize()` method to the `LevelManager` module:

```
#Region "Initialization"
Public Sub Initialize(
    Content As ContentManager,
    gamePlayer As Player)

    _content = content
    _player = gamePlayer
End Sub
#End Region
```

10. Create a new region in the `LevelManager` module for `Public Methods`:

```
#Region "Public Methods"
#End Region
```

11. Add the `LoadLevel()` method to the `Public Methods` region of the `LevelManager` module:

```
Public Sub LoadLevel(levelNumber As Integer)
    TileMap.LoadMap(
        CType(TitleContainer.OpenStream(
            "Content\Maps\MAP" +
            levelNumber.ToString().PadLeft(3, CChar("0")) +
".MAP"),
            System.IO.FileStream))
```

```
        For x As Integer = 0 To TileMap.MapWidth - 1
            For y As Integer = 0 To TileMap.MapHeight - 1
                If TileMap.CellCodeValue(x, y) = "START" Then
                    _player.WorldLocation = New Vector2(
                        x * TileMap.TileWidth,
                        y * TileMap.TileHeight)
                End If
            Next
        Next

        _currentLevel = levelNumber
        RespawnLocation = _player.WorldLocation
End Sub
```

12. Add the `ReloadLevel()` method to the `Public Methods` region of the `LevelManager` module:

```
Public Sub ReloadLevel()
    Dim saveRespawn As Vector2 = RespawnLocation
    LoadLevel(CurrentLevel)
    RespawnLocation = saveRespawn
    _player.WorldLocation = RespawnLocation
End Sub
```

13. In the `LoadContent()` method of the `Game1` class, remove the line that positions the player (`_player.WorldLocation = New Vector2(350, 300)`).

14. Modify the `LoadContent()` method of the `Game1` class by adding the following code to the end of the method:

```
LevelManager.Initialize(Content, _player)
LevelManager.LoadLevel(0)
```

15. Execute the Gemstone Hunter application:

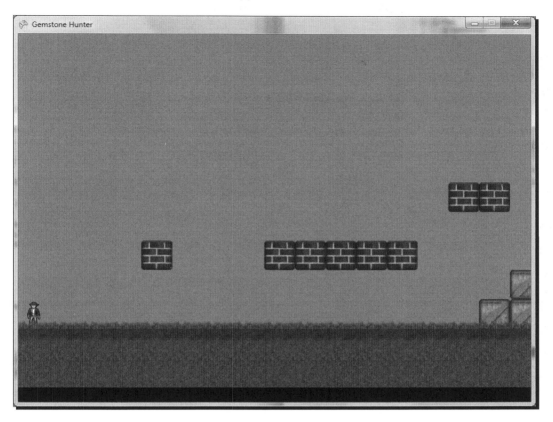

What just happened?

The `LevelManager` holds on to references for the game's `ContentManager` instance and the active instance of the `Player` class. In the case of the player, we need this reference so that we can position the player after a level has been loaded.

The `ContentManager` instance is not used yet, but we will be passing it along to our `Enemy` and `Gemstone` classes when we create instances of them shortly.

To load a map, we use the XNA's `TitleContainer` object to retrieve a stream located within the `Content` folder deployed with our game. We pass this stream to the `LoadMap()` method of the `TileMap`, causing it to load the map for us. The MAP files produced by the **Level Editor** project are named `MAPXXX.MAP`, where `XXX` represents a three-digit number. We use the `PadLeft()` method to fill in any missing leading zeros when determining the name of the map file to load.

After `LoadMap()` has finished, the `LoadLevel()` method examines each square on the map, looking for a `START` code value. If it finds one, the player will be moved to that location on the map. We will expand on this loop later to spawn enemies and gemstones when a level loads.

> **Layer depth and draw order**
>
> In the previous section, when we added the `_player.Draw()` call to the `Game1` class's `Draw()` method, we did not specify where to place it in relation to the existing `TileMap.Draw()` call that was already there, because we are using layer depth sorting. If we draw the map after the player, the player will still appear above the background and interactive layers as we would expect.
>
> Keep in mind, however, that when multiple items with the same layer depth are drawn, the most recently drawn object will appear above any previously drawn objects at that layer depth, just like the default functionality when layer depth sorting is not used and all sprites are drawn at 0.0.

We keep track of the current level and a vector location at which to respawn the player so that we can reload the level if the player dies. Since door transitions will be able to place the player at a location other than that marked with a `START` level code, we track the respawn location separately so we can restart the level at the place the player entered it.

Gemstones

As Gemstone Hunter stands right now, you can explore your first world map, but there is nothing in it. Any `GEM` and `ENEMY` codes assigned to map squares currently do nothing inside the game itself.

The first non-player object we will add to the game world will be the gemstones that the main character is seeking to collect while playing.

Time for action – building the Gemstone class

1. Add a new class called `Gemstone` to the Gemstone Hunter project.

2. Add the following `Imports` directive to the top of the `Gemstone` class file:

```
Imports Tile_Engine
```

3. Add an `Inherits` line to the class declaration to derive it from `GameObject`:

```
Public Class Gemstone
    Inherits GameObject
```

4. Add a constructor for the `Gemstone` class:

```
#Region "Constructor"
Public Sub New(
    content As ContentManager,
    cellX As Integer,
    cellY As Integer)

    WorldLocation = New Vector2(
        TileMap.TileWidth * cellX,
        TileMap.TileHeight * cellY)

    _frameWidth = TileMap.TileWidth
    _frameHeight = TileMap.TileHeight

    _animations.Add("idle",
        New AnimationStrip(
            Content.Load(Of Texture2D)("Textures\Gem"),
            48,
            "idle"))

    _animations("idle").LoopAnimation = True
    _animations("idle").FrameLength = 0.15
    PlayAnimation("idle")
    DrawDepth = 0.875f
    CollisionRectangle = New Rectangle(9, 24, 30, 24)
    Enabled = True
End Sub
#End Region
```

5. Back in the `LevelManager` module, add a declaration to hold a list of gemstones:

```
Private _gemstones As List(Of Gemstone) = New List(Of Gemstone)()
```

6. In the `LoadLevel()` method of the `LevelManager` module, right after the call to `TileMap.LoadMap()`, clear the gemstones list:

```
_gemstones.Clear()
```

7. Still in the `LoadLevel()` method, add a condition to the loop that examines the code values in each square to check for GEM codes. This can be placed right after the condition for START codes:

```
If TileMap.CellCodeValue(x, y) = "GEM" Then
    _gemstones.Add(new Gemstone(_content, x, y))
End If
```

8. Add a new `Update()` method to the `LevelManager` module:

```
Public Sub Update(gameTime As GameTime)
    For Each gem As Gemstone In _gemstones
        gem.Update(gameTime)
    Next
End Sub
```

9. Add a new `Draw()` method to the `LevelManager` module:

```
Public Sub Draw(spriteBatch As SpriteBatch)
    For Each gem As Gemstone In _gemstones
        gem.Draw(spriteBatch)
    Next
End Sub
```

10. In the `Game1` class, call the `Update()` method of `LevelManager` after the player has been updated:

```
LevelManager.Update(gameTime)
```

11. Still in the `Game1` class, modify the `Draw()` method to include a call to draw the level manager right after the player has been drawn:

```
LevelManager.Draw(spriteBatch)
```

12. Execute the Gemstone Hunter application:

What just happened?

Since our `GameObject` class provides all of the behavior we need for gemstones, our `Gemstone` class only needs a constructor, which will load the appropriate `AnimationStrip` and initialize its location and collision area.

We have updated the `LoadLevel()` method in the `LevelManager` class to scan the level for GEM code values and create gems at these locations. Since the `Gemstone` class defines no movement capabilities, the gemstones will remain stationary in the blocks they spawn in, not subject to the whims of gravity.

Scoring

The player needs to be able to pick up the gemstones and receive points for doing so. In order to allow for this, we will need to make a handful of additions to the `Player` class and further modify the `LevelManager` class to detect collisions between the player and the gemstones spawned in the world.

Time for action – implementing score tracking

1. Add a property to the `Player` class to hold the player's score:

```
Public Property Score As Integer
```

2. Replace the current `Update()` method in the `LevelManager` class with the following new version of the method:

```
Public Sub Update(gameTime As GameTime)
    If Not _player.Dead Then
        For x As Integer = _gemstones.Count - 1 To 0 Step - 1
            _gemstones(x).Update(gameTime)
            If _player.CollisionRectangle.Intersects(
                _gemstones(x).CollisionRectangle) Then

                _gemstones.RemoveAt(x)
                _player.Score += 10
            End IF
        Next
    End If
End Sub
```

3. In the `Game1` class, add a declaration for a `SpriteFont` instance that we can use to draw the player's score and a vector pointing to the location on the screen where the score will be displayed:

```
Private pericles8 As SpriteFont
Private scorePosition As Vector2 = New Vector2(20, 580)
```

4. In the `LoadContent()` method of the `Game1` class, initialize the `pericles8` font:

```
pericles8 = Content.Load(Of SpriteFont)("Fonts\Pericles8")
```

5. In the `Draw()` method of the `Game1` class, add a call to display the current score right before the `spriteBatch.End()` call:

```
spriteBatch.DrawString(
    pericles8,
    "Score: " + _player.Score.ToString(),
    scorePosition,
    Color.White)
```

6. Execute the Gemstone Hunter application and collect a few gemstones:

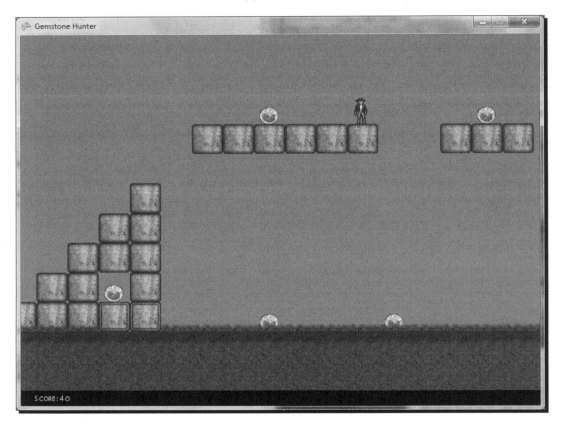

What just happened?

When called, the `LevelManager.Update()` method checks each of the gemstones that exist for the current level and compares their `CollisionRectangle` properties to the same property of the player object. If these rectangles intersect, the gemstone is removed from the `_gemstones` list and the player's score is incremented. Remember that we need to use a reverse-running `for` loop here, because we will potentially modify the contents of the list, and a `for each` loop would throw an exception if the list is modified during the loop.

Enemies

Gemstone Hunter is pretty easy right now. You are free to run around collecting all of the gems you want at your own pace with no chance of ever triggering the dreaded `die` animation. Not for much longer, though—time to add some zombies to the mix!

As with the `Player` and `Gemstone` classes, the `Enemy` class will be derived from the `GameObject` class, allowing it to exist within the world and, like the `Player` class, detect collisions with the tile map.

Time for action – summoning the zombies

1. Add a new class called `Enemy` to the Gemstone Hunter project.

2. Add the following `Imports` directive to the top of the `Enemy` class file:

   ```
   Imports Tile_Engine
   ```

3. Add an `Inherits` line to derive the `Enemy` class from `GameObject`:

   ```
   Public Class Enemy
       Inherits GameObject
   ```

4. Add declarations for the `Enemy` class:

   ```
   #Region "Declarations"
   Private _fallSpeed As Vector2 = New Vector2(0, 20)
   Private _walkSpeed As Single = 60
   Private _facingLeft As Boolean = True
   #End Region
   ```

5. Add a property to the `Enemy` class:

   ```
   #Region "Properties"
   Public Property Dead As Boolean
   #End Region
   ```

6. Add a constructor for the Enemy class:

```
#Region "Constructor"
Public Sub New(
    content As ContentManager,
    cellX As Integer,
    cellY As Integer)

    _animations.Add("idle",
        New AnimationStrip(
            content.Load(Of Texture2D)(
                "Textures\Sprites\MonsterC\Idle"),
            48,
            "idle"))
    _animations("idle").LoopAnimation = True

    _animations.Add("run",
        New AnimationStrip(
            content.Load(Of Texture2D)(
                "Textures\Sprites\MonsterC\Run"),
            48,
            "run"))
    _animations("run").FrameLength = 0.1
    _animations("run").LoopAnimation = True

    _animations.Add("die",
        New AnimationStrip(
            content.Load(Of Texture2D)(
                "Textures\Sprites\MonsterC\Die"),
            48,
            "die"))
    _animations("die").LoopAnimation = False

    _frameWidth = 48
    _frameHeight = 48
    CollisionRectangle = New Rectangle(9, 1, 30, 46)

    WorldLocation = new Vector2(
        cellX * TileMap.TileWidth,
        cellY * TileMap.TileHeight)

    Enabled = True

    CodeBasedBlocks = True
    PlayAnimation("run")
End Sub
#End Region
```

7. Override the `Update()` method in the `Enemy` class:

```
#Region "Public Methods"
Public Overrides Sub Update(gameTime As GameTime)
    Dim oldLocation As Vector2 = WorldLocation

    If Not Dead Then
        Velocity = New Vector2(0, Velocity.Y)

        Dim direction As Vector2 = New Vector2(1, 0)
        Flipped = True

        If _facingLeft Then
            direction = New Vector2(-1, 0)
            Flipped = False
        End IF
        direction *= _walkSpeed
        Velocity += direction
        velocity += _fallSpeed
    End If

    MyBase.Update(gameTime)

    If Not Dead Then
        If oldLocation = WorldLocation Then
            _facingLeft = Not _facingLeft
        End IF
    Else
        If _animations(CurrentAnimation).FinishedPlaying Then
            Enabled = False
        End If
    End If
End Sub
#End Region
```

8. Add a new list declaration to the `LevelManager` module to handle the `Enemy` objects:

```
Private _enemies As List(Of Enemy) = New List(Of Enemy)()
```

9. In the `LoadLevel()` method of the `LevelManager` module, clear the enemies list right after the call to `_gemstones.Clear()`:

```
_enemies.Clear()
```

10. In the `LoadLevel()` method of the `LevelManager` class, add a new `if` statement section to the loop that currently examines each square for `START` and `GEM` code values. Place this section after the check for `GEM` codes:

```
If TileMap.CellCodeValue(x, y) = "ENEMY" Then
    _enemies.Add(new Enemy(_content, x, y))
End If
```

11. Modify the `Update()` method of the `LevelManager` to update enemies. Add the following code below the loop that updates the `_gemstones` list, but inside the `If Not _player.Dead Then` code block:

```
For Each thisEnemy As Enemy In _enemies
    thisEnemy.Update(gameTime)
Next
```

12. Modify the `Draw()` method of the `LevelManager` class by adding a loop to draw each enemy after the gemstones have been drawn:

```
For Each thisEnemy As Enemy In _enemies
    thisEnemy.Draw(spriteBatch)
Next
```

13. Execute the Gemstone Hunter application and observe the enemies as they move through the level:

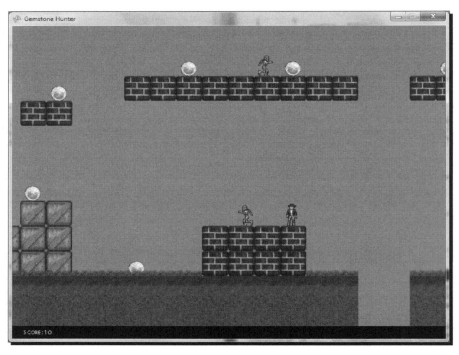

What just happened?

The construction of the Enemy class is very similar to the Player class we built earlier, except that we do not need to handle input for enemies. All of our enemies utilize a very simple artificial intelligence: walk in a direction until you bump into something, and then turn around.

During the Update() method, we store the enemy's current location before any movement takes place. Assuming the enemy is not dead, we then generate a vector pointing in the direction of the zombie's movement—(1, 0) if facing right, and (-1, 0) if facing left.

We multiply the direction vector by the enemy's walk speed (slower than the player—it is a zombie, after all) and add their directional movement to their velocity. We then add the fall acceleration due to gravity to their vertical velocity.

The next step in the Update() method is to call MyBase.Update() to allow the Update() code of GameObject to process the enemy's movement. Again checking to make sure that the enemy is not dead, we compare the enemy's position after MyBase.Update() to the position we stored at the beginning of the method. If the position is the same, we know that the enemy's movement was halted by running into a wall, and negate the _facingLeft variable to turn the enemy around.

If the enemy happens to be dead, we check the currently playing animation to see if it has finished yet. If it has, we know that the die animation, which we will trigger when the player stomps on an enemy, has finished, and we can disable the enemy to remove it from the game. In order for this animation to ever be played, however, we need to be able to determine when an enemy is killed.

Player-enemy interaction

Again, drawing inspiration from the classic platform games, we will decide that when a player collides with an enemy, if the player is landing on the enemy from above, then the enemy will be killed. Otherwise, the enemy will kill the player.

Time for action – interacting with zombies

1. In the Update() method of the LevelManager module, replace the For Each loop that updates the _enemies list entries with the following loop:

```
For x As Integer = _enemies.Count - 1 To 0 Step - 1
    _enemies(x).Update(gameTime)
    If Not _enemies(x).Dead Then
        If _player.CollisionRectangle.Intersects(
            _enemies(x).CollisionRectangle) Then
```

```
            If _player.WorldCenter.Y <
                _enemies(x).WorldLocation.Y Then

                _player.Jump()
                _player.Score += 5
                _enemies(x).PlayAnimation("die")
                _enemies(x).Dead = true
            Else
                _player.Kill()
            End If
        End If
    Else
        If Not _enemies(x).Enabled Then
            _enemies.RemoveAt(x)
        End If
    End If
Next
```

2. In the `Player` class, add a property to hold the lives the player has remaining:

```
Public Property LivesRemaining As Integer = 3
```

3. Add the `Kill()` method to the `Player` class to allow the player to be killed:

```
Public Sub Kill()
    PlayAnimation("die")
    LivesRemaining -= 1
    Velocity = New Vector2(0, Velocity.Y)
    _dead = True
End Sub
```

4. Add the `Revive()` method to the `Player` class, which we will use to respawn the player after they have died. We will implement this functionality when we build the game state structure around the Gemstone Hunter:

```
Public Sub Revive()
    PlayAnimation("idle")
    _dead = False
End Sub
```

5. Execute the Gemstone Hunter application and kill some zombies! If you get killed by the zombies, you will need to end the application and restart it to continue playing.

What just happened?

When we determine that the player has collided with an enemy, we check the Y coordinate of the player's `WorldCenter` vector against the Y coordinate of the enemy's `WorldLocation` vector. The `WorldCenter` vector points to the middle of the object's display area, while `WorldLocation` points to the upper-left corner. If the player's center is above the top of the enemy, we grant the player a kill of the zombie and call `_player.Jump()` to boost them back up into the air. The enemy's `die` animation is played, and the enemy is marked as dead.

Otherwise, the player's `Kill()` method is called, resulting in the player's `die` animation being played, and any current horizontal movement negated. Because the `Player` class `Update()` method checks to make sure the player is not dead before accepting any input, the player will now be unable to move and lies lifeless on the floor.

Level transitions

We have a couple of different door tiles in our tile set that can be used to allow the player to exit the current map and enter a new one. In Chapter 8, *Gemstone Hunter—Put on your Platform Shoes*, we indicated that marking a square with a code in the format T_M_X_Y would indicate that the square contained a transition to map number M at location (X, Y). We will implement this functionality by modifying the Player class.

Time for action – supporting map transitions

1. Add a new helper method to the `Helper Methods` region of the `Player` class:

```
Private Sub checkLevelTransition()
    Dim centerCell As Vector2 = TileMap.
GetCellByPixel(WorldCenter)

    If TileMap.CellCodeValue(centerCell).StartsWith("T_") Then
        Dim code() As String
        code = TileMap.CellCodeValue(centerCell).Split(CChar("_"))

        If code.Length <> 4 Then
          Return
        End If

        LevelManager.LoadLevel(Integer.Parse(code(1)))

        WorldLocation = new Vector2(
            Integer.Parse(code(2)) * TileMap.TileWidth,
            Integer.Parse(code(3)) * TileMap.TileHeight)
```

```
        LevelManager.RespawnLocation = WorldLocation

        Velocity = Vector2.Zero
    End If
End Sub
```

2. Modify the `Update()` method of the `Player` class to add a check for pressing the *Up* key or pressing *Up* on the gamepad to check the current square for an available transition. Place this after the check for pressing the *Space* bar or *A* button to jump:

```
If (keyState.IsKeyDown(Keys.Up) Or
    (padState.ThumbSticks.Left.Y > 0.3f)) Then

    checkLevelTransition()
End If
```

3. Execute the Gemstone Hunter application and move right on the map until you reach the cave door. Stand on the door and press up on the keyboard or gamepad to transition to the next map. Try not to get killed by the zombies on the way! Once you reach the door and walk through it, the second map (`MAP001.MAP`), containing an underground level, will be loaded:

What just happened?

The `checkLevelTransition()` method examines the code value in the cell containing the center of the player's sprite, looking for an entry starting with T_ that indicates a transition square. If found, the text is split into pieces separated by an underscore using the `Split()` method. If the result is not four pieces (T_, the map number, an X coordinate, and a Y coordinate), the method simply returns and does nothing.

If the code is in the proper format, the `LevelManager` is asked to load the desired map. After the map has been loaded (which may contain START code that position the player), the player is moved to the position indicated by the transition code value.

Processing other codes

Now that we have implemented a method that allows the player to be killed, we can handle the final outstanding pre-defined code value—DEAD. This code makes entering the marked square lethal to the player. We will implement this code by building a helper method that will examine the current cell's code value and take appropriate action.

If you define additional code values, you can expand on this method to react to them appropriately.

Time for action – handling codes

1. Add the `checkCurrentCellCode()` helper method to the `LevelManager` class:

   ```
   #Region "Helper Methods"
   Private Sub checkCurrentCellCode()
       Dim code As String = TileMap.CellCodeValue(
           TileMap.GetCellByPixel(_player.WorldCenter))

       If code = "DEAD" Then
           _player.Kill()
       End If
   End Sub
   #End Region
   ```

2. Call `checkCurrentCellCode()` as the first task performed inside the If Not _player.Dead statement in the Update() method of the LevelManager:

   ```
   checkCurrentCellCode()
   ```

3. Launch the game and run to the right until you reach an area where there are floor blocks missing, forming a pit. Jump into the pit, and your character will die when he reaches the lowest level of the pit.

What just happened?

We simply read the code value from the map for the cell where the player's `WorldCenter` point is located. This allows the player to get close to deadly things without actually dying, but one pixel too far will trigger the square.

Game structure

Wrapping our game in a simple game state structure should be fairly familiar by now, and the process is straightforward. Let's put our game state structure together for the Gemstone Hunter game.

Time for action – implementing game states

1. Add declarations to the `Game1` class for our `GameState` enum:

```
Private Enum GameState
    TitleScreen
    Playing
    PlayerDead
    GameOver
End Enum

Private _gameState As GameState = GameState.TitleScreen
```

2. Still in the declaration section of the `Game1` class, add vectors for the display position of our text items, a texture to hold the title screen image, and the delay before respawn when the player dies:

```
Private gameOverPosition As Vector2 = New Vector2(350, 300)
Private livesPosition As Vector2 = New Vector2(600, 580)

Private titleScreen As Texture2D

Private deathTimer As Single = 0
Private deathDelay As Single = 5
```

3. We currently have temporary code in the `LoadContent()` method that loads straight into the first level of the game. Replace the current `LoadContent()` method with the following code:

```
Protected Overrides Sub LoadContent()
    spriteBatch = New SpriteBatch(GraphicsDevice)

    TileMap.Initialize(
```

```
            Content.Load(Of Texture2D)("Textures\PlatformTiles"))

        TileMap.spriteFont =
            Content.Load(Of SpriteFont)("Fonts\Pericles8")

        pericles8 = Content.Load(Of SpriteFont)("Fonts\Pericles8")

        titleScreen = Content.Load(Of Texture2D)("Textures\
    TitleScreen")

        Camera.WorldRectangle = New Rectangle(0, 0, 160 * 48, 12 * 48)
        Camera.Position = Vector2.Zero
        Camera.ViewPortWidth = 800
        Camera.ViewPortHeight = 600

        _player = New Player(Content)
        LevelManager.Initialize(Content, _player)
    End Sub
```

4. Add the `StartNewGame()` helper method to the `Game1` class:

```
Private Sub StartNewGame()
    _player.Revive()
    _player.LivesRemaining = 3
    _player.WorldLocation = Vector2.Zero
    LevelManager.LoadLevel(0)
End Sub
```

5. Replace the `Update()` method with the following code to remove any temporary code and implement the game state logic:

```
Protected Overrides Sub Update(gameTime As GameTime)
    ' Allows the game to exit
    If GamePad.GetState(PlayerIndex.One).Buttons.Back =
        ButtonState.Pressed Then
        Me.Exit()
    End If

    Dim keyState As KeyboardState = Keyboard.GetState()
    Dim padState As GamePadState = GamePad.GetState(PlayerIndex.
One)
    Dim elapsed As Single
    Elapsed = CSng(gameTime.ElapsedGameTime.TotalSeconds)

    If _gameState = GameState.TitleScreen Then
```

```vbnet
        If keyState.IsKeyDown(Keys.Space) Or
            padState.Buttons.A = ButtonState.Pressed Then

            StartNewGame()
            _gameState = GameState.Playing
        End If
    End If

    If _gameState = GameState.Playing Then
        _player.Update(gameTime)
        LevelManager.Update(gameTime)
        If _player.Dead Then
            If _player.LivesRemaining > 0 Then
                _gameState = GameState.PlayerDead
                deathTimer = 0.0
            Else
                _gameState = GameState.GameOver
                deathTimer = 0.0
            End If
        End IF
    End If

    If _gameState = GameState.PlayerDead Then
        _player.Update(gameTime)
        LevelManager.Update(gameTime)
        deathTimer += elapsed
        If deathTimer > deathDelay Then
            _player.WorldLocation = Vector2.Zero
            LevelManager.ReloadLevel()
            _player.Revive()
            _gameState = GameState.Playing
        End If
    End If

    If _gameState = GameState.GameOver Then
        deathTimer += elapsed
        If deathTimer > deathDelay Then
            _gameState = GameState.TitleScreen
        End If
    End If

    MyBase.Update(gameTime)
End Sub
```

6. Replace the `Draw()` method with the following code:

```
Protected Overrides Sub Draw(gameTime As GameTime)
    GraphicsDevice.Clear(Color.Black)

    spriteBatch.Begin(
        SpriteSortMode.BackToFront,
        BlendState.AlphaBlend)

    If _gameState = GameState.TitleScreen Then
        spriteBatch.Draw(
            titleScreen,
            New Rectangle(0, 0, 800, 600),
            Color.White)
    End If

    If ((_gameState = GameState.Playing) Or
        (_gameState = GameState.PlayerDead) Or
        (_gameState = GameState.GameOver)) Then

        TileMap.Draw(spriteBatch)
        _player.Draw(spriteBatch)
        LevelManager.Draw(spriteBatch)
        spriteBatch.DrawString(
            pericles8,
            "Score: " + _player.Score.ToString(),
            scorePosition,
            Color.White)
        spriteBatch.DrawString(
            pericles8,
            "Lives Remaining: " + _player.LivesRemaining.
ToString(),
            livesPosition,
            Color.White)
    End If

    If _gameState = GameState.GameOver Then
        spriteBatch.DrawString(
            pericles8,
            "G A M E   O V E R !",
            gameOverPosition,
            Color.White)
    End If
```

```
        spriteBatch.End()

        MyBase.Draw(gameTime)
    End Sub
```

7. Execute the Gemstone Hunter game!

What just happened?

Much as we did in our previous games, we defined a limited set of game states, beginning the game in `TitleScreen` mode. The `Update()` and `Draw()` methods are segmented to take different actions based on the current `_gameState` value.

Non-interactive game states (`PlayerDead` and `GameOver`) are controlled by our standard timing mechanism, allowing the game to advance after a preset period of time has elapsed (five seconds in this case).

Have a go hero

Of all of the games presented in this book, Gemstone Hunter is perhaps the most open for customization and expansion. Here are just a handful of suggestions for implementing enhancements to Gemstone Hunter based on the things you have learned in this book:

- There are three other types of monster sprites included in the Platform Starter Kit. Modify the `Enemy` class to randomly select a monster type when a monster is spawned.

- Alternatively, modify the `Enemy` type to accept an additional parameter indicating which of the four types of monsters should be spawned, and create new code in the **Level Editor** for each different type of monster. You can then specify exactly which type of monster you wish to appear in each location.

- As with Robot Rampage, Gemstone Hunter is currently silent. Add the sound system from Asteroid Belt Assault to Gemstone Hunter and generate appropriate sound effects for things like picking up gems and squishing zombies.

- Expand on the tile images provided with Gemstone Hunter to add items such as spiked pits and background details such as clouds, hills, and roots for underground areas.

Summary

Gemstone Hunter implements the basics of a platform-style game, allowing the player to move around on a tile-based game world. Key concepts from the Gemstone Hunter game include:

- An alternative approach to sprite-based animation, using animation strips whose dimensions determine the number of frames in the animation instead of specifying the individual frames from a larger sprite sheet

- Deriving multiple game object types from a base type and specializing the behavior of each of the child types while maintaining basic interaction with the game world from the base class

- Implementing gravity and tile map-based collisions to allow the player to explore the game world

- Parsing the map codes we generated in the **Level Editor** to populate the game world with gemstones and enemies when a level is loaded

- Allowing the player to interact with hidden map code for functionality such as level transitions and deadly areas

You've done it! With your first four XNA games completed, I hope that you now have not only ideas for the kinds of games you want to make, but also the knowledge to successfully implement them. The XNA Framework gives independent coders and small development teams a powerful set of tools to bring their creations to life on the PC, the Xbox 360, and now the Windows Phone.

Index

[PACKT]
PUBLISHING

Thank you for buying
XNA 4.0 Game Development by Example –
Visual Basic Edition: Beginner's Guide

About Packt Publishing

Packt, pronounced 'packed', published its first book "Mastering phpMyAdmin for Effective MySQL Management" in April 2004 and subsequently continued to specialize in publishing highly focused books on specific technologies and solutions.

Our books and publications share the experiences of your fellow IT professionals in adapting and customizing today's systems, applications, and frameworks. Our solution-based books give you the knowledge and power to customize the software and technologies you're using to get the job done. Packt books are more specific and less general than the IT books you have seen in the past. Our unique business model allows us to bring you more focused information, giving you more of what you need to know, and less of what you don't.

Packt is a modern, yet unique publishing company, which focuses on producing quality, cutting-edge books for communities of developers, administrators, and newbies alike. For more information, please visit our website: www.PacktPub.com.

Writing for Packt

We welcome all inquiries from people who are interested in authoring. Book proposals should be sent to author@packtpub.com. If your book idea is still at an early stage and you would like to discuss it first before writing a formal book proposal, contact us; one of our commissioning editors will get in touch with you.

We're not just looking for published authors; if you have strong technical skills but no writing experience, our experienced editors can help you develop a writing career, or simply get some additional reward for your expertise.

[PACKT]
PUBLISHING

3D Game Development with Microsoft Silverlight 3: Beginner's Guide

ISBN: 978-1-847198-92-1   Paperback:452 pages

A practical guide to creating real-time responsive online 3D games in Silverlight 3 using C#, XBAP WPF, XAML, Balder, and Farseer Physics Engine

1. Develop online interactive 3D games and scenes in Microsoft Silverlight 3 and XBAP WPF

2. Integrate Balder 3D engine 1.0, Farseer Physics Engine 2.1, and advanced object-oriented techniques to simplify the game development process

3. Enhance development with animated 3D characters, sounds, music, physics, stages, gauges, and backgrounds

Unity 3.x Game Development by Example Beginner's Guide

ISBN: 978-1-84969-184-0   Paperback: 408 pages

A seat-of-your-pants manual for building fun, groovy little games quickly with Unity 3.x

1. Build fun games using the free Unity game engine even if you've never coded before

2. Learn how to "skin" projects to make totally different games from the same file – more games, less effort!

3. Deploy your games to the Internet so that your friends and family can play them

Please check **www.PacktPub.com** for information on our titles

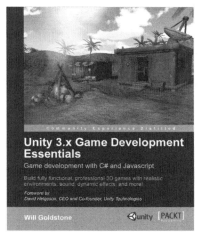

Unity 3.x Game Development Essentials

ISBN: 978-1-84969-144-4   Paperback:420 pages

Build fully functional, professional 3D games with realistic environments, sound, dynamic effects, and more!

1. Kick start your game development, and build ready-to-play 3D games with ease.

2. Understand key concepts in game design including scripting, physics, instantiation, particle effects, and more.

3. Written in clear, plain English, this book takes you from a simple prototype through to a complete 3D game with concepts you'll reuse throughout your new career as a game developer.

CryEngine Cookbook

ISBN: 978-1-84969-106-2   Paperback: 324 pages

Over 90 recipes written by Crytek developers for creating third-generation real-time games

1. Begin developing your AAA game or simulation by harnessing the power of the award winning CryENGINE3

2. Create entire game worlds using the powerful CryENGINE 3 Sandbox.

3. Create your very own customized content for use within the CryENGINE3 with the multiple creation recipes in this book

Please check **www.PacktPub.com** for information on our titles

Made in the USA
San Bernardino, CA
12 December 2012